1/8th Battalion the
Sherwood Foresters
in the Great War

1/8th Battalion the
Sherwood Foresters
in the Great War

W. C. C. Weetman

LEONAUR

1/8th Battalion the Sherwood Foresters in the Great War
by W. C. C. Weetman

Originally published under the title
The Sherwood Foresters in the Great War 1914-1919
1/8th Battalion

Published by Leonaur Ltd

ISBN: 978-0-85706-583-4 (hardcover)
ISBN: 978-0-85706-584-1 (softcover)

http://www.leonaur.com

Publisher's Notes

The views expressed in this book are not necessarily
those of the publisher.

Contents

TO OUR FALLEN COMRADES

In truth they were young gentlemen, yeomen and yeomen's sons, and artificers of the most brave sort, such as went voluntarily to serve of a gaiety and joyalty of mind: all which kind of people are the flower and force of a kingdom.

Sir John Smyth to Lord Burleigh on our men in Flanders in 1589-90

Introduction

It is not only a great honour to have been asked to write an introduction to this book, but it is a real pleasure to me to be linked in this manner to a battalion with which I was so intimately connected for nearly six years and in which I made so many friends, of whom many, alas, have passed the "great divide." The battalion has been lucky in finding in Captain Weetman an author with such a ready and amusing pen, and one especially who was in a position to see the workings of the battalion in almost every phase of its career and from every standpoint, first as a company officer, then as adjutant and finally from brigade headquarters.

To me, perhaps naturally, the most interesting part of the book is the early chapters. From the time, in 1911, when I took over the command of what, I was informed by a staff officer qualified to know, was the best territorial brigade in the kingdom, I was a firm believer in the territorial force. But I hardly think that the most hardened optimist would at that time have thought it possible for a territorial division to mobilise and march complete with equipment and transport to its mobilisation area on the sixth day after receiving the order "mobilise." The amount of work done by battalions and companies was marvellous and only those who experienced it can have an idea of what it meant.

As for the training, I don't believe better work was ever done than during those weeks at Harpenden. True we were lucky in the weather and in the training area, and the 8th Battalion were specially lucky in their excellent staff of sergeant-instructors. All ranks put their heart into the work. I remember particularly the excellent work done by the large batch of recruits which joined the battalion at that time, including surely as good a lot of young officers as ever joined a regiment. The author has described fully the training carried out at Harpenden and in Essex, and that the time and labour spent in it were not wasted is proved by the manner in which all ranks so quickly took on their responsibilities in the trenches, and with such success. That the Territorial Force was in many ways neglected by the higher authorities during those early days is well known, but that the Force amply justified itself is proved by its actions and was fully recognised by those general officers under whose command it came. The following extract from a speech made by Lieutenant-General Sir C. Fergusson, commanding II Corps, to the brigade at Locre, when it left his command, is worth recording to show the high opinion he held of our work in front of Kemmel. "No battalion," he said, "and no brigade could have held the lines better than you have done or have done better work than you have done....Your work during the last three months is work of which any brigade and any battalion might be proud." No higher praise could have been given to any troops by an officer of such standing and repute.

I have written rather at length on this period for I consider the metamorphosis of a territorial battalion into as fine a fighting battalion as ever took the field, is well worth the study of all those who have joined since those days or will join in the future.

It is only fitting that some acknowledgment be made to the memory of the man who did more than any other to make the North Midland Division worthy to take its place in line with the regular army. I refer to the late Major-General Hubert Hamilton, who commanded the division from 1911 to June, 1914, and fell early in the war at Richebourg-St.Vaast. He foresaw that war with Germany must come and worked with all his power to make the division efficient in every way—in training as in organisation. And it was very largely due to his efforts that mobilisation was carried out so successfully.

One word more. I am fully convinced that if every officer and man who joined up in 1914 *after* the outbreak of war, had joined the Territorial Force and made himself efficient *before* August, 1914, there would have been no war. If Germany had known that England could put 1,000,000 men into the field within a few weeks of the declaration of war, instead of only 160,000, she would never have dared to embark on her campaign of spoliation. The risk would have been too great.

If this story of the doings of a territorial battalion in the Great War can do anything to bring that battalion up to strength, to keep it there, and to encourage all ranks to make themselves thoroughly efficient, I am sure that the author will consider himself well repaid for all the time and all the trouble he has spent on it.

C. T. *Shipley*
12th September, 1920

Author's Note

In compiling this history of the 1/8th Sherwood Foresters in the Great War, I have relied for my main facts on the Official War Diary, but from many other sources I have received much help. My thanks are due especially to Lieutenant-Colonel H. Mellish, C.B., for advice on many general points; to Lieutenant-Colonel A. Hacking, D.S.O., M.C., for much help with "The Salient" and "Lens" chapters, and for kindly revising the whole of the book; to Captain A. L. Ashwell, D.S.O., for most of the "Hohenzollern" chapter, and for much general assistance; to Captain A. Andrews, M.C., for much of the detail of the "Gorre and Essars" chapter, and information on many other points, and to Captain A. B. Miners, M.C., for help with the account of the "Battle of Ramicourt" and subsequent fighting.

I have also to thank Captain C. Davenport for some details of transport work; Captain R. H. Piggford for a few notes and the sketch dealing with Mining operations; and Lieutenants C. H. S. Stephenson and E. W. Warner, M.C., for some signalling items, and the diagram of signal communications. I am also indebted to Captain J. D. Hills, M.C., of the 5th Leicestershire Regiment, for many hints on the general arrangement of the work, and to Private A. Hunstone of the 6th Battalion for the excellent plans. To many others who have supplied me with information and helped me on various points, I offer my grateful thanks.

The book is not intended in any way to be a literary effort. All that has been attempted has been a simple narrative of our doings for the use primarily of persons connected with the battalion. My main endeavour throughout, has been to secure accuracy, but it will be understood that in sifting the mass of material placed at my disposal, errors may have crept in. I trust, however, that these are few.

W. C. C. Weetman
Hereford, October, 1920

SUMMARY OF EVENTS

1914.

Aug.	4th	War declared. Mobilisation ordered.
,,	7th	Concentration at Newark.
,,	10th—	} Marched via Radcliffe-on-Trent to Derby.
,,	11th	
,,	15th	Entrained at Derby for Luton.
,,	21st	Moved to Harpenden.

,,	22nd—	} Training in Harpenden	Sept. 29th—Inspection by Lord Kitchener at Luton Hoo.
Nov.	15th	Area.	Oct. 6th—Inspection by Lord Roberts at Sandridge.

,,	16th—	} Marched via Harlow and Dunmow to Bocking.
,,	18th	
,,	19th—	} Trench digging near Bocking.
Dec.	27th	

,,	28th—	By train to Luton for Musketry at Wardown and Galley Hill Ranges, and Field Firing at Dunstable, returning to Bocking.
1915.		
Jan.	5th	

,,	6th—	} Training in Bocking	Feb. 19th—Inspection by H.M. The King near Bishop's Stortford.
Feb.	24th	Area.	

,,	25th	Entrained at Bocking for Southampton.
,,	26th—	} Crossed by detachments to Havre.
Mar.	3rd	
,,	3rd—	{ By train to Cassel and marched to Oudezeele.
,,	4th	
,,	9th	Marched to Merris.
,,	10th	Moved to Bac-St. Maur, for First Battle of Neuve Chapelle. Temporarily attached to 2nd Cavalry Division.
,,	13th	Marched to Neuf Berquin for training.
,,	24th—	} Moved via Vieux Berquin to Romarin.
,,	26th	
,,	27th—	} Trench instruction at Ploegsteert and Messines.
,,	30th	
,,	31st	Marched back to Vieux Berquin.
April	2nd	Marched to Locre.
,,	3rd	Took over Kemmel sector.

13

1915.

April 4th— June 20th	{ In line in Kemmel sector with intervals in rest billets at Locre.	{ April 22nd—Gas used against French and Canadians in Ypres Salient. Traces in trenches held by Battalion. April 24—Heavy trench mortar bombardment of front line held by B, C and D Companies. June 15th—Enemy blew up by mines and raided part of front line.

,, 20th   Marched to huts near Vlamertinghe.

,, 21st— Aug. 28th	{ In line at Hooge and Sanctuary Wood, with intervals at rest in bivouacs near Poperinghe.	{ July 30th—First "liquid fire" attack.

,, 29th— Sept. 30th	{ In line at Middlesex Wood, adjoining Ypres-Comines Canal, near St. Eloi, with rest bivouacs near Ouderdom.	{ Sept. 21st—Inspection by Gen. Plumer. Sept. 25th—Demonstrations in conjunction with attacks on other portions of the front.

Oct. 1st   Marched from Ouderdom and entrained at Abeele for Fouquereuil. Billeted in Béthune.

,, 3rd   Moved to Mont Bernenchon.

,, 4th   Marched back to Béthune, proceeded by 'bus to Vermelles, and took over reserve trenches near Lone Tree, North of Loos.

,, 5th   Moved back to Mazingarbe.

,, 6th   Marched to Fouquières.

,, 13th—
,, 14th   } Attack on Hohenzollern Redoubt.

,, 16th   Moved back to Vaudricourt.

,, 19th   Marched to Lapugnoy for training.

,, 26th   Marched to Béthune.

Oct. 28th   Composite Company with other troops of XI Corps inspected by H.M. The King at Hesdigneul.

Nov. 4th—
,, 5th   } Marched via Epinette to Vieille Chapelle.

14

Nov.	6th—	In line in Richebourg sector, with rest billets at
Dec.	2nd	Vieille Chapelle and Lacouture.
,,	3rd	Marched from Vieille Chapelle to Haverskerque for training.
,,	19th—	Marched via Wittes to Molinghem and continued
,,	26th	training.

1916.

Jan.	7th—	Entrained at Berguette for Marseilles.
,,	9th	
,,	26th—	Returned by train to Pont Remy. Marched to
,,	28th	Ergnies for training.
Feb.	10th	Marched to Ribeaucourt.
,,	20th	Moved by motor lorry to Candas.
,,	21st—	Training and work for R.E.'s on new railway lines
March	5th	in Candas area.
,,	6th—	Marched via Iverny and Maizières to Acq.
,,	9th	
,,	10th—	In line in Vimy sector, with intervals at rest in
April	20th	huts behind Mont St. Eloy. Mining activity.
,,	21st	By 'bus to billets at Tincques and Bethencourt for training.
,,	29th	Moved to Averdoignt.
May	6th—	Marched via Rebreuviette and Gaudiempré to
,,	10th	Bienvillers.
,,	11th—	In line in front of Foncquevillers.
June	4th	
,,	5th	Moved back to Humbercamp.
,,	6th	Marched by night to Le Souich.
,,	8th—	Training in attack practice near Sus-St. Leger.
,,	14th	
,,	15th	Marched to Humbercamp.
,,	16th—	Working parties found for digging cable trenches
,,	18th	and screening approaches near Bienvillers.
,,	19th—	In line in front of Foncquevillers.
,,	27th	
,,	28th—	Rested at Pommier.
,,	29th	
,,	30th	Moved at night to assembly positions in front of Foncquevillers.
July	1st	Battle of Gommecourt.
,,	2nd	Moved back to Gaudiempré.
,,	3rd	Marched to huts at Bavincourt.
,,	4th	Marched back to Pommier and Bienvillers.

15

July	10th	Moved to Bellacourt.
,,	11th—	⎧ In line in front of Bretencourt, with periods
Oct.	28th	⎨ in Support at Bellacourt, and in Reserve at Bailleulval. (Sept. 22nd, Raid by A Company near Blairville.)
,,	29th—	⎫ Marched from Bailleulval via Warluzel, Le Souich
Nov.	3rd	⎭ and Neuvillette to Maison Ponthieu, for training.
,,	22nd—	⎫ Marched via Bealcourt and Neuvillette to
,,	25th	⎭ Humbercourt.
Dec.	6th	Moved to Support billets at Foncquevillers and Souastre.
,,	7th—	⎧ In line in front of Foncquevillers, with intervals in Support in posts in and about Foncque-
1917.		⎨ villers, and in billets at Souastre. (Feb. 16th—
Feb.	18th	17th, heavy bombardment with gas shells and bombs.)
,,	19th	Moved back to St. Amand.
,,	20th	Marched to Iverny for training.
,,	28th—	⎫ Returned via Grenas to St. Amand.
March	1st	⎭
,,	3rd	Took over recently evacuated German trenches at Gommecourt.
,,	4th—	⎧ Followed up enemy to Pigeon Wood, Brayelle Farm and Essarts. (March 4th, heavy counter-
,,	13th	⎩ attack against C Company.)
,,	17th	Moved back to Souastre.
,,	20th—	⎫ Marched via Bayencourt, Courcelles-au-Bois and
,,	24th	⎭ Contay to Bertangles.
,,	25th	Moved by 'bus through Amiens to Revelles.
,,	28th	Entrained at Bacouel.
,,	29th	Detrained at Berguette and marched to Westrehem for training.
April	13th—	⎫ Marched via Vendin-lez-Béthune to Houchin.
,,	14th	⎭
,,	18th	Moved up to Support billets in Liévin.
,,	19th—	⎫ Skirmishing in Cité de Riaumont.
,,	22nd	⎭
,,	23rd	Attack on Hill 65 by C Company.
,,	24th—	⎧ Held sectors in front of Liévin and Loos, with intervals in Support in Liévin and in Reserve
June	30th	⎩ at Marqueffles Farm and Noeux-les-Mines.
July	1st	In Brigade Reserve for attack by 46th Division West of Lens.

July	4th	On relief by Canadians marched to Bully Grenay and by 'bus to Chelers for training.
,,	23rd	Marched to Verquin.
,,	24th—	In line in St. Elie sector and in Support at
Aug.	15th	Philosophe.
,,	16th—	Training in Verquin area.
,,	25th	
,,	26th—	In line in Cambrin sector and in Support at
Sept.	12th	Annequin.
,,	13th—	In Divisional Reserve at Fouquières.
,,	19th	
,,	20th	Marched to Mazingarbe huts.
,,	21st—	In line in Hill 70 sector, in Support in trenches
Nov.	14th	North of Loos, and in Reserve at Mazingarbe.
,,	15th—	In line in St. Elie sector, in Support at Philosophe,
1918.		and in Reserve at Verquin. (Jan. 2nd, Raid
Jan.	20th	on front held by D Company.)
,,	21st	Marched from Verquin to Burbure.
,,	22nd—	Training at Burbure. Large detachment at Mazingarbe digging reserve trenches near Vermelles.
Feb.	8th	
,,	9th	Marched from Burbure to Laires and Livossart.
,,	13th	Moved to Enquin-les-Mines for training.
March	5th—	Marched to Westrehem and by 'bus to Béthune.
,,	6th	
,,	14th—	Held Annequin Fosse "Locality," in view of
,,	19th	heavy attacks expected.
,,	20th—	In line in Cambrin sector. (March 22nd, Heavy
,,	23rd	bombardment and raid on A Company.)
,,	24th—	In Support at Beuvry.
,,	26th	
,,	27th—	In line in St. Emile sector, and in Support in
April	10th	St. Pierre.
,,	11th	On relief by Canadians, moved back to Vaudricourt.
,,	18th	Moved to reserve trenches in front of Sailly-Labourse. Unsuccessful attack by enemy near Givenchy.
,,	20th	Returned to Vaudricourt.
,,	23rd	Marched to Béthune.
,,	24th—	In line in Gorre and Essars sectors, and in Reserve
Aug.	17th	at Fouquières, Vaudricourt Park and Verquin.
,,	18th	Occupied Le Touret after driving out enemy rearguard.
,,	19th—	In billets at Verquin, Vaudricourt Park,
,,	31st	Fouquières, Essars and Gorre.

Sept.	1st	Took over front line near Richebourg St. Vaast.
,,	2nd— 3rd	Continued to drive back enemy rearguards.
,,	4th	Attacked and occupied old British Line in front of Richebourg l'Avoué.
,,	5th— 7th	Moved back via Beuvry to Auchel for training.
,,	11th— 12th	By train from Calonne Ricouart via Amiens to Corbie and marched to La Houssoye for training.
,,	18th	Marched to Bonnay and by 'bus to Poeuilly.
,,	20th— 25th	In line about Pontru and Pontruet.
,,	26th	Moved back to bivouacs near Vendelles.
,,	29th	Battle of Bellenglise.
,, Oct.	30th— 2nd	In dugouts near Lehaucourt and Magny-la-Fosse.
,,	3rd	Battle of Ramicourt.
,,	5th— 7th	In line at Sequehart.
,,	8th	Resting at Lehaucourt.
,,	9th— 12th	Moved via Levergies and Mericourt to Jonnecourt Farm, near Bohain.
,,	17th	Battle of Regnicourt.—The Last Fight.
,,	18th	Moved back to Fresnoy-le-Grand for training.
,,	30th	Marched to Bohain.
Nov.	3rd— 4th	Marched via Escaufort to Catillon.
,,	5th	Crossed Sambre-Oise Canal and advanced to Mezières.
,,	6th	Occupied Prisches and Cartignies.
,,	7th— 9th	At Cartignies.
,,	10th	Marched from Cartignies to Boulogne-sur-Helpe.
,,	11th	Armistice.
,,	14th	Marched to Landrecies.
,, **1919.** Jan.	15th— 2nd	Clearing battlefield in Landrecies area. Demobilisation begun.
,,	3rd	Marched from Landrecies to Prisches and continued clearing battlefield.
Feb.	19th— 20th	Marched via Bazuel to Bethencourt, near Caudry, for completion of Demobilisation.
June	23rd	Return of Cadre and Colours to Headquarters at Newark.

Chapter 1

England

August 4th, 1914—February 25th, 1915

When the 8th Sherwood Foresters concentrated at Hunmanby, at the end of July, 1914, for their usual annual training, the International horizon was clouded with the diplomatic conversations which had followed the murder of the Archduke Francis Ferdinand of Austria by Servians at Sarajevo. Many hoped, no doubt, that the experience of the Morocco incident of 1905 and the Agadir incident of 1911, would again be repeated and that once more the clouds of a world war would be dissipated, but when we reflect upon this period of the world's history it is easy now to see that war with Germany, sooner or later, was inevitable.

The atmosphere was so charged with electricity that it was impossible to settle down to the normal routine of training, and there was little surprise when on August 3rd, bank holiday, Germany declared war on France, and when on the following day, August 4th, Great Britain herself, following upon the violation of the neutrality of Belgium, joined forces with Russia and France.

Territorial camps were at once broken up and all ranks ordered home, with instructions to hold themselves in readiness for any emergency.

The royal proclamation for the embodiment of the 8th Battalion Sherwood Foresters (Notts. and Derby Regiment) was issued at 6.45 p.m. on Tuesday, August 4th, and notified to all units in the briefest possible telegram—"Mobilise." During Wednesday and Thursday, August 5th and 6th, all companies were endeavouring to purchase locally and issue to every man, underclothing and necessaries according to scale. This was a big undertaking, as the scheme for earmarking such goods in the case of embodiment had not been completed, and there was, therefore, some delay in obtaining all requirements. The strength of the battalion on mobilisation was 29 officers and 852 other ranks.

On Friday, August 7th, the battalion concentrated at Newark, under the command of Lieutenant-Colonel C. J. Huskinson, T.D., with Major G. H. Fowler second in command, and Captain E. N. T. Collin, adjutant, companies and their officers at this time being as follows:—

A	Company—	Retford.—Lieut. W. R. Smith, 2nd Lieuts. L. Rose and E. C. A. James.
B	,,	Newark.—Capt. L. C. B. Appleby, Lieuts. C. Davenport and A. H. Quibell.
C	,,	Sutton-in-Ashfield.—Lieut. M. C. Martyn, 2nd Lieuts. H. G. Wright and R. H. Piggford.
D	,,	Mansfield.—Capt. A. C. Clarke, 2nd Lieut. J. W. Turner.
E	,,	Carlton.—Lieut. F. G. Cursham, 2nd Lieut. H. Kirby.
F	,,	Arnold.—2nd Lieuts. G. Clarke and A. F. O. Dobson.
G	,,	Worksop.—Capt. E. W. E. Tylden-Wright, Lieut. W. H. Allen.
H	,,	Southwell.—Capt. J. P. Becher, Lieut. J. K. Lane, 2nd Lieut. H. B. S. Handford.

Lieutenant A. L. Ashwell was machine-gun officer; Captain F. W. Johnson, and Surgeon-Captain H. Stallard, medical officers, and Rev. J. P. Hales, chaplain; Major W. N. Sarll was quarter-master, but, being medically unfit, at once handed over his duties to Captain R. F. B. Hodgkinson, who joined from the Territorial Force Reserve. Captain R. J. Wordsworth mobilised with brigade headquarters.

The battalion was billeted for the most part in schools: B Company were detailed for various duties in the town, and H Company found guards on bridges and other points on the Great Northern Railway, the most important being the tubular bridge. Nothing of interest happened except that a too keen sentry one night loosed off at some suspicious looking persons, who turned out to be innocent platelayers returning home from work. Fortunately there were no casualties.

On Monday, August 10th, at 9.30 a.m., we paraded in the Market Place ready to begin our move to concentration areas. The mayor (Mr. J. C. Kew) and corporation were present, accompanied by Canon Hindley, vicar of Newark, and other clergy, and there was a dense crowd of onlookers. After an address by the mayor, who wished us God speed, and a short service, we marched off *via* the Fosse Way to Radcliffe-on-Trent, leaving behind H Company under Captain Becher, to guard the railway.

For the first time in its history the battalion had complete first line and train transport with it, this being under the command of Lieutenant Davenport, who had been appointed transport officer. The vehicles were not exactly regulation pattern, but little fault could be found with the horses, all of which had been purchased locally. Floats from Warwick and Richardson's and Hole's formed the majority of the small arm ammunition and tool carts, whilst Dickens's Mineral Water drays and Davy's Brewery drays made fairly good general service wagons, when fitted with light wooden sides. A furniture van full of blankets, two corporation water carts, and a bread cart with a large red cross on each side, completed the collection. We feel sure that few regimental transports can have looked more like a circus than did ours as we left Newark.

The march of 14 miles to Radcliffe-on-Trent was completed about 4 p.m., and after a good night's rest we left early on August 11th, and proceeding *via* Nottingham, arrived at Derby at 6.30 p.m., after a 23 mile march. This was a very severe test for all, as few were really "hard" enough at that time for such a long trek. Route marches were accordingly carried out, on each of the three extremely hot days spent at Derby, as the main part of our programme.

Whilst at Derby the main subject of discussion was that of imperial service for territorial units. So far as we were concerned a considerable number of officers and men had already volunteered. There were many others who had not actually done so, but there was no doubt as to what their answer would be. Of the remainder many were practically disqualified from serving abroad by reason of age, unfitness, family and business ties, and other reasons, and for them, in the light of the little we knew then, the decision was most difficult, and the need for it we hardly thought fair. The demand for volunteers was in the first instance put rather baldly, with little notice, and with apparently little realisation of the enormous difficulties under which so many were labouring, and it was not surprising that this appeal met with little response. A second earnest appeal, reinforced by the feeling that the honour, even the existence of the battalion was in danger, resulted in over 800 volunteering, which was eminently satisfactory, though it is impossible to avoid the feeling that many who volunteered then did so against their better judgment, and that the decision should have been made for them.

All the other units in the division having more or less similarly settled this vital question, training was started in earnest.

The first area allotted to the division was Hertfordshire, and we

21

entrained on August 15th, for the first time, and by no means the last. Hours went by after our scheduled time before there was any sign of the train. In an adjoining field, however, the various company entertainers had full scope and played to large audiences. Eventually we got off in two trains, and detraining at Leagrave marched the last three miles to Luton, where we arrived in the early hours of August 16th. Here we stayed for six days and carried out a little training, mostly at Luton Hoo and Markyate. We cannot say that we regarded this as the most pleasant of our experiences, as our billets were not of the best either for officers, who were mostly crowded into a few cottages, and took turns at bathing in small tin baths in the sculleries, or men who were also crowded in somewhat unwholesome schools, while our menu consisted monotonously of bully beef and pickle, and army biscuit and cheese.

Better things fortunately were in store, for on August 21st, we moved on a few miles to Harpenden, where we were destined to stay for three months, and where we received on all sides the greatest possible hospitality. We are sure that all who were billeted at Harpenden will look back with the greatest pleasure to the time spent in that delightful district. The men for the most part were billeted in small houses, three or four together, and with the more than ample rations and billeting allowances then in force, both men and billet owners were exceedingly well off.

Here we had also the 5th, 6th and 7th Sherwood Foresters, which, with ourselves, formed the Notts, and Derby Infantry Brigade, under the command of Brigadier-General C. T. Shipley, who had Major E. M. Morris as brigade major, and Captain R. J. Wordsworth as staff captain. The Stafford and Lincoln and Leicester Infantry Brigades completed the North Midland Division, which was commanded by Major-General The Hon. E. J. Montagu Stuart-Wortley.

Fortunately the weather for some time was splendid, and the battalion soon began to show the result of constant and regular drill, and the turnout and smartness improved rapidly. Training comprised almost every possible form that could be required to make both officers and men efficient, and went so far as to include the detailing of Sergeant-Instructor Mounteney to carry out the by no means easy task of trying to turn officers into swordsmen. It is no disparagement of his efforts to congratulate ourselves that we never had to put our lessons to the test of stern reality. "Infantry training" and "field service regulations" were studied and more or less followed out in practice in all we did. Most of our drill, musketry instruction, bayonet fighting, physical exercises, and outpost drill were carried out on the splendid common at Harpenden, but our training area extended to most of the surrounding parks and farms, where the bulk of our more advanced work in attack practice and tactical exercises was carried out. Perhaps some of the best remembered places are High Firs, where we first spent a night in bivouacs, Sandridge, where there was a small range, Rothamstead Park, Redbourn, Ayre's End, Hammond's End Farm, Annable's Farm, Mackery End, Thrale's End Farm, where barbed wire entanglements were put up, the like of which we never saw in France or anywhere else, and Cold Harbour. At Sundon, not far from Dunstable, we dug and occupied our first real trench system, which after a preliminary skirmish at night, when rockets were used to guide the attacking troops, had to withstand a heavy dawn attack by the Lincoln and Leicester Brigade.

Classification practices were fired at Wardown and Galley Hill ranges, near Luton, on thoroughly wet and disagreeable days, with ammunition not intended for the rifle we were using, and altogether under such adverse conditions, that good scores were impossible.

In addition to brigade and divisional schemes in the neighbourhood of Harpenden we had big shows on two days at Kinsworth, near Dunstable. Of our indoor classes, probably the most entertaining were the French lessons given after mess sometimes by a kind friend from the Y.M.C.A.; he did his best, but we fear that it was not quite the right time of day to find a class of officers in a mood for imbibing instruction.

Meanwhile there were many changes in personnel: Lieutenant James took over A Company from Lieutenant Smith, who was unfit; Captain Appleby and Lieutenant Cursham proceeded to Dunstable to take charge of home service men; Lieutenant Quibell went to the depot at Newark; Captain Tylden-Wright being unfit, G Company was handed over to Captain Allen; Lieutenant Turner took over the machine-gun section on Lieutenant Ashwell becoming assistant adjutant; Lieutenant G. Clarke was musketry officer; Lieutenant H. B. S. Handford, signalling officer; and Lieutenant Piggford, scout officer. Subalterns who joined during these early days included 2nd Lieutenants W. H. Hollins, J.V. Edge, A. Hacking, E. M. Hacking, W. N. Wright, J. R. Eddison, B. W. Vann, J. M. Gray. J. S. C. Oates, R. E. Hemingway, A. P. F. Hamilton, and W. C. C. Weetman. Hamilton soon left us to join the divisional cyclists and afterwards served with the Tank Corps, winning the M.C. In other ranks there were also changes: Sergeant-Instructors Hancock, Holmes and Walker went to other units, a number of men

OFFICERS AT HARPENDEN; NOV., 1914.
BACK ROW: 2ND LIEUTENANT A. F. O. DOBSON, 2ND LIEUTENANT J. S. C. OATES, 2ND LIEUTENANT E. M. HACKING. 2ND LIEUTENANT A. HACKING, 2ND LIEUTENANT W. C. C. WEETMAN, LIEUTENANT H. B. S. HANDFORD, CAPTAIN J. K. LANE, 2ND LIEUTENANT J. R. EDDISON, 2ND LIEUTENANT H. KIRBY.
MIDDLE ROW: 2ND LIEUTENANT J. M. GRAY, 2ND LIEUTENANT W. N. WRIGHT, LIEUTENANT H. G. WRIGHT, 2ND LIEUTENANT B. W. VANN, 2ND LIEUTENANT J. V. EDGE, LIEUTENANT G. CLARKE, 2ND LIEUTENANT W. H. HOLLINS, 2ND LIEUTENANT E. C. A. JAMES, 2ND LIEUTENANT J. W. TURNER, LIEUTENANT C. DAVENPORT.
FRONT ROW: CAPTAIN AND QTR.-MTR. R. F. B. HODGKINSON, CAPTAIN W. H. ALLEN, MAJOR A. C. CLARKE, REV. J. P. HALES, CAPTAIN AND ADJT. E. N. T. COLLIN, LIEUTENANT-COLONEL C. J. HUSKINSON, MAJOR G. H. FOWLER, CAPTAIN J. P. BECHER, CAPTAIN M. C. MARTYN, CAPTAIN A. L. ASHWELL, SURGEON-CAPTAIN H. STALLARD.
ON GROUND: 2ND LIEUTENANT R. H. PIGGFORD 2ND LIEUTENANT A. P. F. HAMILTON.

went to Dunstable, and a good many were discharged medically unfit, but our numbers were constantly being swelled by the arrival of recruits who kept coming in batches at frequent intervals from the depot, and made up our strength practically to establishment.

Lieutenant-Colonel G. S. Foljambe, who had joined from the Territorial Force Reserve, was in charge at the depot, and later commanded for some time the 3rd Line, with the unenviable task of getting together and training in an extraordinarily short space of time, personnel to replenish the 1st and 2nd lines. Many young officers and others who passed through his hands in those days look back with pleasure and affection to the happy times spent under his kindly care at Newark and Belton Park.

Recreations in these early days were run on the usual lines. Padre Hales had a reading room and organised battalion concerts from time to time, at which much local talent was displayed, but with everyone living in houses organised entertainment was not so necessary as we later found it to be in isolated camps, or at out-of-the-way villages in France.

We were inspected three times during this period; once at Harpenden by Lieutenant-General Sir Ian Hamilton, commanding the Central Force, again on September 29th, by Lord Kitchener in Luton Hoo Park, when we thought we made a very creditable display, and lastly, on October 6th, after we had carried out an attack scheme ending up on the Sandridge rifle range, when the battalion had the honour of marching past Lord Roberts.

The air, of course, was full of rumours. As early as September 1st, we were told that we should be off to France in a month: later the date was fixed for October 30th, and then November 7th, Bordeaux being mentioned as the elusive objective. On this last occasion it seemed so certain that we were going that a farewell sermon was preached, which turned out to be decidedly premature. We heard with every conceivable detail the delicious stories of the thousands of Russians who kept pouring through Nottingham, and like others we had the usual excitements of spy scares, all of which were very entertaining, and one at least highly dangerous, when one of our chases took some of us over the railway embankment armed with loaded revolvers.

Whatever the possibilities of our going out early may have been, one step was taken which could have had only that object in view, *viz.* inoculation against typhoid. We can only hope that the medical officers who operated on us got more fun out of the operation than we did.

Marching orders came eventually, and as ever, when least expected. Late on Sunday evening, November 15th, we were told to be ready to move at an hour's notice. This was presumed to be due to a feared raid and landing on the east coast—at any rate one hopes there was some equally good reason for it, for quite a number of officers and men had been allowed to go on week-end leave, and had to be recalled by telegram, whilst the following day was to have been a holiday.

We shall not easily forget that night—the energy we expended in packing valises, brows sweating, tempers bad, language beyond description,—all trying the impossible feat of making the wonderful collection of kit we had got together on the advice of one friend or another keep within the allotted allowance of 35lbs.

Apart from our own individual troubles, we had the additional enormous task set of issuing new equipment to everybody. The 1908 bandolier pattern had been withdrawn, and new leather equipment (pattern 1914) had arrived on the previous Friday and Saturday, and the quarter-master's staff had been busy marking it and getting it ready for issuing. This all had to be issued during the Sunday night, and was carried round to billets in blankets. The language of something like 900 men all trying to put together an entirely new set of equipment, the like of which they had never seen, may well be imagined. We were the first battalion to be issued with this equipment, which on the next day's march proved very unsatisfactory, many buckles and straps pulling right out of the webbing of the packs and haversacks. We were glad when a month later it was all withdrawn, and we were issued with the much more popular and lasting web equipment.

Eventually the battalion paraded at 9 a.m. on November 16th, one hour late, and in consequence instead of leading the brigade we had to march in rear. We got to Harlow, a distance of something like 26 miles, about 8 p.m. This was a very trying march, and as many men had only been issued with new boots during the night, it was not surprising that several fell out. On this march we first realised what a difficult and technical job "supply" can be. The supply and baggage wagons appear to have been hopelessly overloaded, and in consequence both rations and blankets failed to reach us that night. It was largely owing to the extreme kindness and hospitality of the inhabitants of the delightful little village of Harlow, amongst whom was the evergreen veteran Sir Evelyn Wood, V.C., that we were fed and breakfasted and able to continue the march the following day, 14 miles to Dunmow. This proved more trying than the previous day, and the medical officer and stretcher-bearers had a busy time attending to those who fell out.

On the 18th, we finished the journey by a nine mile march to Bocking, and there settled down into billets for the rest of our time in England. Though we were spoilt at Harpenden, we are sure that all ranks have nothing but pleasant recollections of the time spent at Braintree and Bocking, where one and all treated us with the greatest kindness, and we hope were sorry to lose us. Where all were so kind it is almost invidious to mention names, but one feels (though they themselves would be the first to deny it) that a special debt of gratitude is owed to the nuns of the convent at Bocking, whose kindness and care for those who were billeted at the convent, and for all with whom they came in contact, were beyond all praise.

In order to prepare for any possible German landing on the Essex coast orders had been issued for a series of trenches to be dug to form defensive lines for the protection of London, and we were at once set on to this work, which was pushed on as rapidly as possible, systems of trenches, redoubts, gun positions, and other defensive works being put in hand. Our work was mainly at Panfield, Marks Farm and Black Notley. It was not an ideal season for trench digging, especially in the clay of Essex, which was the "genuine" article, and we were glad when the bulk of it was finished by Christmas. This work was carried out under Royal Engineers' supervision and was in some ways instructive, although we thought that the principles we had been taught in the military manuals were frequently violated by the siting of trenches along the sides of prominent hedgerows. Nevertheless, what we did was more after the nature of what we were to meet in France, and therefore of considerable practical value. That our work was satisfactory was testified to by the insertion in Central Force Orders of January 23rd, 1915, of the general officer commanding-in-chief's keen appreciation of the soldierly spirit and enthusiasm shown for the work by all ranks. All the same, we have no regrets that it was never necessary to occupy the trenches for actual warfare.

Owing to another scare Christmas leave was cancelled. Scarborough had been bombarded on December 22nd, and there was apparently a bit of a "breeze." According to one writer this was due to a little lack of liaison between our naval and military authorities. The former had apparently spread a rumour that an invasion of the German coast was to take place, and the enemy concentrated numbers of troops there in case it happened. This concentration came to the knowledge of our military spies, who, however were not told of the cause, and their report appears to have caused our War Office to think that an invasion of England was contemplated. We were not, however, by any means dull at Christmas. On December 24th, we beat the 6th Battalion 2—1 in the first round of the divisional football competition, Vann being skipper, and in the evening the warrant officers and N.C.O.'s had a dance at Braintree Corn Exchange. On Christmas Day there was church parade at Braintree, when the Bishop of Derby preached. Later, dinners were issued on a sumptuous scale, and in the evening the officers were entertained at the White Hart by the colonel and Major Fowler.

In a later round of the divisional cup competition, we beat the divisional mechanical transport column 3—0, and got into the semi-final, when, however, we were badly beaten by the 4th Leicesters at Bishop's Stortford, by 3 goals to nil. In a brigade paper chase which was held on December 26th, Private Allen of E Company came in first.

On December 28th, we returned to Luton by train to carry out final firing practices at the Wardown and Galley Hill Ranges, and field

27

firing practice at Dunstable in appalling weather, when frost, snow and rain made accurate shooting perfectly impossible, and we were glad indeed to get back to Bocking on January 6th, 1915.

The rest of our time was spent in final training, mainly carried out at Gosfield Park and Abbot's Hall, and in preparations for going out, in which the inspection and completion of equipment of all kinds played a prominent part. This was not too easy a job for the young company or Section commanders, as the men by this time were up to all the "old soldier" tricks, and were very clever at making one article appear almost simultaneously in half-a-dozen different kits. Drill included a certain amount of new bayonet fighting and other exercises under Major A. C. Clarke, who had attended a course at Chelsea. Mules arrived in January and were objects of much interest; our miscellaneous transport vehicles were discarded and replaced by new ordnance pattern issues, to which were added two Lune Valley cookers, kindly presented by the ladies of Nottinghamshire. At the end of January the battalion had to be completely reorganised in order to come into line with the regular battalions: the old 8-company system was abolished, and the 1914 double company organisation introduced, entailing an immense amount of work and keeping us busy right up to the time of our departure. The situation was not helped by the absence of Major Fowler with eight subalterns and 407 recruits, who were away carrying out musketry classification practices at Luton from February 3rd to 20th.

Our chief relaxation at Bocking in the early part of 1915 was night searching for elusive spies, who were supposed to carry on lamp signalling; more often than not when these were tracked down they turned out to be innocent stable guards doing their nightly rounds. At other times we picketed the roads to hold up motor cars which were supposed to be acting as guides to Zeppelins, but it is doubtful whether either of these occupations did a great deal towards bringing about the more rapid conclusion of the war.

One also remembers the excitement caused by the first Boche aeroplane dropping bombs within a mile of the village, which we, of course, imagined had been dropped for our especial benefit. One of the scouts secured a "dud," which was the object of much interest to everyone, up to the divisional commander.

It was about this time that the first distinguishing patches were allotted to battalions. Our first was a square green patch worn behind the cap badge, undoubtedly very smart, and the envy of the other battalions in the brigade. When we got to France the officers of the battalion had to wear two short vertical green stripes at the top of the back of the jacket, to enable them to be picked out from behind, as all ranks were more or less similarly dressed and officers' swords were discarded. Later still these marks were worn by all ranks in the battalion, and the practice was continued up to the end of the war.

On February 15th, confidential orders were received that we were to proceed abroad at a very early date. Final preparations were put in hand, equipment, stores and clothing were issued to complete, and everything was made ready for a move.

On February 16th, Colonel Huskinson received notice of his appointment as commander of base details on lines of communication with Captain G. Clarke as his adjutant. Colonel Huskinson had been to a great extent responsible for the recruiting of the battalion to full strength before the war, and his keenness and enthusiasm throughout the difficult times of reorganisation and training during these first six months of the war, contributed largely to the high standard of morale and general efficiency reached in England. One and all were sorry to lose him, but we were glad indeed to find that Major Fowler was to succeed him in command of the battalion.

On February 19th, we had the honour of being inspected with the rest of the division by H.M. the King, at Hallingbury Place, near Bishop's Stortford.

Into the last few days was crowded an immense amount of work, for the final arrangements never seemed to finish, and changes took place right up to the last. We were made up to establishment in officers by the arrival of Lieutenants G. S. Heathcote and F. B. Lawson, and 2nd Lieutenants C. L. Hill and T. H. F. Adams, whilst large reinforcements from the 2/8th Battalion on February 22nd, brought us up to full strength, and when we left Bocking on February 25th, we were 31 officers and 996 other ranks. Second Lieutenant R. E. Hemingway was left behind with 100 men as the first reinforcement, and the orderly room was handed over to the care of Colonel-Sergeant Instructor F. Kieran. We left by two trains at 7.50 and 9.15 a.m., and by 4.0 p.m. had all detrained at Southampton Docks.

On the whole the battalion was well equipped, and physically everyone was fit. The chief drawback appeared to be that we had rather a large percentage of young and inexperienced officers and N.C.O.'s, but as all had much to learn of the kind of warfare actually going on, this was no great disadvantage. With so many late additions and the very recent reorganisation, few commanders had had the opportunity of getting to know their men. So far as training was concerned we had covered in a way the whole of what the books had to say, and were fairly well acquainted with ordinary methods of fighting. There was a tendency towards staleness at the moment, and it is doubtful whether prolongation of our training in England would have been beneficial. We felt somewhat ignorant of many practical points affecting trench warfare, into which the fighting on most of the western front had degenerated, and though we had received useful hints from Major Hume, who had been out, we yet had a great deal to learn; this we did in France, in the hard school of bitter experience. Whatever our shortcomings, we felt proud indeed to belong to the first complete Territorial Division to embark for France.

At this time the personnel of battalion and company headquarters were as follows:

Commanding Officer.—Lieut.-Colonel G. H. Fowler.
Second-in-Command.—Major A. C. Clarke.
Adjutant.—Capt. E. N. T. Collin.
Medical Officer.—Surg.-Captain H. Stallard.
Chaplain.—Rev. J. P. Hales.
Quarter-Master.—Capt. R. F. B. Hodgkinson.
Transport Officer.—Lieut. C. Davenport.
Machine-Gun Officer.—Lieut. A. F. O. Dobson.
A Company—(formerly E and F Companies).
    Capt. A. L. Ashwell; Lieuts. G. S. Heathcote, H. Kirby, and F. B. Lawson; 2nd Lieuts. J. V. Edge, and E. M. Hacking; Comp. Sergt.-Major A. Mabbott; Comp. Quar.-Master Sergt. E. Haywood.
B ,, (formerly B and H Companies).
    Capt. J. P. Becher; Capt. J. K. Lane; Lieut. J. W. Turner; 2nd Lieuts. W. H. Hollins, J. R. Eddison and B. W. Vann; Comp. Sergt.-Major W. Mounteney; Comp. Quar.-Master Sergt. S. C. L. Shelton.
C ,, (formerly C and D Companies).
    Capt. M. C. Martyn; Capt. H. G. Wright; Lieuts. H. B. S. Handford and R. H. Piggford; 2nd Lieuts. A. Hacking and T. H. F. Adams; Comp. Sergt.-Major E. Hopkinson; Comp. Quar.-Master Sergt. J. R. Dench.
D ,, (formerly A and G Companies).
    Capt. W. H. Allen; Lieuts. E. C. A. James and W. C. C. Weetman; 2nd Lieuts. J. M. Gray, C. L. Hill and J. S. C. Oates. Comp. Sergt-.Major F. Spencer; Comp. Quar.-Master Sergt. F. A. Pritchard.
Acting Regimental Sergt.-Major.—E. A. Westerman.
Regimental Quar.-Master Sergt.—D. Tomlin.

Armourer Quar.-Master Sergt.—R. A. G. Loughman.
Signalling Sergt.—W. Burton.
Machine-Gun Sergt.—F. Parker.
Transport Sergt.—C. Green.
Sergt. Drummer.—W. Clewes.
Provost Sergt.—G. Phillipson.
Sergt.-Cook.—S. Wiffen.
Pioneer Sergt.—J. Caddy.
Acting Sergt.-Tailor.—H. A. Huckerby.
Sergt.-Shoemaker.—G. H. Fletcher.
Orderly Room Sergt.—F. Torrance.
Orderly Room Sergt. (Base).—E. Kirkby.
Orderly Room Clerk.—Corpl. R. Harvey.
Non-Commissioned Officer i/c Stretcher Bearers.—Corpl.
　　R. F. Bescoby.
Medical Orderly.—Corpl. B. Sissons.

CHAPTER 2

France

February 25th, 1915—June 20th, 1915

As soon as the detrainment was completed, we proceeded on board the *Mount Temple*, with certain Royal Field Artillery details, the ship being under the command of Major Kent, R.F.A. At 6.30 p.m. we dropped down to Netley, imagining we were off, instead of which we anchored there for the night. The greater part of the next day, February 26th, was spent on board in physical and other exercises and inspections. Late in the afternoon, much to our surprise, orders were received that 21 officers and 763 other ranks were to disembark, presumably because it was not desirable for so many troops to cross on a slow going boat like the *Mount Temple*. Having left on board Major Clarke, Captain Ashwell, and Lieutenant Heathcote with two-and-a-half platoons of A Company, and Captains Hodgkinson and Davenport with the signal, transport and machine-gun sections, the remainder of us disembarked about 6.30 p.m., and proceeded to a rest camp about three miles outside Southampton. It was very disappointing to be split up, but there was nothing to be done but to make the best of it. We cannot say that our two days' stay at the rest camp was exactly enjoyable, for the camp was uncomfortable, and no passes were allowed to the town. We therefore fully appreciated the kindness of the ladies of the St. John Ambulance Association, who had huts near the camp, and gave us most excellent meals.

On February 28th, a further contingent of 101 men under Captain Becher embarked on the *Caledonian*, and later in the day the rest of us went on board a small Clyde pleasure steamer, the *King Edward*, where we were crowded beyond description. Neither party sailed, however, that day, and we spent the night on board. The next day those on the *King Edward* had to disembark once again! This took place early in the morning, and after a little wandering we ultimately obtained billets for the officers at the Central Hotel, and for the men at the Watt Memorial Hall.

In the end we embarked on the *King Edward* on the afternoon of March 2nd, and sailed the same night. There was so much to interest everyone until we got out to sea that we had little time in which to indulge sentimental feelings. That gliding down Southampton Water in silence broken only by the throbbing of the engines, with lights out, sentries posted, and in some cases machine-guns mounted, the sudden appearance out of the darkness from somewhere off the Isle of Wight of a destroyer to pilot us across the Channel, the challenge to the ship as to who we were, and the order to "carry on," the numberless rays of searchlights sweeping around on all sides—such was the start of our great expedition, precisely the same, no doubt, as that of most other troops who crossed during the war.

We had an excellent crossing and anchored off Havre early the following morning, disembarking about 7.30 a.m. The morning was spent amongst the hangars at the docks, drawing sheep-skin coats and other equipment. Here we were met by Major Clarke who reported that Captain Ashwell with two platoons had already proceeded up country, and that they had all had a very uncomfortable time at Havre, sleeping in trucks or wherever they could. They had been joined by M. Lacolle, who was to be attached to the battalion as Interpreter. After dinner we marched down to our entraining point, and were able to entrain more or less at leisure during the afternoon—our first experience of a French troop train. Later on we got accustomed to their ideas, but certainly for the men, and often for officers too, the French way is not quite in accordance with our own ideas, and we must confess it went very much against the grain to have to crowd 36 to 40 men in nothing more or less than a cattle truck. *Hommes* 40, *chevaux* 8, may be all right for the *chevaux*, but for the *hommes* we consider a revised number is required.

During these first few hours spent at Havre we learnt to appreciate the Y.M.C.A. huts, which supplied much excellent refreshment, and the officers will certainly not forget the delicious tea and cakes so generously provided by Mrs. Pitt.

We left for the north at 5.15 p.m. At Rouen a halt was made for the engine to take in water, and ourselves coffee and rum. The taste of the latter was new to most of us, but we liked it well enough to hope that we might make its acquaintance again. Early in the morning of March 4th, we had a short *halte repas* at Abbeville for breakfast, and continuing *via* Calais and St. Omer we eventually, about 1 p.m., after a 20 hours journey, detrained at Cassel, which if tradition does not lie, was the happy hunting ground of the good old Duke of York, who

Had ten thousand men,
He marched 'em up to the top of the hill,
And he marched 'em down again.

If the English Tommy of those days was anything like the modern "Old Bill" he probably had something pointed to say about the hill of Cassel, and was equally unappreciative of the magnificent view one got from its summit!

Captain Ashwell met us at the station and acted as our guide to the little village of Oudezeele, which we reached about 5 o'clock after a trying seven miles' march. The men were tired after their long, cramped journey; many wore new boots, whilst all were weighed down with enormous packs, which had been added to by the newly drawn sheep-skin coats. It was not surprising that under such conditions many fell out, and that most of us were thoroughly weary by the time we reached our destination. Ashwell and his party too, had not had a pleasant time. Strangers in a strange land without battalion, brigade or divisional headquarters—or any of the other luxuries which make life worth living—they had found existence rather precarious. Ashwell himself had walked 45 miles in three days in search of rations, so that our arrival with the transport was more than welcome.

We found our billets rather strange after the houses and cottages to which we had become accustomed in England, as they consisted mostly of scattered farms, several platoons and sometimes a whole company or more being billeted at one farm, generally in barns.

Captain Becher and his party arrived late the following day, having been kept three days on the *Caledonian*, and the battalion was once more complete. As the rest of the brigade had crossed before us and had already gone up for trench instruction, we were temporarily attached to the Lincoln and Leicester Brigade.

We spent a few days training at Oudezeele, including one or two route marches to get accustomed to the *pavé* roads, and Edge, as newly appointed sniping officer, gave a little special instruction in that branch of warfare. We had a visit from Major-General Stuart-Wortley, who discussed the training to be carried out, and our coming duties in the trenches. The weather was very cold, and a good deal of work was in the shape of lectures in billets, and the reading of various routine and other orders issued to troops on arrival.

It was during one of our route marches in this district, which took us through the little village of Wormhoudt, that we made our first acquaintance with French troops. Many of them were back resting in billets, and the warm welcome they gave us as we passed through the narrow streets of the village crowded with French *poilus*, the whole battalion whistling the *Marseillaise*, was an experience which will not be readily forgotten.

On March 9th, we marched with the Lincoln and Leicester Brigade *via* Cassel, Caestre (where General Smith-Dorrien saw us march past), and Strazeele to Merris, where we joined up with the rest of our brigade, back from their course of instruction in the trenches. Fortunately the fur coats which had caused us so much trouble on the last march were now carried for us by motor 'bus. At Merris we saw our first real signs of fighting, both the church and the hospice having been hit several times by shells, whilst there were isolated graves of both French and English scattered about the surrounding country. Here too, we saw our first fighting aeroplane (armed with one short French rifle), which had crashed just outside the village. It was also at Merris that we had our first experience of paying a company "in the field." Instructions on the subject had led us to believe that this was a complicated performance, but in practice it turned out to be quite easy. Company imprests were at a later date done away with and a battalion imprest instituted, which was much more convenient, as also was the very handy "Officer's Advance Book," which was introduced later. At first there seemed but little check on the money that was drawn, and field cashiers appeared to issue money to all and sundry on the flimsiest authority.

Preparations were being made about this time for a British offensive at Neuve Chapelle, and our brigade was attached temporarily to General Gough's 2nd Cavalry Division, with the object, if the attack succeeded, of breaking through in the region of the Bois du Biez. In order to be nearer the scene of operations we were moved from Merris at an hour's notice at noon on March 10th, and marched *via* Rouge Croix to Bac-St. Maur. This was a memorable experience, but later on we became accustomed to rapid movement, and the great concentration of troops which was necessary when fighting was imminent. Transport marched brigaded, and in passing through Sailly-sur-Lys in the darkness seemed to be so mixed up in the seething mass of men that we almost began to doubt if they would ever extricate themselves. Under the guiding hand and voice of Captain Davenport, however, our transport eventually got clear. During this operation "Davvy" evidently made a great impression on one soldier (a regular), by his forcible language, as the latter was heard to remark "There's a bloke what knows 'is job." Confusion was great in Bac-St. Maur too, for when we got there, the billets which we had been allotted were still occupied by Canadians. Eventually, we all got shelter of a kind, in probably the dirtiest and poorest billets we ever had either in France or Belgium. This was our first meeting with our Canadian friends, and we can hardly say we were impressed, though we all knew well what they were made of. We have specially vivid recollections of one Canadian sentry on duty at night opposite D Company's billet, evidently "well away," loosing off his rifle at intervals, apparently to let us know that he was "present and correct." One bullet was close enough to be unpleasant, and fetched a lump off the tree just outside the window. In this area we were nearer to the line than we had yet been, some of our guns firing from quite close to the village, and we found it an interesting experience to see for the first time an aeroplane being shelled.

We stood by for two days, ready to move at a moment's notice, hearing much of the noise of the battle. The attack, however, was not successful and the Bois du Biez plan, therefore, fell through. On March 13th, we got orders to move to fresh billets. We had to travel light as we were still regarded as a "flying column." Much superfluous kit was left behind, to be sent for later on, and the weird bundles left at the *estaminet* at Bac-St. Maur will not readily be forgotten. We marched that afternoon *via* Estaires to Neuf Berquin, where we had again to be content with rather crowded, if somewhat more comfortable billets than we had left.

One or two changes in personnel had already taken place. Captain Hodgkinson gave up the appointment of quarter-master owing to some technicalities, and for the moment acted as Censor. In this capacity he was obliged, to our great annoyance, to carry out the order to relieve us of our cameras, which were sent home,—no doubt on the whole a wise and necessary precaution. Captain Hodgkinson was succeeded as quarter-master by Lieutenant Torrance, who was destined, with a short break in 1918, to carry out the duties up to the end of the war. He performed them with much success, and in a way that only Torrance could. On his appointment as quarter master, the orderly room came under the charge of Corporal R. Harvey, who carried out his difficult task with the utmost devotion, without a break until the last man of the battalion was demobilised. Second Lieutenant G. W. Fosbery, who received his commission as we were about to cross to France, took over his platoon from Handford, who as signalling officer had enough other work to keep him busy.

We stayed at Neuf Berquin for ten days and did a considerable amount of useful training, but unfortunately at this time many men were sick, owing to the bad water, so that parades were somewhat small. In addition to continued route marches to keep feet in condition we practised formations for advancing through woods in the Bois d'Aval, open warfare attack under the watchful eye of General Gough, and several trench-to-trench attacks on the leap-frog principle, the first line capturing and holding the front trench, and other lines passing through them to attack the support trenches. We also began to practise making and throwing the old "jam-tin bomb," the beginning of the attack of "bomb fever," which unfortunately was to play such a prominent part in the warfare of the next two or three years, undoubtedly to the detriment of all sound training and tactics.

Arrangements had meanwhile been made for our initiation into the mysteries of real trench warfare, and with that object in view we were moved on March 24th, to Vieux Berquin, and on the 26th, across the frontier to Romarin in Belgium, being once more attached to the Lincoln and Leicester Brigade. Much to our regret the rum issue was stopped the next day!

We were attached for instruction to the 10th Infantry Brigade, 4th Division, and the programme arranged allowed each company to spend two nights in the trenches, with a break of 24 hours in billets. The battalions to which we were attached included the Royal Irish Rifles, 2nd Royal Dublin Fusiliers, Argyll and Sutherland Highlanders, 2nd Seaforth Highlanders, and 2nd Royal Warwicks, who held the trenches about Ploegsteert and opposite Messines.

The first night each officer and man studied the work of his counterpart in the battalion to which he was attached, and the second night platoons were allotted definite lengths of trench, for which they were held responsible. This first experience was not exactly full of incident, as on the whole we had a very quiet time, but for us, as for all others on their first visit to the line, many little incidents of everyday trench routine were novel and exciting. Recollection lingers on the long, slow tramp to the trenches, along corduroy tracks in thick darkness lighted up from time to time by Very lights from our own trenches and by the infinitely superior ones from the enemy (we recollect that some of us, faithful to our instructions, but slightly misguided, began ducking quite five miles behind the line when a flare went up), the constant order to keep closed up, the *whizz* of bullets, at every one of which we ducked instantly, the cracking of rifles, the 'dead cow' smell which afterwards became so painfully familiar, the arrival at the trenches and the posting of sentries. Later the cautious creeping over the parapet to look at the wire and at dawn stand-to, followed by the frizzling of bacon and the brewing of tea (in these days each side had a more or less respectable breakfast, evidenced by the columns of smoke that went up from the respective front line trenches directly after stand-down). Such incidents we feel sure were sufficiently novel at the time to impress themselves vividly on the memories of those whom a kindly fate has preserved to read these recollections.

Probably the most uncanny feeling some of us had was, when on starting from battalion headquarters for the trenches, we met a stretcher party carrying out one of our own men, Company Sergeant-Major Hopkinson, who had been wounded by a sniper, and was our first casualty. It was an experience that everyone had to go through, but it was not pleasant. Hopkinson and two men of D Company wounded by shell fire were our only casualties during our instructional tours. That we did not make a bad impression is attested by a letter written from an officer of the 2nd Seaforths, who says:

> I thought your officers and men most awfully keen, and I was immensely struck by the way your men came into the trench— no noise at all, and perfect discipline and quietness and keenness. They were awfully willing to act up to any small suggestions you made as to what they ought to do. They came in so much better than regulars, and I was genuinely filled with admiration for them. They were a splendid body of men.

It is, perhaps, needless to say that we on our part much appreciated the great kindness shown us by the units to which we were attached. Those of us who happened to be in or near Petit Douvre Farm during this attachment were much interested in finding some of the early drawings of Bairnsfather, as done for the *Bystander*. The interior walls of the farm were covered with his charcoal sketches, in some cases to the order of commanding officers who were to follow! It was at the same farm that Private Cottam, of D Company, acted as head butcher in the slaughter of an abandoned pig, causing a good deal of excitement before final despatch. Most of the men brought away with them "souveneers" of this first visit, none more unaccountable than the dud 77 mm. shell carried about in his pack for several days, by a sturdy sanitary man of A Company—in fact, until discovered by a rather alarmed company commander.

On March 31st, we left Romarin, and marched back to our old billets at Vieux Berquin, being met at Doulieu and escorted from there by the 6th Battalion band. Only one band had been allowed to come out with the brigade, and after some discussion that of the 6th Battalion was selected, and carried on up to the end of the war, virtually as a brigade band.

Orders were received on April 1st, for our division to take over its first portion of the British front in relief of the 28th Division, and on April 2nd we marched with the rest of the brigade *via* Bailleul to Locre, in Belgium. As few, if any of us, had ever studied Flemish, the language question in some of the villages of Flanders presented a little difficulty, but with his guiding principle of *tout-de-suite*, and the *tout*er the sweeter, the British Tommy never seemed to have any trouble in getting what he wanted. We were disposed to think sometimes that the Belgians did not look very kindly on us. Perhaps it was because in our early days we were rather inclined to take too much notice of the frequent reports we heard of supposed Belgian spies, and of Belgians being in communication by various means with the Boche on the other side of the lines. One well remembers the suggestion made from time to time that signalling was carried on by means of the windmill on Mont Rouge, or by the display of washing laid out to dry on the ground by Belgian housewives. At any rate we did find a house at Locre, where a number of pigeons were kept, a fact which aroused the suspicions of some of the officers of D Company, and in the same house were discovered quantities of British stores of all kinds, which must have been got from our troops in a not too straightforward manner. Some of the inhabitants, too, treated us with scant courtesy. It was here that the lady of the establishment removed the handle from the pump where Sergeant Markham's platoon was billeted, and not content with that went a step further, and for some reason best known to herself, gave him a cold douche when asleep one night. Some of us, on the other hand, were more fortunate in our billets, and all who went to the hospice can have nothing but the most pleasant recollections of the great kindness of the mother superior and other ladies. Padre Hales, who left us to be attached to brigade headquarters, when we crossed to France, was billeted there with our field ambulance, and we were allowed to go there for baths when out of the line, and always received much kindness and hospitality. Unfortunately during the German onslaught in 1918, this delightful place was completely destroyed. The bathing arrangements in general at this time were somewhat poor, the nearest military baths being at Bailleul, about four miles away, so that we were very delighted at receiving during our stay at Locre, from Miss Gilstrap, of Winthorpe, Newark, three galvanised iron baths, with boiler complete. With these and other local devices we were able to get the men bathed at their own billets, which was a great boon. Another similar consignment from Mrs. John Becher, unfortunately got lost in the post, but we trust was of benefit to some other unit.

THE AVENUE, KEMMEL, 1915

In the afternoon of Easter Eve, April 3rd, we attended a church parade, taken by the bishop of London, of which many of us have bitter recollections, as owing to a mistake in divisional orders, we were rigged out in full marching order. Further, as it was a damp and windy day, few of us could hear a word of the address, and all wanted to get as much sleep as possible in view of the great adventure before us. The same night, which turned out to be miserably wet, we left Locre, to take over the trench sector in front of Kemmel held by the 1st Devons. Company commanders had already been in the trenches for 24 hours to get the lie of the land, and they, together with the guides of the Devons, met us at the appointed rendezvous, the celebrated band stand at Kemmel. There were, of course, no lights; rations and trench fuel, which had been taken up by the transport, were issued in sandbags, and water in petrol tins, and each platoon was then led off by itself. When one looks back on trench reliefs, one is inclined to wonder how on some occasions they were carried out at all, the possibilities of going wrong seemed so great. In the present case, however, nothing untoward happened, and we set off by our various routes to the front line, passing such favourite spots as the Sahara Desert (the final resting place of every bullet fired within a radius of five miles, or so it seemed), the Willows, Irish Farm or The Orchard, and into the G and H trenches. In our heavy greatcoats and with full packs, which we continued religiously to carry for many months for no apparent reason, the journey was not pleasant, and we were not sorry to get into the trenches, where the relief was completed about 11 p.m. C Company being mainly composed of miners and under the command of a mining engineer, were put in the right sector where was our only mine, much to the relief of, at least, one company commander, who had mental visions of a mine as a large black cavern, where hand-to-hand fighting went on incessantly! A Company had the centre and D Company the left, B Company occupying the two supporting points and billets in Kemmel village. Battalion headquarters were at the doctor's house in Kemmel, and the transport and quarter-master's stores remained at Locre.

There was practically only one trench line at this time, and this, like most of the trenches in Belgium and the low lying districts, was a line of breastworks with very little wire in front, and only one or two small supporting points. The opposing front lines varied from 25 to about 300 yards apart, being closest at Peckham Corner, on the right. Shelters were built mostly of timber and corrugated iron, strengthened with sandbags, and were generally in the *parados* of the trench.

Easter day—our first day holding a bit of line on our own—was fairly quiet, except for a little shelling of D Company on the left during the afternoon. On the right, some men of C Company sang hymns, and the enemy made overtures for a truce by showing a white flag. About 40 of them appeared on the parapet, and a brisk conversation ensued for several minutes across No Man's Land. A somewhat unflattering remark from one of the enemy who had a wonderful knowledge of forcible English, ended the armistice rather hurriedly.

On most nights during these early days of the war, each side had its turn at five or ten rounds "rapid" to relieve the monotony of things. In this we were on equal terms with the enemy, but during the day we were hopelessly outclassed owing to the great shortage of periscopes, and the lack of telescopic rifles and well constructed loophole plates, of all of which the Hun seemed to have an abundant supply. It was long before we got anything like adequate numbers of these very necessary trench requisites. It was not surprising, therefore, that for some time the Boche snipers had the upper hand and could do almost what they liked. Their shooting was extremely accurate, and as the trenches were enfiladed on all sides, and there was in many cases little *parados*, we soon had casualties, most of which were sentries shot through the head. Our first fatal casualty was Private Hyde, of A Company, shot in this way on April 6th. We were also short and entirely inexperienced in the use of rifle grenades and trench mortars, with which the enemy made very good practice. A large trench mortar certainly did find its way up to the trenches by some means one day, and provided considerable amusement to our men. It is reported to have dropped its first bomb into the enemy trench, and its second into our own—its erratic behaviour ultimately making it no doubt more annoying to ourselves than to the enemy. Lieutenants A. Hacking and Hollins were the pioneers in the use of rifle grenades, with which they eventually did good work at Peckham Corner.

After a tour of four days which were most uncomfortable owing to constant rain, we returned to Locre. The system of four days in trenches and four in billets, taking turns with the 6th Battalion, continued for some time with little variation. When out of the line we, of course, had to find those never-to-be-forgotten working parties, which had become part of the normal trench warfare system. Having had a hard four days in the trenches, it was never a pleasant duty to have to march up three or four miles on one or perhaps two nights out of our few days' rest, to do a job for the Royal Engineers or some other specialists in the trenches. Otherwise, our stays at Locre were fairly pleasant. There were no great attractions, but we had enough to do as a rule in general training and cleaning, and the country round about was extremely pleasant, either for walking or riding. Perhaps the greatest excitement was to go down to Bailleul to shop and call on "Tina." Such luxuries as canteens for supplying the wants of the inner man were quite unknown in these early days, when we had to rely mainly on parcels from home or purchases in the local towns.

Work in the trenches consisted mainly of strengthening or rebuilding the parapet and *parados*, and in putting out barbed wire defences. As a rule, we wanted far more sandbags than were ever forthcoming, but in these days they were used indiscriminately, and in consequence many very weak structures were built, which could not possibly stand without support through a single wet season. The barbed wire defences were very poor, and as soon as we got into the way of doing it much time was spent in that not too pleasant work, for Boche snipers did execution by night as well as by day, and made themselves very objectionable. Our entanglements consisted mainly of "knife-rests"— wooden frames strung with barbed wire. These were made by the men in the brigade workshop at Kemmel, run by Major Wordsworth, the staff captain, to which each battalion contributed a quota of pioneers and trade specialists. One officer learnt a very practical lesson in their use from the enemy. He had some carefully placed in position one night, where he thought his wire particularly weak, but his spirits fell to zero the following morning, when on looking over the top he saw his precious knife-rests in position guarding the Boche trenches opposite! From that time onwards knife-rests were securely fastened to each other and to the ground. Our brigade (hereafter known as the 139th Infantry Brigade) had a good reputation for trench work, and the digging element was used to great advantage by the 6th Battalion commencing what was one of the first long communication trenches dug on the British front. It extended from the front line nearly back to Kemmel and was for ever known as the "*Via* Gellia." In its later stages it was worked on by ourselves. This trench was a great convenience, as it enabled reliefs to be carried out much more securely by avoiding going over the open, and permitted of visits of inspection to be made by daylight, and the wounded to be carried back to the dressing station at Kemmel. In the early days they remained in the trenches until it was dark enough for the journey to be made over the top.

On April 22nd, we experienced a little of the backwash of the first Hun gas attack against the French and Canadians in the Ypres Salient a few miles north of us. During most of the time we had been in this area there had been considerable activity in that quarter, and the shelling and burning of Ypres could be plainly seen from the Kemmel trenches. This attack was the beginning of the second battle of Ypres. The only effect on ourselves of the gas used on this occasion, was to make our eyes smart and a few men sick. It did, however, cause a commotion on all sides, and with unaccustomed speed, the first consignment of respirators was sent out to us—pieces of gauze which had to be filled with tea-leaves, damped, and fastened round the mouth in the event of attack. These were improved from time to time, and a little later we got a gas-proof smoke helmet—the earliest form known as "P," and the later as "P.H." Vermorel sprayers were also provided in due course, and some solution for spraying the trenches to clear them of gas. Bells and gongs formed of shell cartridge cases or pieces of iron were also hung in the trenches to be sounded by the sentry if any sign of cloud gas was seen. There was perhaps a natural tendency to imagine gas when there was none, and an official report of gas by C Company on the night of May 8th, was found to be due to the proximity of a dead cow.

April 24th witnessed our first serious bombardment. We had already had several somewhat severe baptisms, but they were trifling in comparison. About 6 p.m., after an exceptionally quiet day, and just before we were to be relieved, the enemy began an organised trench mortar bombardment of G1 and 2, occupied by platoons of C and D Companies, and H 4 held by Lieutenant Vann and his platoon of B Company. It lasted for about an hour, and made large breaches in the parapet of G1 and 2, and practically demolished the whole of H4, a small isolated trench on the extreme left, opposite Petit Bois. Both these trenches were completely enfiladed by the Boche, so that their shooting was extremely accurate. It was thought at one time that the enemy might attempt a raid on G1 and 2, but this did not develop. A machine gun team consisting of Lance-Corporal Sharrock and Privates Hopewell and Davis, which was posted in G1, behaved most coolly, and Sergeant A. Phillipson, of D Company, did very gallant work in the same trench under heavy fire with Privates Coombes and Durand, all in a more or less dazed condition, helping to dig out the wounded. On the left Vann and his platoon had a very bad time. Whilst he was digging out wounded a bomb fell close by, killing four and burying three others, and blowing Vann himself several yards across the open at the back of the trench, and practically wiping out the garrison. Major Becher brought up reinforcements and helped Vann to get the position made good, and great assistance was given by 2nd Lieutenant Hollins and Lance-Corporal Humberstone. Privates F. Boothby and A. Gleaden of B Company also did excellent work, helping to dig out and dress the wounded, most of the time in full view of the enemy, not more than 70 yards away. The 2nd Royal Scots on our immediate left, also gave us valuable assistance. Our total casualties during the hour's bombardment were 14 men killed and two officers (Vann and Gray), and 14 men wounded. When we were back at Locre after this tour, General Shipley spoke to the battalion on parade and thanked them for the good work done, especially congratulating Vann, and on the following day the general officer commanding our division also congratulated the battalion on its behaviour under fire.

Several changes took place during April, owing to casualties. Captain Allen went down sick on April 6th, and Lieutenant James took over the command of D Company until the 14th, when Captain Hodgkinson was appointed. He, however, also had a short stay there, for on April 22nd, when in an excess of zeal to see what was going on opposite G1, where some suspicious work was reported, he apparently thought he could sufficiently camouflage himself behind a pair of field glasses to gaze over the top of the parapet, the almost immediate result was a bullet which just grazed his head, and he, too, had to leave us. D Company then came under Captain Lane. Second Lieutenant Eddison, our first fatal officer casualty, was killed on April 21st, being hit by a bullet whilst out wiring, and though help was instantly rendered by Drummers Newton and Robb, who pulled him out of the shell-hole of water, into which he had fallen, and carried him into the trench, he died in a few minutes. Four officers were down for a short time with measles, including Captain Martyn, who unfortunately was invalided to England, and was succeeded in command of C Company, by Captain H. G. Wright. Martyn served later in Ireland and France, as second-in-command of the 2/8th Battalion and in command of the 2/7th Battalion, and won the D.S.O. and M.C. Lieutenant Lawson got a shell wound in the shoulder and had to leave, and 2nd Lieutenants Gray and Vann also had to be in hospital for a short time from what was later known as "shell-shock." A great loss, too, was Sergeant Wilmore, a very gallant soldier, who was sniped one day when outside his trench.

May found us beginning to feel our feet. The commanding officer had talks with officers as to a more aggressive attitude being taken up; we had a lecture from Major Howard, R.E., at Kemmel as to the construction of an invisible loophole, low down in the parapet, and so built as to afford a good field of fire and permit of our replying better to the Hun snipers. Sergeant-Drummer Clewes also got into action with his telescopic rifle from sniping posts cunningly placed behind the front line, the only possible position from which really successful sniping could be done, and was not long in getting quite a good "bag." Shortly afterwards he was put in charge of the newly-formed brigade sniping section. A trench mortar was actually got into use, and did a certain amount of damage to the Boche trenches, but naturally produced considerable retaliation. Further efforts to fire rifle grenades met with some success, whilst a Gamage catapult introduced to throw bombs provided, at any rate, a little amusement. In patrolling considerable progress was made. Second Lieutenant A. Hacking did some very daring work at Peckham Corner, and near Petit Bois; 2nd Lieutenant Hollins and Lance-Corporals Heath and G. Gadd of B Company made splendid reconnaissances of the enemy's wire; and 2nd Lieutenant Edge, who was always to the fore in wiring, no matter how bright the night, carried out a daring daylight reconnaissance, the first attempted in the battalion, getting nearly up to the German front line in company with Private C. E. Bryan, of A Company. Private W. O'Brien, of the same company, was another who knew no danger; in fact, at night it was difficult to keep these two men in the trench at all. Daring patrols were also carried out by 2nd Lieutenant Vann, Sergeant Pickering and Lance-Corporal Humberstone. Perhaps the most successful was a fighting patrol, which went out on the night of May 9-10th under 2nd Lieutenant Oates, with the object of rounding up a Hun patrol. Oates, who had a party of six men with him, went forward with Private Nicholson, leaving the remainder behind, to within about 50 yards of the German wire. On their way back they ran into a Boche patrol. Oates promptly shot one man, Nicholson bayoneted another, whilst two others who were wounded got away. Oates and his party got back safely.

On May 14th, we carried out one of those little manoeuvres which may have been of immense importance, but appeared to us at the moment to be so much waste of time, trouble and energy. Instead of proceeding to the trenches that night according to programme, we got sudden orders to embus for Hill 60, in the Ypres Salient, to dig there under Royal Engineers' supervision for the 5th Division. The net result was that of the 600 who went, 400 dug for one-and-a-half hours, and 200 for three-quarters-of-an-hour, after which the party returned to Locre in the 'buses. The idea, doubtless, was a good one, as it was necessary to dig more trenches where part of our line had given way during the recent fighting, but the organisation of the work seemed to leave a good deal to be desired. It was the remnants of a Canadian battalion returning from this fighting in the salient shortly after midnight on one occasion, whilst we were back at Locre, which made us think we must have had more than an ordinary nightmare, for we awoke with a start to hear the strains of a brass band coming along the *pavé*,—at 1 a.m. such a proceeding seemed decidedly strange. It was not long, however, before we found that all was well, and that it was our own brigade band playing the Canadians through the village. This was evidently appreciated by them, for one of their number in a letter to the *Daily Telegraph*, after describing the magic effect of the music on his men, concludes with the remark:

The Canadians will remember how the band of the Sherwood Foresters played them through the darkness at midnight out of 'Bloody Ypres.'

About the middle of May we began reliefs with the 7th Battalion, and our sector was extended slightly left to include some of the J trenches opposite Petit Bois. An interesting entry in the war diary is that May 16th, the day following relief, was the first day absolutely free from casualties since we took over our portion of the line. This, however, must have been an exceptional day, for bad luck so far as casualties went pursued us with great regularity. Captain Lane was badly wounded on May 26th, when out wiring, and the command of D Company then passed to Lieutenant James. Captain H. G. Wright, to the great regret of his friends in all ranks was killed on June 6th, being shot, through the double loophole plate from which he was firing, and was succeeded in command of C Company by Captain G. S. Heathcote. Lieutenants Kirby and Weetman and 2nd Lieutenant Fosbery were wounded in May, and 2nd Lieutenant Oates early in June, and all had to leave the battalion. Captain Ashwell and 2nd Lieutenant Edge were also slightly wounded. Our only reinforcement officers were 2nd Lieutenants N. L. Hindley and G. G. Elliott. Company Sergeant-Major Mabbott, of A Company, was invalided to the base, and was succeeded by Company Quarter-Master Sergeant Haywood, Sergeant G. W. Godfrey being promoted Company Quarter-Master Sergeant in his place. Company Sergeant-Major Mounteney, B Company, was invalided to England and Sergeant Chappell was appointed company sergeant-major of that company. Sergeant J. A. Green was appointed company sergeant-major of C Company in place of Company Sergeant-Major Hopkinson wounded, and Sergeant T. Powell became company sergeant-major of D Company after Company Sergeant-Major Spencer left, also wounded. The latter obtained a commission some time later, only to be killed in France when doing excellent work in command of a company of another battalion of the Regiment. A change had also taken place in the brigade staff, Major E. M. Morris, the brigade major, who had worked so strenuously all through our period of training in England, and done so much to help us in learning our job in France, having left on June 1st, to take command of the 2nd Royal Irish Rifles. He was succeeded by Major W. G. Neilson, D.S.O., of the Argyll and Sutherland Highlanders.

Early in June we moved still further left and took over more of the J and K trenches, with the reserve company at Siege Farm, and battalion headquarters at Rossignol Farm. Our numbers at this time were swelled by the presence of a company of the 8th King's Royal Rifle Corps who were attached for instruction—the first of Kitchener's Army that we had seen.

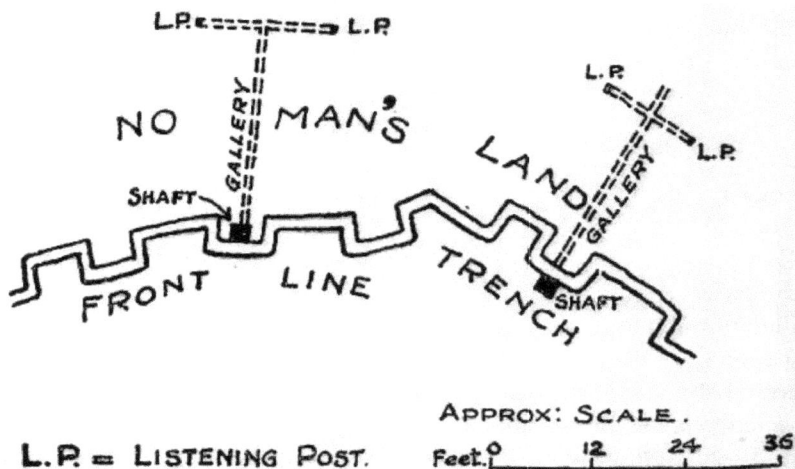

L.P. = LISTENING POST.

APPROX: SCALE.

SKETCH SHOWING ARRANGEMENT OF MINE GALLERIES

Our severest handling in the Kemmel area occurred on the last day of our last tour there, and was begun by the blowing of enemy mines, a form of warfare which had already developed considerably at various points along the battle front. Tunnelling companies of the Royal Engineers had been formed, but their numbers were not sufficient to cope with all the work, and in order to help them mining sections were formed in some of the infantry brigades as well. From the miners of the 139th Brigade, it was not difficult to select suitable men for this purpose, and towards the end of May, a small party was taken from the battalion to join the brigade mining section, which was put under the command of Captain Piggford. Included in the party were Corporals Boot and Attenborough, both of whom later received decorations for gallantry in underground work. These brigade sections were normally used for defensive mining only—broadly to prevent the enemy blowing up our trenches. The Royal Engineers' tunnelling companies on the other hand, were employed for offensive work in blowing up the enemy. Where mining was feared, sentries in the front line had to report at once if any suspicious sounds were heard, which might indicate that the enemy were mining in the neighbourhood, in order that protective measures might be taken. The J trenches, which varied from 30 to 70 yards away from those of the Boche, were mostly built on water-logged ground, where to sink shafts and drive galleries was not an easy task. Nevertheless, for some time signs and sounds had been reported which seemed to indicate that mining on the part of the enemy was going on in this very region. Attempts had, therefore, been made by us to sink shafts and take counter measures, but these had proved unavailing owing to the bad nature of the ground. The enemy, however, succeeded where we failed, and on June 15th, exploded three mines, one of which blew up a portion of J3 Right. This took place at 9.10 p.m., when the 7th Battalion were just beginning to arrive to relieve us. At the same time a terrific fire was opened with artillery, trench mortars, rifle grenades, machine guns and rifles, and for over an hour an incessant cannonade was kept up on our front line, support company and battalion dump. Telephone wires were broken—an occurrence looked on later with less anxiety as it happened so often, and we had no S.O.S. signal; pigeon service, which had been established in the trenches just before this time, was, of course, of no avail for night work, and battalion headquarters were out of communication with the trenches except by runner. Our reply to the bombardment was almost negligible, and whatever the politicians and their statistics may prove, we know that our supply of gun ammunition at this time was totally inadequate. Some of the enemy got into the mine crater, but were driven out by C Company at the point of the bayonet. Private J. Sharman, of B Company, who was practically the only man left in the trench when the enemy tried to occupy it, shot one and drove off another, both of them having attacked him at the same time. He was hit on the leg by a dud bomb, and got a bullet through his haversack. Excellent work was also done by Corporal Humberstone in reorganising the garrison, and by Lance-Corporal Templeman and Private Tongue in repairing telephone wires. Eventually things quietened down, and when the relief was complete, we returned to Locre for a few days' well-earned rest. Our casualties were unfortunately heavy, and included two excellent officers, Eric Dobson and Humphrey Hollins, also Corporal Wilcox and eight men killed, and 29 wounded, whilst the 6th King's Own Yorkshire Light Infantry, some of whom were in the trenches with us for instruction, also lost several men.

This was one of the earliest raids that ever took place, and was planned doubtless to inflict casualties and secure prisoners, but not to capture trenches. One man of D Company is reported to have blamed this affair for the loss of a pair of boots, as he assured his platoon com-

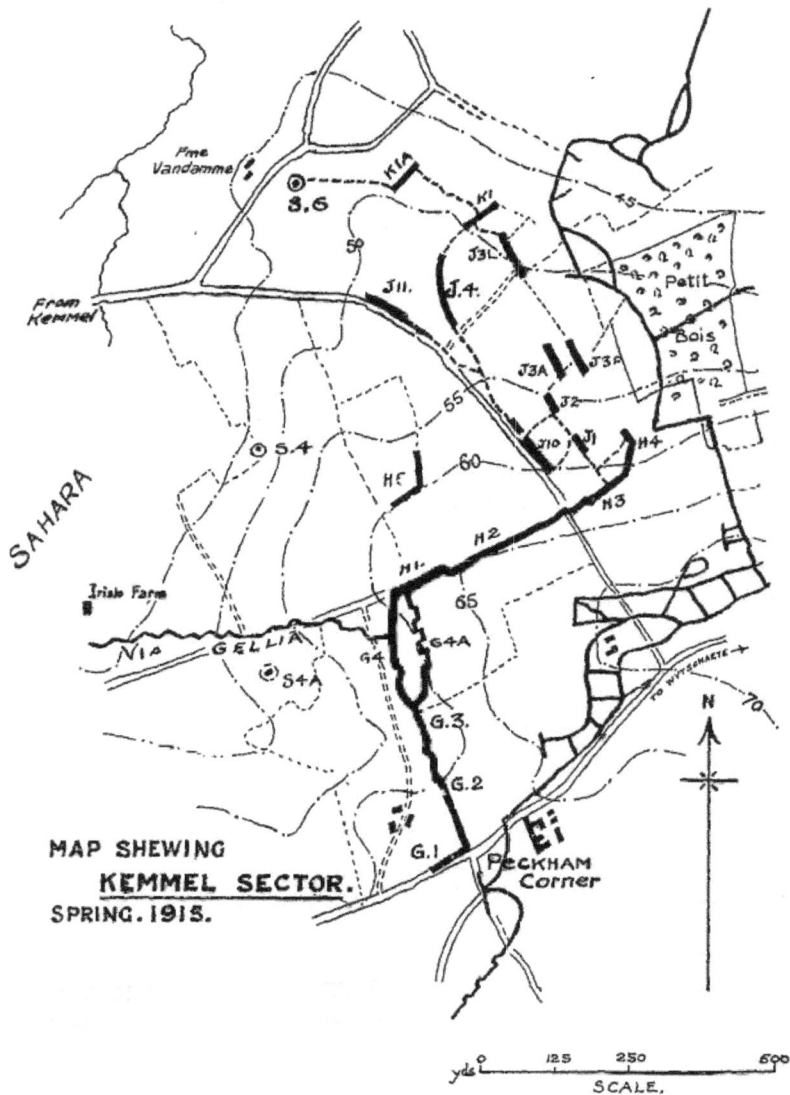

MAP SHEWING
KEMMEL SECTOR.
SPRING. 1915.

yds 0   125   250   500
              SCALE.

mander at a kit inspection a little later "that they were lost when that
there mine at Kemmel went up!" As no man had more than one pair
at a time the platoon commander scratched his head.

Thus ended our stay in the Kemmel sector, which was taken over
by the 50th (Northumbrian) Division. We were now beginning to
feel quite old hands, but our experience had been dearly bought. We
had lost heavily and were sadly in need of a draft, for to balance our

total casualties in other ranks of 49 killed or died of wounds, and 120 wounded, we had so far received only 20 reinforcements.

The corps paid a tribute to the work performed by the brigade during our stay at Kemmel. Far more valuable, however, were our first experiences of trench warfare. The meaning and importance of responsibility and discipline were for the first time really impressed upon the minds of officers and men alike. Gradually, if imperceptibly, they had learnt something of what would be required of them in the times of fighting ahead.

Sometimes one is tempted to compare conditions at Kemmel with trench routine three years later. In the Kemmel days the platoon commander lived with his platoon, and seldom even visited his company headquarters and he undoubtedly acquired an intimate knowledge of every man of his platoon, which was never equalled in later days. This further bred a sense of responsibility and initiative which was all to the good at a time when comfort, safety and enterprise depended so largely on individual initiative. At the same time it must not be forgotten that in later days officers and men alike were called upon to undertake more patrols and raids, and had to suffer far heavier and more incessant shelling and trench-mortaring than was our general experience at Kemmel.

As a school of instruction our time at Kemmel undoubtedly provided a very valuable lesson not only to officers, N.C.O.'s and men of the battalion, but to officers of the brigade and divisional staffs, whose experience of the new form of warfare could hardly have been learnt under better conditions than those which obtained during our first two months of trench routine.

CHAPTER 3

The Salient
June 20th, 1915—October 1st, 1915

The Canadian's description of it as "Bloody Ypres," referring doubtless to the salient in general, was very apt, and will be endorsed by all who ever had the misfortune to sample it at any period of the war. We have never met anyone who boasted of having found a "cushy spot" in it, and so far as we ourselves were concerned, the three months spent in the salient were very nearly, if not quite, the hardest months of the war.

Leaving Locre on the evening of June 20th, we marched with the rest of the brigade to the Ouderdom Huts on the Reninghelst-Vlamertinghe road. These were the first "huts" ever occupied by the battalion; they were absolutely exposed to view, the surroundings being open ploughed fields, and when the Boche "Sausage" went up "Silent Percy," a German long-range gun, warned anyone walking about that movement must cease. There were, however, deep shelter trenches round the huts, which afforded good protection, and we escaped without casualties, though the transport having had a few shells in the horse lines, deemed it wise to move back a little. We left there on June 23rd, and marching *via* Kruistraat and Zillebeke proceeded to Sanctuary Wood, where we relieved the 5th East Yorkshires in trenches 7 to 12. These trenches were good, being both narrow and deep. There was a good deal of liveliness on both sides, and things were anything but pleasant in the region of a wood. whose title was something of a misnomer. The transport too, had many good runs for their money when bringing up rations and stores. The congestion on the road each night was intense. Only one bridge, 14, over the Ypres-Comines canal was available for the transport of all units occupying the centre of the salient, and the journey from the transport lines to the dump and back, took something approaching seven hours. We were not particularly envious of their job here on many occasions, though never once did they fail to get supplies up to the dump. This was at the south-west corner of Sanctuary Wood, and a very unhealthy spot, where we were lucky indeed in not getting very heavy casualties. There was hardly any water fit for drinking in the front area, so that one of the water carts had to be brought up full every night and left in the shelter of the wood, and the empty one taken back.

Rain made the trenches very uncomfortable, and we had plenty to do in keeping them in order, and in building shelters, of which we were very short. These consisted for the most part of two or more waterproof sheets laced together, and held in position across the trench, by stones placed on the ends on the parapet and *parados*. Little was done by us in the way of active operations during our first tour, except a certain amount of patrolling, in which 2nd Lieutenant Adams and Private Needham were the leading lights, and got some useful information. A Company had rather a bad time, suffering over 20 casualties from *whizz-bangs* (77 mm. shells) and salvoes of 5.9's.

We were relieved on the night of June 29/30th, after a seven days' tour, by the 5th Lincolns, and moved back to bivouacs at a charming camp near Poperinghe, where we spent 12 of the most enjoyable days we ever had in France. The weather was glorious, and we made the most of it. We were spared strenuous work as far as possible on the very hot days, but carried out much useful training of a general kind, and reorganised and refitted all the units in the battalion. Two new officers, 2nd Lieutenants R. E. Hemingway, and E. S. Strachan joined us, the former eventually succeeding Lieutenant A. Hacking, who had just been appointed our first battalion grenade officer. A draft of 69 men also arrived, together with 11 rejoined men,—a most acceptable addition to our numbers. Several quite interesting cricket matches were played, the last of which, officers v. N.C.O's., was won by the officers. We managed one concert, which was given entirely by our own artistes, and went off very successfully. Poperinghe was quite close, and though possessing no great attraction, yet it was a change to walk or if possible get a horse for the afternoon and ride over there sometimes to see what was going on, and call on our little friend "Ginger" at the café, and do any shopping that was wanted. Here for the first time we encountered a divisional troupe, and enjoyed many a pleasant evening with the 6th Division "Fancies," with their Belgian artistes "Vaseline" and "Glycerine." But perhaps the greatest source of pleasure to all ranks now, was that great institution "leave" which had just been started. True it was but four days, and for an extremely small number, but it was something after all, and encouraged those who were not lucky enough to have it at the moment, that their turn would eventually come to get out of the war for a brief space, and return to their families at home. Captain Ashwell left us whilst we were here to take charge of reinforcements at St. Omer. During his absence of five or six weeks A Company was commanded by Lieutenant J.V. Edge.

We left camp with much regret on the afternoon of July 11th, and proceeding *via* Kruistraat, where a halt was made for tea, at the White Château, we eventually took over trenches B 2, 3, 4, 7 and 8, in the Hooge sector, from the North Staffords. The trenches here were close together, at some points not more than 25 yards apart. This nearness necessitated in some cases the erection of small-mesh wire netting to prevent the enemy throwing hand-grenades into our trenches. Mining was carried on unceasingly, and with both sides displaying abnormal activity with every kind of war machine invented, life was not at all pleasant. Possibly we had the greatest dislike for the rifle grenades which the Hun was in the habit of showering over on every possible occasion, but his shelling of the whole of our sector, which he carried out with great regularity, was extremely uncomfortable, and casualties mounted rapidly. To the more normal means of trying to wear down the enemy, we were now able to add fixed rifles and rifle batteries. These were laid on definite targets, and fired according to a time table specially arranged, and we hope had the effect desired. Sergeant-Drummer Clewes too, in charge of the brigade sniping section, was always worrying the Huns on every possible occasion, and made some splendid bags. Work in the trenches was of a more or less normal kind, consisting chiefly of strengthening fire and support trenches and putting out wire, not forgetting the never-ending efforts to drain away the water. Good patrols were carried out by Lieutenant James and Corporal Hotson.

After a heavy tour of 12 days we were relieved on July 23rd, by the 7th Battalion, and marched back to bivouacs near Ouderdom, a long trek, the last company not getting there until 7 a.m. the following morning. We were shelled out of this camp almost immediately, doubtless because a staff officer anxious for the comfort of the officers had had four beautiful white tents put up. Unfortunately they had been pitched on the eastern slope of the field in full view of the Sausage already mentioned, and Silent Percy soon got busy! On July 25th, we took over another field near Busseboom, where we were left in peace, so far as the Hun was concerned, though as the field had just previously been used by gunners for horse lines we had in other ways quite a lively time. Here we were joined by 2nd Lieutenant Everard Handford and an excellent draft from the 2/8th Battalion.

We had little time during this six days' rest to do more than the usual refitting and cleaning, as large fatigue parties were required on two days for divisional work. Bathing was an easier matter, as we were now able to use the new divisional baths at "Pop." So far as the washing of clothing was concerned, the men did their own, laundries being very few and far between.

We had now in front of us what turned out to be the longest and most trying of all the battalion's experiences in the trenches, for after relieving the 7th Battalion in trenches B 3, 4, 7, and 8 at Sanctuary Wood on the night of July 29/30th, we did not get out for 19 days.

Colonel Fowler at this time was on leave, whilst Major A. C. Clarke was unfit, and a little later had to return to England. Major Becher, who succeeded him as second-in-command was, therefore, in temporary command of the battalion. Much to our regret our old friend "Doc" Stallard had also just left us for a tour of home duty. Well had he stuck it all through, but he was beginning to feel the strain of his strenuous duties, which were now taken over by Surgeon-Lieutenant C. B. Johnstone. The latter had a memorable journey to join the battalion, which was then in the line, riding up on the front of the horse ambulance that used to go nightly to Maple Copse to evacuate the previous twenty-four hours' wounded. The road was very rough and mostly shell holes full of water, and he had a decidedly rough passage. Other arrivals about this time included three new subalterns, Lieutenant C. M. Houfton, and 2nd Lieutenants R. V. Harvey and A. H. Date, whose first experience of trench warfare was to be rather more exciting than the average! Company Sergeant-Major J. A. Green was temporarily acting as regimental sergeant-major in place of Sergeant-Major Westerman, who had just left for England.

The trench system taken over ran partly on the outskirts of Sanctuary Wood, and partly through the wood itself, which in those days was most picturesque, with delightful wild flowers and thick undergrowth. The right was held by B Company (Lieutenant J. W. Turner) and C Company (Captain G. S. Heathcote) and the left by D Company (Lieutenant E. C. A. James), whilst A Company (Lieutenant J. V. Edge) were in reserve. By a very happy coincidence, we had with us A Company of the 10th Sherwood Foresters, sent into the line for the first time for instruction. Captain G. P. Goodall, subsequently killed at St. Eloi, was in charge of this company, amongst whom our men found many friends.

We occupied the left of the 46th Divisional sector, with the 5th Battalion on our right, the 7th Battalion in immediate support in Maple Copse, and the 6th Battalion in brigade reserve.

The 14th Division, which had only been in France a few weeks, and had been with us for instruction at Kemmel, had recently taken over the sector on our left, where there had been much fighting during the past few weeks for the possession of Hooge, which centred about the stables and wall running near the *château*. It was there that in our last tour we had seen a brilliant assault by the Gordons and Middlesex, after a terrific mine explosion.

At 3.30 a.m. on July 30th, immediately after stand-down, and within a few hours of our arrival in the trenches, on a perfect summer morning, the whole of the wood was suddenly surrounded by a ring of fire, while at the same time a heavy bombardment was opened, concentrating apparently on the trenches around Hooge crater. Under cover of this bombardment, and behind *flammenwerfer*, the enemy attacked the point of the salient held by C Company, at the same time throwing the greater weight of his forces against the Hooge sector occupied by units of the 14th Division. The latter, who like ourselves had only come into the line the night before, were undoubtedly surprised by the sudden attack, and by this first use of *flammenwerfer*. Their men, dead tired, had just got down to sleep, and the rapidity of the enemy attack left little opportunity for organising successful defence.

The result was that the enemy succeeded at once in gaining the whole of the front and support trenches on our left, pushing forward into the north end of the wood, and threatening to cut off the whole of the salient, and leaving the trenches held by D Company in imminent danger of being turned from the rear.

The first attack on the point of the salient was driven off by rifle and machine gun fire. Here Private Grantham displayed conspicuous gallantry in remaining at his post, in spite of being surrounded by flames, and killing several of the enemy at close quarters. Very few of the enemy succeeded in getting into our lines, though for a short space of time there was a dangerous gap on the left of C Company, which was filled up by the presence of mind of 2nd Lieutenant Hindley and Seargeants Sheppard and Smith, and a platoon of B Company, one of whom, Private Tyne, did particularly fine execution by throwing back unexploded enemy bombs. This platoon lined the parapet, and by opening rapid fire prevented the attack from developing. Unfortunately, an enemy machine gun traversed the parapet, killing many of the men of this gallant platoon, until a bomb thrown a prodigious distance by Sergeant G. F. Foster appears to have fallen on the top of it, evidently knocking it out, and by the volume of smoke produced wrecking a *flammenwerfer*. Several of the enemy were seen to be killed or wounded by this lucky bomb.

Further attacks by the enemy on the point of the salient were made during the day, and a more serious one early next morning, but they were readily driven off with loss. We should like here to pay a tribute to the magnificent courage and coolness of the men of the 10th Battalion, which contributed very largely to the entire defeat of the enemy's attack on this front.

Meanwhile the position on the left was uncertain and very alarming, and Sergeant A. Phillipson in particular, in command of the left platoon, No. 13, had a most anxious and trying time. Elements of the 14th Division straggled from the left with stories of the German advance. These accounts might easily have demoralised our battalion but for the magnificent example of Lieutenant James, his second-in-command, 2nd Lieutenant Vann and Sergeant A. Phillipson, and the coolness and courage of every man of D Company. The situation on this flank was serious indeed. All the trenches on the left had been captured, and the enemy were reported as pushing into the wood in the rear of our trenches. James acted promptly, and immediately pushed out a left flank-guard. Major Becher at headquarters sent forward reinforcements from the reserve company, and eventually the 7th battalion from Maple Copse were despatched by brigade and did splendid work in spite of heavy shelling, in digging a switch line connecting the trenches in the neighbourhood of Zouave Wood to our left flank.

Early in the afternoon the reserve brigade of the 14th Division, who had only reached bivouacs near Poperinghe at three in the morning, returned and made a gallant but fruitless counter-attack to recover the lost trenches. Could it have been expected that men, who had been in the trenches for a week, marched back during the night no less than 12 miles, only to turn once more, march back those interminable 12 miles, part of the time under heavy shell fire, dog-tired, without sleep or food, could without adequate artillery preparation perform a feat which later required a division of fresh troops, after one of the most carefully planned and destructive bombardments at that time known? The brigade could but have failed, and to the onlooker it seemed a tragic blunder, but to those who have read the pathetic story of a tragic day, the title given by *The Student in Arms* of *The Honour of the Brigade* alone provides the excuse for an operation which from every other point of view, was one of the costly blunders of the war.

On August 9th, the 6th Division attacked after a very heavy bombardment and re-established the situation. No troops could have done finer work. The enemy who had manned the redoubtable Hooge crater in great strength, suffered very heavily, but the total prisoners captured in a hard fought attack amounted to five. The 2nd Sherwood Foresters, under that magnificent officer Colonel Hobbs, who in pre-war days had at one time been adjutant of our battalion, eventually endeavoured to hold the crater on our left, but this was soon found to be untenable, and remained in No Man's Land.

An incident which is not without its humour, while illustrating the tiredness of our men, may be worth recalling. During the bombardment preliminary to the counter-attack, when the noise of our own artillery was deafening, and the proximity of the enemy shelling far from assuring, a platoon commander discovered one of his men fast asleep on the firestep. With some difficulty he was aroused and, rubbing his eyes, he exclaimed, not without a certain degree of indignation that his slumbers had been cut short—"What's oop?"

Our casualties during the activities of July 30th and 31st, amounted to 21 killed and 40 wounded, and the 10th Battalion had ten casualties in addition. This total was increased from day to day by incessant shelling, trench mortars and rifle grenades, and by the unfortunate inaccuracy of one of our 6-inch naval guns, which persisted in firing into our trenches until its identity was eventually discovered. During the first fortnight in the line here, our casualties were no fewer than four officers wounded (Vann, E. M. Hacking, Hindley and G. G. Elliott); 36 other ranks killed, or died of wounds, and 90 wounded. Included amongst the killed were Sergeant A. Phillipson, who throughout had shown the utmost coolness and gallantry, and Sergeant E. Layhe, who had done very good work as Scout Sergeant. "Jimmy" James, who had struggled on manfully in spite of being very unfit, eventually had to give up and go to hospital, D Company being taken over by Vann.

During these days there was much active patrolling in order to make certain of the dispositions of the enemy, and much daring work was carried out by Lieutenants Vann, Turner, and H. B. S. Handford, 2nd Lieutenants A. & E. M. Hacking, Corporal Gadd, Lance-Corporal Wilson, and Privates Nicholson and Thompson. Vann in particular was much in the good books of General Allenby, the corps commander, for his splendid work, though he was once the cause of his very nearly spoiling an immaculate pair of breeches when showing him with much glee a particularly *un-get-at-able* loophole plate

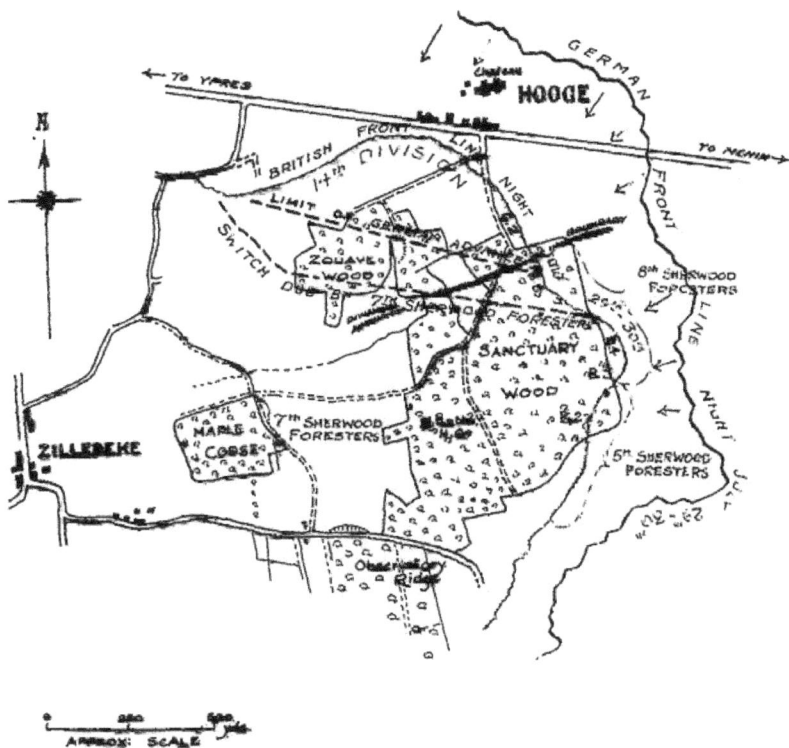

Arrows indicate direction of German attack July 30th 1915.

in a very muddy trench. We are led to believe, however, that this crime was forgiven, as Vann was later honoured by the general with an invitation to dinner.

Apart from shelling, which continued intermittently, the rest of our stay in the line was uneventful. It was not, however, until August 17th, that the battalion, reduced in numbers but tried at last in real fighting, were relieved by the 7th Battalion, and marched back to bivouacs near Ouderdom, dead tired but happy in the thought that they could hand over intact the trenches which they had taken over three weeks before.

The attack had evidently not been an attempt to break through. The enemy no doubt had hoped to seize our front line system from the right of B4 trench northwards. There can be no doubt that had this succeeded the difficulty of the counter-attack would have been largely increased. Indeed, at a time when troops could ill have been spared, it is probable that the Ypres Salient would have been considerably reduced, and the morale of the enemy proportionately increased. This was pointed out by General Allenby, who, addressing the battalion on parade on August 25th, said: "I have read with great pleasure and pride the report of the general commanding your division, telling of the arduous work which you recently did in the neighbourhood of Hooge. By your boldness, tenacity, and gallantry, you did work of very great importance. Perhaps you do not know that not only did your action have an important bearing on that particular bit of line, but on the whole campaign, because of the political reason for holding the salient. The town of Ypres is nothing to us, but if the Boche took it they would publish it to the world that they had captured the fortress of Ypres, which we have held since November, 1914."

The battalion also received the special thanks of the field marshal commanding-in-chief on their efforts during the tour. To the delight of everyone, especially all ranks of B Company, John Becher was awarded the D.S.O., a very well-deserved honour for most splendid work whilst in command of the battalion, during one of the most anxious periods in its history; Vann for his gallantry here and previously at Kemmel got the M.C. Mention must also be made of the splendid work of our new medical officer (Johnstone), his assistants Corporals Sissons, Martin, and Bescoby, and all the stretcher-bearers, who worked indefatigably day and night, often in circumstances of great personal risk in dressing and evacuating the wounded, not only of our own battalion, but of the King's Royal Rifle Corps, the Rifle Brigade, and the 2nd Sherwood Foresters. In these operations they established a reputation for gallantry and devotion to duty which in the whole brigade was conspicuous throughout the war.

Our bivouacs were in a nice spot sheltered from view by a small wood. Our rest was not a long one, and was much of the usual type, but had an additional interest in that we were fortunate in getting two very good entertainments from the 46th Divisional Concert Party, the Whizz-Bangs, which had lately been formed, and was to be a source of much pleasure from now on to the end of the war. Whilst there we were joined by two new officers, 2nd Lieutenants A. H. G. C. Moore and P. C. Hemingway, and 107 other ranks, but we wanted men badly now, as in addition to our heavy casualties in the line, we lost during the month of August 41 N.C.O's. and men, whose term of enlistment expired on the completion of one year's war service. These included many old hands who were difficult to replace.

On August 29th, we took over trenches at Middlesex Wood, where the brigade were holding the line astride the Ypres-Comines canal, near St. Eloi, and there we stayed, with one short rest in bivouacs, for a month of more or less normal trench warfare. Perhaps the main points of interest were that we were covered by Belgian gunners, who were not too particular where or when they fired, that we were now getting a supply of sniperscopes (specially constructed rifles, fitted with periscopes, for firing from a trench without looking directly over the parapet), which formed most useful additions to our trench stores, and seemed to cause the enemy considerable annoyance, and that we were able on one or two occasions to make good practice with Colonel Fowler's elephant gun against some of the enemy's loophole plates. On September 25th, in conjunction with attacks by the French and British, on various other parts of the Western Front, we had to demonstrate by means of artillery, machine gun and rifle fire, and a dummy gas and smoke attack, which was to be provided by burning on the parapet of the front line trenches large quantities of damp straw, which had been carried up with much labour, and a good deal of very frank comment. Much to the relief of those intimately concerned with this bonfire, the wind on the day of the attack was unfavourable, and the straw at least did not end in smoke. The demonstration provided some amusement to our grenadiers, who, with the assistance of a Gamage catapult, and two west spring throwers succeeded, to their immense delight in bursting the old Béthune bomb as shrapnel over the German trenches. It was only when the last bomb was thrown that Sergeant G. F. Foster, the stoutest bomber that ever lived and fell, ended a demonstration which can hardly have caused a flutter in the dove-cotes of the German higher command.

Here, as on many other occasions, all ranks would have worked more intelligently, and with greater personal satisfaction, if they had known something of the general plan, and the part they were being asked to play. This plan really must have been a big thing, for some one was kind enough to send us a lot of literature on such subjects as "How to guard against spies in newly captured territory," and generally how to behave there; whilst maps and other documents gave us the most intricate detail of every well, and other supply of water for at least 20 miles east of where we were. Evidently the sender was an optimist!

On the 30th September, the 8th Lincolns took over from us in support in the canal dug-outs. The enemy having already given us an extremely unpleasant afternoon chose this very inconvenient occasion for "putting up" a mine under the trenches held by the 6th Battalion, on the south side of the canal. This operation and the accompanying bombardment involved a stand-to, and caused a certain number of casualties both in the trenches and among the troops in the support dug-outs. The relief was, however, duly carried out, and the battalion marched back to tents near Ouderdom in the early hours of October 1st, where a little later in the day General Allenby came to say good-bye and wish us luck in our new sphere of action.

We had previously, on September 21st, had the honour of being inspected by General Plumer, commanding the Second Army, who expressed himself as very satisfied with the smart turnout of the battalion. We were still very weak, though we had continued to receive small drafts of reinforcements, and had been joined by five new officers, 2nd Lieutenants G. H. F. Payling, R. T. Skinner, R. A. Abrams, G. H. Fisher, and C. Pickerell; "Dolly" Gray also came out again and rejoined. We had, however, lost Captain Collin, the adjutant, who had just left to take up a staff captaincy, and his place after being held for a few days by Lieutenant A. Hacking, was now taken by Lieutenant Weetman, who had just rejoined. Captain Piggford had gone home sick, and 2nd Lieutenant P. C. Hemingway wounded; and we had also recently lost M. Lacolle, our one and only battalion interpreter. Henceforth we were not to be allowed this luxury.

It is, perhaps, not out of place to mention here an interesting little episode which had taken place at home, namely the depositing of the colours in Newark parish church. This ceremony was carried out on July 24th, and was attended by the mayor and corporation of Newark. Lieutenant-Colonel G. S. Foljambe was in charge of the parade, and Captain R. F. B. Hodgkinson commanded the escort to the colours, which were carried by 2nd Lieutenants R. J. Shipley and C. Pickerell.

CHAPTER 4

Hohenzollern Redoubt
October 1st, 1915—October 17th, 1915

We packed up during the afternoon of October 1st, and in the evening marched to Abeele, where we entrained for a destination unknown to most of us, but presumed to be somewhere in the far south. We made ourselves as comfortable as we could for the expected long journey, only to be rudely awakened after what seemed to be a five minutes' sleep, and turned out into the cold dark night at Fouquereuil, a suburb of Béthune. The remainder of the night was spent at a somewhat elusive Orphanage in the town itself. On the following day we moved into billets at the northern end of the town on the banks of the La Bassée canal, where we were joined by the transport which had come from Ouderdom by road. October 3rd saw us once more on the move to Mont Bernenchon, a clean, attractive little village, a few miles N.W. of Béthune. Our hopes of spending a day or two in peace were soon shattered, for on the following day we made what seemed to be another emergency move to Béthune, where we embussed for regions unknown. Shortly after dark we arrived at Vermelles, and picked up guides, who led us as only guides can, to what proved to be a portion of the German front line system captured in the fighting a few days before. The trenches, which were near the Lone Tree, and within sight of the famous Tower Bridge at Loos, were little damaged, and seemed to have been captured without a great deal of fighting, but the incessant rain and scarcity of habitable dug-outs made our stay as uncomfortable as the most hardened stoic could have desired. Our work consisted of reversing portions of the original German support trench to form a fire trench facing the other way. Owing to the distance to the then German line (1,000 to 1,500 yards) and the low visibility, we were able to work openly and practically unmolested. Our only casualties were the result of an unlucky shell which fell on the morning of October 5th, amongst a party of signallers, killing Lance-Sergeant C. E. Harrison, signalling sergeant, and three men, whilst another man died of wounds a few days later.

The same evening we got orders to leave the trenches, and after a thoroughly unpleasant tramp, in heavy rain and thick darkness over the slippery chalk tracks, which were guess-work to most of us, we arrived soon after midnight at Mazingarbe, which for dirt, damp, and general cheerlessness, almost rivalled our never-to-be-forgotten billets at Bac-St. Maur. So ended a beastly, tiring, and, for all we ever learned, quite purposeless expedition.

After a short meal and much needed rest we felt fit for anything, and made light of the trek on the early morning of October 6th, to our rest billets, which we found at Fouquières, a nice clean little village about a mile west of Béthune. Here we found ourselves, for a short time, in peace and something approaching luxury.

Our move south had brought us into the First Army (General Haig) and XI Corps. (Lieutenant-General Haking), which had been busy in the recent fighting, and we now learned definitely for the first time that in the further fighting that was shortly to take place we were to play a prominent part. On Saturday, October 9th, preliminary orders and plans were issued, and we learned that our task was to be the capture of the Hohenzollern Redoubt and Fosse 8, an admirably constructed scale model of which had been made on the ground outside divisional headquarters at Gosnay, where officers and N.C.O.'s (and stray inhabitants) spent some time in a careful and interested examination of it.

In addition, a somewhat hurried reconnaissance of the position itself was made by Colonel Fowler and the company commanders from our trenches in front of Vermelles, from which the attack was to be made. In the short space of a couple of hours they endeavoured to get a working knowledge of the maze of communication trenches, and the hostile ground over which, if all went well, we should have to advance. Sunday was spent in church Parade, and in going again through the preliminary orders and plans, and in the afternoon the corps commander interviewed the officers of the division at divisional headquarters. We were then told something more as to the reason and general plan of the attack, and were informed that we should be supported by the heaviest concentration of artillery yet known in the war—400 guns of all calibres,—that all contingencies had been provided for, and that in spite of the strength of the position, we should probably encounter very little opposition before reaching our objective.

The object of the attack, which was to be undertaken by the XI

Corps, was to establish the left flank of the First Army, and to render possible a further advance in conjunction with the French on the south. The objective included the quarries and Fosse 8, the 46th Division being allotted the task of capturing the Hohenzollern Redoubt and Fosse 8, whilst the 12th Division was to attack on our right, and be responsible for the quarries. The Fosse and surroundings had already been in our hands once, having been attacked and captured during the last week in September by the 9th Division, who unfortunately, however, had been compelled to withdraw, and a subsequent attempt by the 28th Division to recapture it had also proved a dismal failure. What, we wondered, was in store for the 46th Division?

Fosse 8 is, or rather was, a typical colliery pit, with the usual winding and head gear and other plant, and pit-head pile of slag (called in this case the Dump), which like its neighbour, the famous Tower of Wingles, overlooked the whole position, whilst in rear there were the usual rows of miners' cottages. These cottages (called *corons*) had cellars, and were thus very easy to defend with machine guns, which could fire with great effect, and comparative safety, from ground level. In front of the Fosse and protecting it lay the Hohenzollern Redoubt, consisting of a salient trench system shaped rather like a big bean, and projecting well in front of the German main system, to which it was connected by communication trenches, and by two flank trenches known as Big Willie and Little Willie. The importance of the position lay in the fact that it was on the top of a gentle rise, giving command and good observation of our position on either side. Its capture was rendered difficult by the fact that the ground in front of it was level, and almost devoid of cover, affording a very fine field of fire, which could be swept from practically every direction. From our trenches very little could be seen except the Dump, and the roof of the manager's house.

The attack was to be carried out by the 137th Brigade on the right under Brigadier-General E. Feetham, C.B., and the 138th Brigade on the left under Brigadier-General G. C. Kemp, whilst the 139th Brigade were to be in divisional reserve under Brigadier-General C. T. Shipley. To the 137th Brigade were attached 100 grenadiers from the 139th Brigade, two sections divisional Cyclist Company, and the 1/2nd Field Company, Royal Engineers (less one section), and to the 138th Brigade, the 1st Monmouthshire Regiment (divisional Pioneer Battalion), 125 Grenadiers from the 139th Brigade, two sections divisional Cyclist Company, and the 1/1st Field Company, Royal Engineers (less one section), whilst General Shipley's divisional reserve consisted of the 139th Brigade (less 225 Grenadiers), one platoon divisional Cyclist Company, and two troops Yorkshire Hussars. The covering artillery consisted of three groups of heavy artillery under the corps commander, and one group of divisional artillery (six brigades of 18-pounders, and one brigade of 4.5 Howitzers).

To his immense pleasure, 2nd Lieutenant R. E. Hemingway, our battalion grenade officer, was put in charge of the grenadiers attached to the 138th Brigade, the party also including the battalion grenadier sergeant, G. F. Foster. Bombing was now entering on the period of its greatest importance—always in our humble opinion greatly exaggerated. The Mills bomb was rapidly ousting all other kinds, and shortly became almost the only one in normal use. Much time was put in at throwing practice, and every kind of artifice was adopted by instructors to make it interesting, and at the same time improve the aim and distance thrown. A "platoon" of "grenadiers," as they were at first called, was formed in each battalion, consisting of a grenadier officer, a sergeant and 32 men, (eight from each company), and to show how much we respected them, we put them when on the march at the head of the battalion. There was a brigade grenadier officer too, who made himself generally responsible for the training and work of grenadiers throughout the brigade. The first officer appointed to this post in our brigade was Lieutenant A. Hacking, who had taken over the duties just before the Hohenzollern battle. The task allotted to the Grenadiers in this fight, was to bomb the various communication trenches leading from West Face to Fosse Trench, clear dug-outs and establish blocks in Fosse Alley.

Information regarding the enemy, gained by corps intelligence during the attacks of September 25th, and following days from our own officers, and from the examination of prisoners, was to the effect that the enemy trenches in the redoubt, with the exception of Dump Trench and South Face, were badly damaged and not strongly wired, that previous attacks had been exposed to heavy enfilade fire from Mad Point or Madagascar, that it was not thought there would be much enfilade fire from the south-east, and that it was not necessary to waste a lot of heavy shell on the Dump, as it could be made untenable by both sides. How far this was justifiable will be seen.

Our few days at Fouquières passed very quickly in the bustle of completing equipment, going again and again with all ranks through the maps and plans of attack, detailing and organising bombing squads in the place of those detached for duty with the other brigades, and writing last letters home "in case—" There was little or no excitement. We had most of us seen too much by this time to be either unduly pessimistic or over-confident about our own chances, so that everything seemed to go quietly and smoothly. The first steel helmets had just arrived—quaint, antique, Japanese looking things, with ingenious corrugations to catch the bullets—and were issued to the machine gunners, who had also received the first supply of the new box respirator, issued in place of the smoke helmet. The machine gun section was now commanded by Lieutenant Adams.

It was at 3.45 p.m. on October 12th, after making our final inspections and collecting blankets, packs and other surplus stores at a convenient barn, that we moved off from Fouquières on a fine Autumn afternoon, leaving behind only 2nd Lieutenant Gray, and a few odd men, who were not fit to go into action. Transport marched in rear of the battalion to temporary lines behind Noyelles, where it remained until after the battle.

We had a very pleasant and easy march up to Vermelles, where a halt was made for tea. Here we were passed by one of the Stafford battalions who were to make the assault. It was too dark to see their faces, but their voices were full of confidence and cheeriness, which it did one good to hear. A temporary quarter-master's stores was fitted up at Clarke's Keep, Vermelles, where companies picked up their rations for the 13th, water in petrol tins, grenades, Vermorel sprayers, and other odds and ends likely to be required. An emergency ration of cold bacon and bread was also issued.

Eventually after a very slow march through Vermelles, which was a seething mass of men and transport, we arrived about 11 p.m. at our assembly position in Sussex Trench, where space was allotted to us by Lieutenant C. L. Hill, signalling officer, who had gone on ahead with a few signallers for that purpose. We soon settled down and made the best we could of what remained of the night. This was not long, for the carrying parties for the 138th Brigade, and others had to report for duty at Clarke's Keep at 6 a.m. on October 13th. In all we provided a total of five officers and 300 other ranks for this duty, and they were busy most of the morning taking up to the front line such necessary articles as rations, water, grenades, and rum. His devotion to the last-named duty was too much for one bloodthirsty, but very ill-disciplined member of the battalion, who became "non-effective" in consequence, and was reported by someone, who saw him lying in the bottom of a communication trench, as "dead—shot through the head." He was "dead" right enough, but he lived to fight—and, it is feared to "die" again—another day!

Our artillery fire during the morning was normal, "so as not to arouse the suspicions of the Germans," who, as a fact, probably knew quite as much as most of us about the time and nature of our attack. But at 12.0 noon, every gun began in real earnest, and it was possible to stand on the firestep of our trench, and get an undisturbed, if rather distant, view of the shells bursting all over the German trenches. After half-an-hour of this most unusual, but very pleasing spectacle, one felt that there would be little left for us to attack.

At 1 p.m. the greenish yellow clouds of smoke and chlorine gas (known for some time as the Auxiliary) discharged from cylinders in our front line began to roll towards the enemy lines, the breeze being exactly right both in strength and direction, and we became happier still at the thought of paying the Germans back in their own coin. During the whole of our bombardment we could hear very little reply from the German guns, though from time to time we could see a few "woolly bears" and other shell-bursts, at odd points about the forward trenches. Probably they were saving most of their fire for the actual assault, and except for a stray machine gun bullet or two, we ourselves were in no kind of danger. One of those, however, which must have dropped at a steep angle, slightly wounded Regimental Sergt-Major Mounteney, who was standing in the trench with the officers of battalion headquarters. He had only rejoined from England a few days before, and was our first casualty in the attack.

At 1.50 p.m. the gas discharge ceased, but the smoke was continued until 2.0 p.m., when our guns "lifted" from the enemy front line, and the 137th and 138th Brigades began the assault. As the smoke cleared away, we could get a fair view of a portion of the attacking troops (Staffords) on the right as they went steadily, and apparently in excellent order over the top, but, almost at the same time we heard with surprise and dismay, the somewhat slow *tap-tap* of numbers of those enemy machine guns, which were to have been so completely silenced by our bombardment! We watched the Staffords for a few moments until they disappeared from view.

Then followed a period of anxious waiting, and the only information we got was to the effect that the 138th Brigade on the left had practically gained their portion of the redoubt.

Soon after 3 o'clock, we received orders to move forward, and began to proceed by way of Inverness Trench, Bomb Alley and Left Boyau to Reserve Trench. Movement was very slow, owing to the congestion of the traffic, and the narrowness of the trenches, and took a long time to complete. There we were destined to remain for several hours, and suffered a few casualties from shell fire, apparently directed at the junctions of the trench with Central and Right Boyaux. We were now nominally at the disposal of general officer commanding 137th Brigade, but never received any orders from him, and eventually drifted to the command of general officer commanding 138th Brigade.

Traffic became more and more congested by the stream of wounded which was now pouring down Central Boyau and Barts Alley, and by carrying parties and supports endeavouring to get along the reserve trench up to the redoubt.

Soon we began to gather scraps of information from those who were coming down, and to realise that things were going far from well. The usual answer was "Don't ask me, all I know is it's Hell up there!" It was now getting too dark to see, and we could only gather that at any rate we were holding the West Face and having a pretty bad time in doing so; also that our Grenadiers attached to the 138th Brigade, had suffered heavily. Sergeant G. F. Foster was carried down dying from wounds in the body, and Hemingway was reported to be dangerously wounded, if not already dead.

Things had not gone well. As we learned afterwards the attack of the Staffords on the right had been held up almost immediately by machine gun fire, and very little ground had been made. On the left, the Lincolns and Leicesters at first were more fortunate, and reaching West Face with comparatively few casualties, began to make their way up to Fosse Trench. But the further they advanced, the more heavy became their losses, until eventually the advance came to a standstill, the furthest point reached being about 100 yards from Fosse Trench. From these more advanced positions they were gradually forced back, until only the West Face was in our hands. It is abundantly clear that the effect of our bombardment did not come up to expectations, and that many machine guns were untouched, and, worst of all, that the Dump, on which "heavy shell need not be wasted, as it could be made untenable by either side," proved to be a miniature Gibraltar, honeycombed with shafts and galleries leading to concealed machine gun emplacements. Small wonder that little ground could be made or held in the face of such defences.

The news that things were going badly induced a battalion commander of another brigade, whose battalion had been taken from him piecemeal and scattered to the four winds of heaven, to order A Company, in the absence of Colonel Fowler, to go across to the redoubt to reinforce the troops there. Information, however, was brought by Lance-Corporal Simpson of A Company (killed a few hours later), who made a rapid and courageous journey over the open to West Face, to the effect that that trench was already overcrowded, and that the troops there required thinning, rather than reinforcing.

It was now getting late and things seemed to be in a very unsatisfactory state, when orders were issued by Colonel Fowler, who had met General Kemp in the trenches, and received verbal instructions to be prepared to carry out an attack at short notice on the right portion of the redoubt, for companies (except B who were detached for other work) to begin to move up in readiness to our front line trenches. This movement began about 9.0 p.m. very slowly along Reserve Trench and Hayward's Heath. The difficulty of moving a battalion at night, in single file, through a maze of unfamiliar trenches without losing touch, may be better imagined than described, and it was after midnight before we had covered the 400 or 500 yards, which was all we had to do.

Whilst this was going on Colonel Fowler and the adjutant, accompanied by the staff captain, Major Wordsworth, made a hasty reconnaissance of the position, and found that elements of the 138th Brigade and Monmouths were holding the north-western portion of West Face, whilst the eastern portion of Big Willie was held by the 6th Battalion. Except for a short distance near the barricade on each flank, the trench between these points was held by the enemy.

At 2.45 a.m. on October 14th, we received from general officer commanding 138th Brigade, written orders to attack and consolidate "as soon as possible" the south-eastern portion of West Face, the junction of South Face and Big Willie (shown on the map as point 60), and if possible the "chord" of the redoubt. The order stated that the 6th Battalion in Big Willie would co-operate by a bombing attack along that trench "at the same time." Owing to the difficulty of getting messages to and fro, in the maze of unknown trenches in the dark, it was quite impossible to get in touch with the 6th Battalion so as to give them any idea when our attack would begin, so that we were not able to rely on getting much help from them. The commanding officer decided that two companies would be sufficient for the attack, which was of course going to be without artillery support, and A Company (Major A. L. Ashwell), and D Company (Captain B. W. Vann), were detailed. A hasty conference was arranged at a small dug-out at which Colonel Fowler, who intended himself to lead the attack, gave the few orders that were possible in the circumstances:—"A quiet advance, no firing, and in with the bayonet."

Owing to the darkness and the unfamiliar ground, it was necessary to make some arrangement for keeping direction. Major Becher was, therefore, sent across to the West Face, with instructions to stay at the extreme right flank of the 138th Brigade position, and there to show a light from a flash lamp on which the left flank of our attack would be directed.

As soon as this was settled, and company commanders had issued their instructions, we began to deploy in front of our original front line trench, as nearly as possible opposite our objective.

It was again a very slow job getting the men out of the deep and narrow support trenches, and over a single duck-board bridge across the front line into position; indeed many men of D Company never received the order at all, and remained in the support trench in ignorance of what was going on. The men were extended to about four paces, D Company on the right, A on the left. This movement was carried out very quietly, with entire absence of hesitation or confusion, and the men were then dressed as nearly as possible on the required alignment—no easy matter when one has only a map, and has never seen the objective or the ground in front of it. Rifles were loaded and bayonets fixed, Colonel Fowler with characteristic unselfishness, giving his rifle to an officer who had a bayonet, but no rifle to put it on. All these preliminaries were carried out without attracting the attention of the enemy, who were about 250 yards away. Finally at about 3.45 a.m. the order was given to advance, keeping our left flank on Becher's lamp, which we could see from time to time across the intervening ground. It was a strange experience, this slow night advance through the darkness and mist in the almost uncanny stillness which, sooner or later, always follows heavy fighting; so like what many of us had done in peace-time "night-ops," that it was difficult to realise that this was war, and would end in hand-to-hand fighting; that, however quietly we went, we must eventually be discovered, and perhaps swept away by machine gun and rifle fire. The ground was for the most part level, and not badly cut up, and there was little wire. A few of our dead, one or two severely wounded still struggling painfully back to our lines, and a number of abandoned rifles were all that were left to show what had happened on the previous day. When we were about half-way across it was realised that we were getting too far to the left, and direction was changed half-right. It was not until the right of the line was close up to the old German wire, that we were discovered. Fire was opened from somewhere half-right, probably in the neighbourhood of Point 60, but it was not severe, and only a few casualties were caused. On arriving at West Face it was found to be practically empty on the right, the few Germans who had been there having probably left hurriedly as we approached. On the left we found a mixed crowd of Lincolns, Leicesters, and Monmouths, with a few Robin Hoods, all under the command of Colonel Evill, of the Monmouths. Many of them were wounded, and nearly all were exhausted by their dreadful experiences of the previous day. Our arrival was, therefore, very opportune and put fresh life into them.

It was now quite evident that we had come too far to the left, and although we had gained 100 yards or so of the West Face, our right flank was not in touch with the 6th Battalion in Big Willie. In their eagerness to get at the Germans, and urged on by the shouts of the Lincolns and Leicesters, the left half of A Company ran through the West Face and began pushing on. The enemy, however, were waking up, and our men were met with much heavier fire, which, although unaimed, caused a number of casualties. Edge was severely wounded in the arm and chest, and Everard Handford was killed instantaneously by a bullet in the head, whilst numbers of men also fell. It was then seen that any further advance was out of the question. The only thing to be done was to consolidate what we had, and try to extend our gains laterally by bombing along the West Face. Grenadiers and grenades (English and German) were collected, parties were organised by Ashwell and Vann, and several more yards of trench were gained. Strachan leading one of these along the trench with utter fearlessness was never seen again, and was probably killed at once. Shortage of grenades soon made it clear that we must stop and build a barricade to hold up the Germans, who as usual seemed to have a never-ending supply.

On the extreme right, Vann and others of D Company had come across some Boches out of the trench, apparently preparing to make an attack over the open. Most of these were slaughtered, and the rest made all possible haste back to their trench. This appears to have been part of an organised counter-attack, as the enemy tried a similar attack on the left as well, which also failed. Nothing was heard of the bombing in Big Willie by the 6th Battalion, but we learnt afterwards that they had made several attempts to progress along that trench without success.

All available tools and sandbags were got together in the trench to build a barricade at the right flank. It was now getting light, and this was attended with much danger, and in the work of filling sandbags and placing them at the barricade, we had several men killed in a very short time.

Vann had already been wounded by a bullet in the left forearm, and had gone down to be dressed, returning with his usual courage and tenacity, after having his wound attended to. The commanding officer, however, would not let him stay, and he had to go down again to hospital. Ashwell was hit by a bullet in the right shoulder a few minutes after Vann, and he, too, had to leave us.

The enemy were not more than fifty yards away, and the least exposure brought a bullet with deadly aim, though in this respect they did not have things entirely their own way. We could distinctly see the tops of their helmets over the parapet, and at one time there was such a collection that we thought they were going to attack, but nothing came of it, and we settled down to work again. There was no wire or obstacle of any kind between the two trenches. We were too close to get our guns on to them, otherwise we could have done much execution. Practically all the work on the right was done by men of D Company, who eventually made a barricade, which was more or less bullet-proof, and dug a length of trench to protect that flank. Here Sergeant W. L. Green did excellent work, encouraging everyone by his fine example. For nearly 24 hours he stuck to his post in spite of bombs and rifle fire. He was ably assisted by Sergeant Turgoose and Privates Keeling, Hubbard, Dickinson, Offord and Sly of D Company, also Private F. Attenborough of A Company, whilst Lance-Corporal Skelton did splendid work in attending to wounded.

Meanwhile Colonel Fowler had made arrangements for the defence of the trench on the left, from which, much to their relief the Lincolns, Leicesters, and Monmouths, had been withdrawn during the early hours of the morning. Their place had been taken by A Company, which having lost all its officers, was now commanded by Sergeant L. Bell. Parties were set to work to improve the trench, which was badly knocked about, and during the following night the company dug a new trench a few yards in front, in order to get a better field of fire and for better protection. The northern end of West Face was all this time held by the 7th Battalion.

C Company (Captain H. B. S. Handford, in place of Captain G. S. Heathcote, who had left to do duty at the base) who had been left behind in Hayward's Heath when A and D Companies went over to attack, stayed there until 5.0 a.m. when 2nd Lieutenant R. A. Abrams and a party of 15 were detailed to carry grenades up to A Company in the redoubt, where many of them remained. The rest of the company moved up to a communication trench near the original front line, where they received orders from a battalion commander of another brigade, to carry water and grenades over the open to the redoubt. They started shortly after 7.30 a.m., but as it was quite light, they were seen immediately, and heavy machine gun and rifle fire was opened on them at once. Basil Handford and several others were killed instantaneously, and several were wounded. The attempt was foredoomed to failure, and the men were ordered back into the trench. For the rest of the day they helped to carry stores to the redoubt by way of a new communication trench and to fetch in and attend to the wounded. Very gallant work was done in this operation by Company Sergeant-Major Haywood, Seargeants Leivers and Bexton, and Privates Winterbottom, Allen, and Eyre.

B Company (Captain Turner) had been detached about 5.0 p.m. on October 13th, and ordered to proceed over the open to reinforce the garrison of our original front line. They remained for some time in the old support line, from which all the company grenadiers were sent up to reinforce the men in the redoubt. One of these, Lance-Corporal G. W. Moore, did very gallant work in remaining alone for three-quarters-of-an-hour on the enemy's side of a barricade, which was being built up behind him, and then continued to bomb the enemy for eight hours. The company was later ordered to dig a communication trench to link up the redoubt with our old front line. They started about 9.0 p.m., and worked continuously on it throughout the night, much of the time under heavy rifle fire, and by dawn a serviceable trench had been dug, and a very important communication established. Captain Turner was congratulated by the officer commanding the 7th Battalion on the very good work of his company, in the supervision of which he had been most ably assisted by Sergeant Rawding.

October 14th seemed a never-ending day for those in the redoubt. Fortunately in a way, the lines were too close together for us to be shelled, but bombing went on almost uninterruptedly, and our casualties mounted rapidly. Grenadier reinforcements were sent along from time to time from every company in the battalion, also from the 5th Battalion, whilst 2nd Lieutenant G. H. Fisher, who was acting as grenade officer in the absence of Hemingway, came up during the morning, and at the right barricade displayed the greatest courage until he was badly wounded and had to leave, dying a few days later. Bombing was also going on at the left barricade, and throughout the day from one flank or the other, the cry was ever "more bombs" or "more bombers." We had fortunately been able to get a signal line up to the redoubt, and a station established there, in a fairly deep dug-out, so that most of the time we were in telephonic communication with those behind.

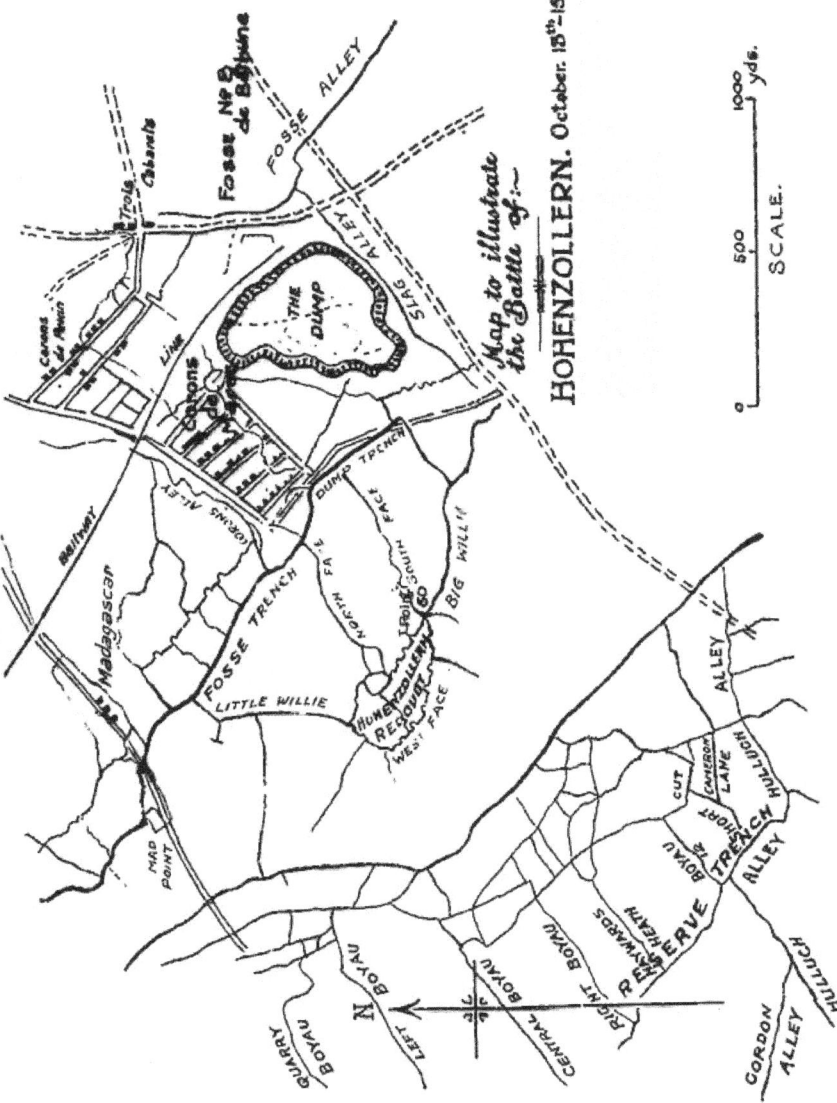

Map to illustrate
the Battle of:—
HOHENZOLLERN. October. 13th–15th 1915.

SCALE.

0   500   1000   yds.

Fosse No 8
de Béthune

FOSSE ALLEY

SLAG ALLEY

THE DUMP

FOSSE ALLEY

Corons

Line

Corons de Pekin

Railway

Trois
Cabarets

LORON'S ALLEY

DUMP TRENCH

Dump South Face
North Face

Dump Trench

HOHENZOLLERN
REDOUBT

West Face

BIG WILLIE

LITTLE WILLIE

FOSSE TRENCH

Railway Madagascar

MAD POINT

QUARRY BOYAU

LEFT BOYAU

N

CENTRAL BOYAU

RIGHT BOYAU

REAR BOYAU

NORTHWARDS

RESERVE TRENCH

CUT

CAMBRIDGE LANE

SHORT ALLEY

HULLUCH

HULLUCH ALLEY

GORDON ALLEY

Our relief promised for the night of October 14th, never came, and we were compelled, alas, to remain in the redoubt. Everyone was tired out, having had little or no sleep, and very little food, for 48 hours. As soon as it was dark the Sappers put out some wire in front of West Face, which encouraged us considerably, and we got through the night without any untoward incident. About 6.30 a.m., on the morning of October 15th, we were relieved in West Face by portions of the 5th and 6th Battalions, and by Grenadiers of the Irish Guards, and withdrawn to Railway Reserve Trench, where we joined up with the remainder of B and C Companies. By the tragic irony of fate, as the Guards were actually filing into West Face and the relief was nearly complete, Colonel Fowler, who was taking a last glance over the top to see if he could find any trace of Major Becher, the last signs of whom had been the flashes of his lamp, to guide us across to the redoubt—was killed instantaneously by a sniper's bullet. So determined had he been to find Becher, that he had himself gone out during the night with Sergeant Stokes in a gallant but unsuccessful endeavour to find him.

Major J. E. Blackwall of the 6th Battalion took over the remnants of the battalion the same evening, and shortly before midnight we were devoutly thankful to be relieved by the Irish Guards. As the relief was taking place, the enemy attempted an attack against the garrison of West Face, but as this was now swelled by the relieving troops, they got rather more than they bargained for, and were beaten off with heavy loss. At the same time they put down quite a barrage on the reserve trenches, and made our relief distinctly unpleasant, but eventually we got it completed without further casualty.

Much to our delight, just before leaving, we heard that Becher had been found. It appears that whilst we were going over to the attack, he had been bombed by the Boches, and badly wounded, as also had Daniels, his batman, who was with him. They got separated, but both managed to crawl away, though Becher eventually had to lie by in an old bit of trench near the German lines. It was from here that, after having been discovered by an officer of the Leicesters, he was eventually rescued on October 15th, by Company Sergeant-Major Haywood, and Lance-Sergeant T. Martin, who carried him a distance of 200 yards under more or less continuous rifle fire. Alas, however, he was not to recover, and after lingering on for ten weeks, he died in hospital on January 1st, 1916. In John Becher the battalion lost one who was beloved by all, who had throughout ever had at heart the welfare of his men, whether in or out of the trenches, at work or at play. What he did in the early trench days at Kemmel, was known to few. Often and often he was out on patrol at night in No Man's Land, mainly for the sake of example, for it was part of his creed never to tell a man to do anything that he would not dare to do himself. He lies buried in the British cemetery at Abbeville. It was a hard fate that struck down John Becher and his two brothers-in-law, Basil and Everard Handford—two of the most promising young officers in the battalion—within a few hours of each other.

Much untiring energy and devotion were shown by many during these strenuous three days, not by any means the least by our medical officer, Captain C. B. Johnstone, and his stretcher bearers. Johnstone himself worked almost incessantly for over 48 hours in attending the wounded, and in many cases helped to carry them long distances, often under heavy fire. To him and all his helpers are due our grateful thanks for their work on that occasion.

On relief we marched out to the transport lines behind Noyelles, where, in the early hours of October 16th, we got some most welcome and refreshing tea, supplied by Torrance and his followers, and then moved on, most of us more asleep than awake, to Vaudricourt, where we arrived about 6.30 a.m., and at once got down to sleep in some of the poorest billets it was ever our misfortune to strike.

Thus ended the more or less fruitless battle of Hohenzollern Redoubt. Though we held a portion of the redoubt as a result of the fighting, it was of no tactical value, and indeed later on was evacuated or blown up. The 12th Division fared no better, and we can only look back on the whole attack as, through no fault of our own, a dismal failure. The battle caused us enormous casualties, all to no purpose. Our battalion alone lost seven officers and 35 other ranks killed or died of wounds, three officers and 132 other ranks wounded, and 14 missing, all of whom were afterwards found to have been killed. Amongst the casualties were Sergeant H. Hall, killed, and Seargeants Archer, Burn, Barrow, and I. B. Bell and Corporal Bruerton wounded.

It was a pleasure to all to hear a little later that for his gallantry and splendid work in this attack, and on many other occasions, "Pat" Ashwell was awarded a well-deserved D.S.O.

At 5.0 p.m. on the afternoon of October 17th, the whole battalion and many officers of the brigade and division, attended the funeral of our beloved colonel in the English cemetery, under the church at Fouquières, the service being taken by his old friend Padre Hales. Some 18 months afterwards the battalion arrived in billets six miles away from this spot, after a long and tiring march. They were expected to move into the line the next day, and some officers who were lucky enough to be mounted, rode over to see the colonel's grave. Around the grave, which had been carefully looked after by the *curé* and other kind friends, and was covered with snowdrops and daffodils just in bloom, they found a number of the old warrant officers and N.C.O.'s of the battalion paying a silent tribute to their old commanding officer. Such a tribute, surely is the finest testimonial to the character of a man who ever inspired in all ranks an affection and respect, which can never have been exceeded in any unit of the army.

CHAPTER 5

Richebourg—Marseilles—Candas
October 18th, 1915—March 5th, 1916

We were now little more than a skeleton of a battalion, so that the arrival of 103 reinforcements, including Sergeant E. E. Deverall, was very welcome, but so far as officers were concerned we remained for the moment very depleted. Captain Turner remained in command of B Company; Lieutenant E. M. Hacking took over A; Lieutenant Abrams C, and Lieutenant Gray D.

Major-General Stuart-Wortley came to see us on October 18th, when the battalion paraded in a field just outside Vaudricourt, and thanked us for our work in the battle, and spoke to a few of the N.C.O.'s and men, whose names had been forwarded as having done specially well.

The following day we were not sorry to leave our wretched billets and march to Lapugnoy, where we got very comfortable quarters, and stayed for a week. Here we were able to do a little reorganising, and were fortunate in getting several new subalterns, *viz.*: 2nd Lieutenants A. Andrews, H. R. Peerless, who shortly became battalion grenade officer, F. E. Kebblewhite, C. H. Powell, A. H. G. Cox, E. Hopkinson (formerly company sergeant-major of C Company) and H. B. Hammond. With their welcome arrival. Companies got more or less into shape. We were unfortunate in having to send a large party by 'bus one day to Sailly Labource, to help to fetch out the empty gas cylinders from the Hohenzollern trenches, but on the whole the few days spent at Lapugnoy were very pleasant. The Whizz-Bangs were in the same village, and gave several good shows, which after our recent gruelling were very refreshing, the more so as on this occasion they were assisted by two French ladies, who, needless to say, added enormously to the attraction.

The *vin blink* of Lapugnoy was also most attractive, and apparently rather more than usually potent, for it was undoubtedly the cause of casualties amongst all ranks. We left there on October 26th, and marched to Béthune, where we were again fortunate in being comfortably billeted at the Orphanage, with officers' billets and headquarters' mess in the Rue de Lille.

Two days later, on October 28th, a review of troops of the XI Corps, was held by the king and the prince of Wales at Hesdigneul. Representatives of all units of the 46th Division were included in the parade, to which we contributed a composite company of six officers and 250 other ranks, under Captain Davenport. The parade ground was a newly ploughed field, and as for several days previously there had been heavy rain the conditions were extremely unfavourable. After taking the salute, the king went on to inspect another unit in an adjoining field, where, unfortunately, he had a nasty accident, and the last we saw of him was driving away from the parade ground and looking very ill.

Further reinforcements joined us at Béthune, mostly from entrenching battalions, making our strength up to more normal figures, though for many months to come, we seldom exceeded 600 to 700 all told. Captain Hill was appointed to command D Company, 2nd Lieutenant Cox succeeding him as signalling officer. Mounteney rejoined and resumed his duties as regimental sergeant-major.

Our next move was to the Richebourg sector—probably the most miserable trenches we ever met with, and then held by Indian troops. Leaving Béthune on November 4th, we proceeded *via* Epinette, where we spent one night, to Vieille Chapelle and relieved the 58th Rifles (Meerut division) in front line trenches on November 6th, with battalion headquarters in Edward Road, just behind Richebourg L'Avoué, and the front line a little in front of that village, and just south of Neuve Chapelle. This was a bad country for trenches, being flat and low lying, with the water level even at normal times very near the surface. The Boche as usual had such high ground as there was. This was mainly in the region of the Bois du Biez on our left, from which he got a fair view over much of our area. The Indians had done little trench work, and all that was taken over was a very poor front line, with a few scraps of support trenches, and one or two communication trenches, mostly full of water. It was during our first tour that a waggish Hun called out one night, after one of our Very lights had made rather a worse display than usual, "Better luck next time. I'll show you how to send them"—which he promptly did, adding later, "I don't want to fight, I've had enough of the war." Towards the end of our stay in this area, we came across another talkative lot of Boches, who had a good deal to say one night, enquiring what regiment we were, and making various remarks about cigarettes and plum puddings.

It was towards the end of our first tour that we had the first of our happily few casualties in this area, Lieutenant Houfton being killed early in the morning of November 11th. He was endeavouring to make his way with Lieutenant Abrams along an absolutely water-logged trench to Boar's Head, the extreme right of our battalion sector, and they were evidently being carefully watched by a Boche sniper, who was doubtless able from time to time to catch a glimpse of their caps above the parapet. Eventually, when they got to a spot where the parapet was particularly low, he fired, the bullet killing Houfton, and passing through the peak of Abrams' cap. Sergeant T. Martin gallantly went to Houfton's aid, across 400 yards of very difficult and exposed ground.

The front we held was changed somewhat after a time, and we side-stepped to the left, with battalion headquarters in dug-outs, at the side of the Rue du Bois. The few odd houses left along this road were mostly used by the gunners as observation posts, the principal being Ritz, Carlton, Princes, and Trocadero, and as the Boche gunners probably had a very shrewd suspicion of this, the neighbourhood of the road was often not a healthy spot, and on one or two occasions was shelled fairly heavily. It was on one of these, when we had some men wounded near Factory Corner, that Private Redfern, the old bandsman, coolly went to their aid in the midst of the shelling, and was dressing one of the men when he was himself mortally wound-ed. Lance-Corporals W. H. Lacey and S. Matthews also showed great bravery in rescuing wounded men at the same time. In connection with this shelling of areas behind the front line, a somewhat unhappily worded order was received to the effect that daily reports frequently omitted to mention the activities of hostile artillery, and that as an ex-ample at a certain time on a certain day, Guards Trench was subjected to a sharp bombardment, and that had it not been for the fact that "a staff officer was accidentally in the front line at the time," nothing would have been known of this at divisional headquarters!

The Boche machine gunners gave us a certain amount of trouble too, particularly at night, when they regularly sprayed all the area from the Rue du Bois to Windy Corner, doubtless hoping to catch trans-port and carrying parties. One particular artiste used to try to play tunes with his gun and we had no difficulty in recognising his favour-ite as an attempt at *Yip-y-addy*. It was a very unlucky burst from one of these one night that killed that very brave soldier Sergeant Sheppard, who had previously been awarded the D.C.M. for gallantry at Hooge. Lieutenant Adams, our machine gun officer, did his best to get his own back against them, and used to stalk out nightly alone, contrary to all regulations, and fire off his guns at odd times in the hope of catching someone. He was rewarded one night, after patiently lying in wait for a search light that the enemy had used occasionally from their front line parapet, by knocking it out with a burst of fire almost the instant it showed itself. But on the whole there was very little excitement; in fact, we hardly had time for much, as we only spent a total of 16 days in the trenches here altogether. Cold winter weather had set in, and there was little or no comfort possible for the men holding the front line. It was here that we first really found it necessary to use "gumboots thigh" when they could be got, and to dress legs and feet daily with whale oil to try and ward off that horrid complaint "trench feet," which might easily have caused many casualties in such trenches as these. A most complicated form had to be filled up with every case sent down to hospital suffering from trench foot, and no mercy was shown to any commanding officer who did not take every precaution to prevent it. Fortunately we had a very good record. Every effort was made to relieve the men in the front line every 24 hours, and to take them back as often as possible to the billets near Windy Corner, where they were able to get their clothes dried, and a good night's rest before going back to the line.

Our rest billets and transport were at Vieille Chapelle. The field where the latter had their lines was nothing but a mass of mud, in most places knee-deep. The transport at this time showed remarkable activity, limbers going backwards and forwards all day to Lacouture on some mysterious duty, which was by no means unconnected with the excitement which arose in "A" branch of divisional headquarters towards the end of our stay, about some houses missing from that village! They had been removed piecemeal to the transport lines, where they were used to form standings.

During one tour spent in brigade support, battalion headquarters and two companies were in that village, and two companies in billets in Richebourg St. Vaast, or finding garrisons for St. Vaast, Grotto and Angle posts. An interesting discovery in the rafters of a ruined house at Richebourg St. Vaast was a pepper box found to contain several gold *louis*. Captain E. M. Hacking was the means of their being handed over to the French authorities and, we hope, eventually restored to their owner. The billets at Lacouture were not very good, but we had a great find there in the shape of what had once been a billiard table in the remains of the Village Institute. At the same time curiously enough, and for some time afterwards, the quarter-master reported that the demand for green cloth for putting behind cap badges was extraordinarily small!

The main drawback to our periods of rest was those wretched working parties, which seemed to pursue us everywhere. Here the work in hand was the building of a solid breastwork in continuation of Guards Trench, just east of the Rue du Bois. Two nights out of each four we were at rest, we had to send large parties to Richebourg to carry on this work, which was being done "by the piece." A certain number of sandbags were issued to each man about half-a-mile before he got to his work, and he was told that when these had been filled and laid he could return. It is perhaps needless to say that many of the sandbags found a resting place in the nearest ditch, not far from the Royal Engineers' dump, where they were issued, and that the building of the breastwork did not proceed very rapidly.

During our stay here several new officers joined, including 2nd Lieutenants H. K. Simonet, G. A. P. Rawlings, and A. H. Michie from the 2/8th Battalion, and 2nd Lieutenants A. Bedford, G. G. Elliott, and W. W. Pitt. We were also given as second-in-command, Major E. H. Heathcote, from the 6th Battalion, whilst his brother Captain G. S. Heathcote, rejoined at the end of November and resumed command of C Company. At the same time Captain E. M. Hacking went to brigade headquarters to learn staff duties, leaving A Company under Lieutenant Andrews, until taken over a little later by Captain A. Hacking, who rejoined from brigade. We also lost 2nd Lieutenant Pickerell, who was invalided home. Our losses in other ranks during our stay amounted to three killed and 15 wounded.

On December 2nd—we retain most pleasant memories of that night—we were relieved by the 7th Battalion in the left sector, and on one of the darkest nights known, made our way back in the usual way to Vieille Chapelle. About 9.30 p.m. a message was received from brigade that the commanding officer or adjutant was wanted at once. The adjutant was sent and came back with the news that we were to be "prepared to move at short notice to an unknown destination." At 5.0 a.m. the next morning further orders were received and we left Vieille Chapelle at noon the same day, marching *via* Merville to Haverskerque, where we got very good if scattered billets. There we proceeded to clean off some of the mud of the Richebourg trenches. During our march we met units of the 19th Division, moving up to relieve the troops in the trenches, and could not help feeling a touch of sympathy for them having been suddenly fetched away from comfortable billets, to take over such water-logged trenches, and we felt that for once fortune had favoured us.

Rumours of all kinds began to float around, and of all quarters of the globe that were mentioned Egypt was believed to be "it," and it was not long before we found out that that indeed was our intended destination.

Everyone was happy, and we were soon looking smart once more; in fact, so splendid was the effort at cleaning up, that the battalion was congratulated by our divisional commander at his inspection on December 7th, as being the smartest battalion of the eleven he had inspected.

Odd men who had been detached for duty with other units rejoined. We had a few small drafts, and one new officer, 2nd Lieutenant W. H. B. Rezin.

We now settled down for drill, interior economy, and lectures. Particular attention was given to guard drill and guard mounting ceremonies, as the divisional commander expressed a wish that we should turn out like the Guards Division, who were in the same corps. Fur coats and other winter kit were handed in. A horrid *pro forma* certificate reached orderly room, and the commanding officer found he had to sign a certificate to the effect that the battalion was in possession of every article enumerated in A.F.G. 1098 (Mobilisation Store Table). This document contained such items as *screws—brass, buckle roller 1 in.* $\times$ $^7/_8$ *in.—2, awls, brad—1, cordage, tarred spun yarn,—lbs. 14*, and other luxuries which had long been considered superfluous, and mostly lost in the salient. We had been told to indent for anything we wanted in the way of clothing or equipment, so that there was some consternation on the arrival of a new and fierce deputy assistant director of ordnance services just at this moment, who told quarter-masters that during the last month, the whole of the Guards Division had not used the number of articles they were indenting for. Formal indents for *awls, brad, etc.*, were therefore out of the question. The quarter-master accused the transport officer, and the transport officer accused the quarter-master, but in the end the mess cart, which had a good cover, was requisitioned, and made two or three secret journeys by night to Merville, and when surprise was expressed that everything on the Mobilisation Store Table was present, both the individuals concerned looked supremely innocent, and no more was said about it. It has since transpired that a jar of rum played a prominent part in this incident.

Here we parted with Big Ben, Old Bob, and other heavy draught horses, which had been with us since leaving Newark, and received in exchange mules from the Guards Divisional ammunition column, two of which rejoiced in the aristocratic names of Harry Thaw, and Legs Eleven.

We were inspected by the assistant director of medical services; we had lectures on "duties on board ship" and "entraining." Special short leave was granted to a few lucky ones, and all preparations were made for a big move. Our billets were very comfortable. We could get good dinners at the corner café, and those of us who were there, will never forget the wonderful concert given by the 19th Divisional Ammunition Column who were billeted there, in which two ladies from Merville assisted.

On December 19th, we marched to Wittes, a small village on the La Bassée canal, near Aire. This was a short march on a bright Sunday morning, chiefly memorable for a wonderful equestrian feat on the part of a certain company commander, who went with his horse into a dyke at the starting point, and instead of coming out with the animal, stayed in by himself, and for the fact that an unfortunate mistake in map reading, caused the battalion to perform a most startling and snake-like turning feat in a lane only a few feet wide, the mistake being discovered just as the last transport vehicle had entered the lane. However, as it was a bright day and we were going away, great good humour prevailed, and each company played "Here we go round the water cart" in its own good time, and the tangle was soon sorted out.

Our before breakfast parade at Wittes on a few occasions took the novel form of the whole battalion doubling up and down along the canal side to the accompaniment of the drums. This was entertaining for a brief space, but the novelty soon wore off. Ordinary training was continued, and included several route marches. It was during one of these that the C Company "wag" brought forth a spontaneous remark one day when passing one of those little dog-carts one used to see so often. It was very heavily laden and the dog was straining every nerve. A big, powerful looking woman was walking at the side carrying a horse whip, but taking no share in the burden. As the company passed, our friend remarked "Eh, mum, you've forgotten your spurs!"

Christmas, 1915, spent at Wittes was a very cheery one. All sorts of good things had been received from home, including a present for every officer and man from the Nottingham Comforts Fund, and altogether we had a most enjoyable time. Football matches and sports of all kinds were indulged in, and one has vivid recollections of Sergeant Deverall giving a wonderful boxing display, and of a poor Frenchman waking up one morning to find his best wagon at the bottom of the canal.

MAJOR J. P. BECHER, D.S.O.
DIED OF WOUNDS, JAN. 1ST, 1916

On Boxing-Day we marched *via* Aire to fresh billets at Molinghem, which were probably the most verminous we ever found. In spite of this drawback we had a very good time, and on January 6th, 1916, had the pleasure of welcoming the 11th Sherwood Foresters, who marched over from a neighbouring village and played us at football. After a good game we beat them by two goals to one. A brigade inter-battalion football competition was also played, in which after beating the 5th Battalion one—none, and the 7th Battalion three—none, we won the brigade championship and some very neat medals.

Whilst at Molinghem, we got our long expected orders to move south, and on January 7th, A and C Companies, and half the first line transport vehicles, under Major E. H. Heathcote entrained at Berguette, and were followed by the remainder of the battalion on January 9th, except the horses, which were entrained at Lillers on January 11th. Eventually, after a train journey of nearly three days, the battalion was concentrated at Marseilles, where after some re-arranging, battalion headquarters and B and D Companies were billeted at Camp Moussot, and A and C Companies under Major Heathcote, at Camp Borely.

At Marseilles we spent what was probably our happiest fortnight in France. It is not difficult to imagine the pleasure everyone experienced at being transported to the shores of the Mediterranean in January after the filth and mud in the trenches, and wet and fogs of northern France. The change was marvellous, and the turnout and appearance of the men splendid, and indeed the subject of comment by English people arriving from abroad, who said they could not help being struck on landing at finding the place full of well set-up and healthy English Tommies. Truly the change was delightful, though the officers who had the misfortune to be billeted for a time in the draughty bathing establishment opposite Borely Camp, are not likely to forget the cold nights they spent there. Sea bathing, which we got almost next door to the camp, was a great delight, and of course the town itself was full of attractions. We need only mention such names as the Cannibière, Theresa's Bar, Lindens, The Alcazar, Castell Muro, The Palais Crystal, The Bodega, and the Novelty, to recall many incidents to all those who were fortunate enough to be with us. It was certainly delightful, but played havoc with our banking accounts, and must have given Mr. Cox a very busy time. We did a certain amount of training in our more serious moments, which were not many, ordinary work normally finishing about 1.0 p.m., and the men being allowed out from 2.0 p.m. onwards. Many guards and camp and town fatigues had to be found, however, almost daily, which much depleted our numbers on parade. Training was mainly of the barrack square type. There was a certain amount of interest for those at Moussot Camp, in watching the Indian troops, whilst those at Borely spent much time either in dodging the loose horses and mules, which wandered at will about the camp, or the camp commandant, who had a violent dislike to orange peel, and if he found any at once arrested the nearest man, whether guilty or not!

Four new officers joined us there, *viz.*, 2nd Lieutenants C. G. Tomlinson, E. C. Marshall, A. A. Hodgson, and W. S. Jones, and a draft of 39 men, all of whom no doubt thought it a very *bon* war.

Plans for our sea journey had got so far advanced that our transport vehicles had actually been taken down to the docks for loading, when, alas for us, our hopes of going east were shattered on January 24th, by the receipt of orders to entrain the next night.

What exactly caused the sudden change of plans we did not know at the time, but subsequently heard it was due to the unexpected ease with which Gallipoli had been evacuated. Needless to say there was much regret on all sides, especially when we found that we were to go back to the north of France and join the Third Army on the western front. On the evening of the 25th January, we marched down through cheering crowds of French people to the Gare d'Arenc, where after waiting about for four hours, we entrained at 4.10 a.m. on the 26th. It is sad to think that this wait gave an opportunity once more for light-fingered people in the transport section to annex eight or nine P.L.M. goods sheets, which were carefully stowed away, one on each limber, and later proved of great value in several places where there was a scarcity of billets.

We detrained at Pont Remy on the morning of January 28th, after a peculiarly uncomfortable journey, and owing to our guide preferring to go three miles uphill to one on the flat our march to Ergnies was a somewhat lengthy business. In this area we followed the Ulster Division, and we are glad to add that the billets taken over from them were invariably scrupulously clean, and had evidently been vastly improved under their able medical authorities. We stayed here for several days, and had an opportunity of resting the men after their long journey, and of carrying out a little training. Some of this was in preparation for a brigade ceremonial parade, which took place on February 3rd, when General Shipley spoke of the splendid work done by the brigade in France up to that time, and read out a list of the honours and decorations awarded, of which we had had a fair share. At Ergnies we had flying visits from Colonel Huskinson and "Doc." Stallard, both of whom we were delighted to see looking very fit.

On February 10th, we marched to Ribeaucourt, where we stayed for a little over a week. Here on February 16th, we parted with Lieutenant Adams, 2nd Lieutenant Rezin, and 35 N.C.O.'s and men of the machine gun section, who went to form part of the newly created brigade machine gun company. In place of the Vickers gun thus withdrawn, we were issued with the new light Lewis machine gun, air cooled, mounted on a bipod and easily carried. Each company had two of these and the whole were supervised by a battalion Lewis gun officer, 2nd Lieutenant Simonet being the first to be appointed to this duty. Musketry was carried out on a 300 yard range, which we fitted up near the village, and bombing practice under the guidance of 2nd Lieutenant Peerless, who made considerable progress in the use of the west spring thrower. Captain A. Hacking had been again taken to brigade headquarters, to act as grenade officer, and Captain Lawson who had rejoined at Wittes, was appointed to command A Company in his place. All this time we were well in the back regions out of harm's way. The only journey made to the front area was that by a party of officers, who one day had to reconnoitre some reserve lines of trenches near Forceville and Mailly Maillet. We once had orders to be prepared to take over the line at Beaumont Hamel, but this fell through.

Ribeaucourt we shall always remember, owing to the exorbitant claims made by the inhabitants for damage to billets. Never before nor after did we receive such demands as those made by the good people of that village, headed by the *miare*, who after showing much hospitality to a few of us, seemed to want to give the villagers a lead in their demands! How they were eventually settled we never found out. Here, too, Captain Davenport and Sergeant Blunt were chased down the village street one day by two infuriated women armed with broomsticks, their store of bully beef and army shirts having been discovered by the former, when looking for odds and ends to hand into the deputy assistant director of ordnance services in exchange for new articles. The D.A.D.O.S. had just issued an ultimatum to the effect that he would issue nothing except on the return of the old article. Transport men, therefore, scoured the country side for bottoms of nose-bags, backs of dandy brushes, pieces of rope, etc., which were cleaned and handed in and quite a good stock of new articles was obtained in return.

On February 20th, we were taken in motor 'buses by a somewhat circuitous route to fresh billets at Candas, where we stayed until March 6th. Most of this time the weather was extremely cold and there were several heavy snowstorms. Navvying on new railways was our chief work, under the supervision of the 112th Company Royal Engineers, either about Puchevillers, or the station at Candas, in preparation for the offensive that was to take place later on. Our fortnight at Candas completed three whole months of what was practically "rest" in the back areas. We were now to play a more active part in the war.

CHAPTER 6

Vimy Ridge
March 6th, 1916—April 21st, 1916

Vimy Ridge will always bring up in the minds of those of the 8th Sherwood Foresters, who were with us at that time the word *mines*. Everyone seemed somehow or other to have heard that that part of the line was famous for mining warfare, and as the news was passed on from one to another that Vimy Ridge was our destination, a kind of whisper of "mines" passed with it. The area proved to be a mass of mines, and we found that mining warfare was extremely unpleasant, though most of our own experience was confined to the latter part of our stay there.

The front line in this sector, in the early part of 1915 had run through the east end of the Lorette Ridge to Carency, and thence to La Targette, but on September 25th of that year, the French had driven the enemy back nearly a mile, practically to the foot of the Vimy Ridge itself. In this area were portions of the front having such well-known names as The Labyrinth, and Souchez Sugar Refinery—reminders of the fact that some of the most savage fighting of the whole war took place there, owing to the struggle of the enemy to retain a footing on that splendid line of observation, the Lorette Ridge. The Arras-Béthune road, known as the Route de Béthune, and bordered by a few scraggy trees, ran through the sector more or less from north to south—about a mile behind the front line, and two miles in front of Mont St. Eloy. The forward area was a scene of desolation—trenches and wire, shell-holes everywhere, mine craters here and there, showing more or less where No Man's Land was, and beyond them the gently sloping ridge, with little variation except a few shattered trees marking the site of La Folie Wood.

Such was the sector that our advance party of officers went up to reconnoitre on March 5th. The French were holding the line, and this was the battalion's only experience of taking over from them. We were not let into the secret of the why and wherefore of the move, but doubtless we relieved in order to allow them to send much wanted help to their friends at Verdun, who were now so hard pressed owing to the enemy's continued attacks. It was hoped that the fact of our taking over this part of the line could be kept from the Boche, at least until relief was complete, and to further this object the advance party were given French "tin hats" to wear so as to maintain the deception. We fear that despite our efforts, the enemy knew just about as much of the relief as we did, and rumour says that a Boche scout, on getting across to the French front line two days before we relieved them, openly expressed his surprise to the French sentry that the English had not already arrived! We were shown the greatest kindness by the French when we went up to reconnoitre, and they did all they could to explain the situation, and many an officer drank confusion to the enemy in a glass of sweet sparkling wine. Those who were there will doubtless well remember the group of officers being assembled just behind the Arras-Béthune road, in full view of the German lines, under the French brigade major, who was acting as guide, when the Hun gunners, not being able to let such an opportunity slip, at once put over a few "pip-squeaks," and we discovered with a considerable amount of pleasure, that our gallant allies were just about as good in getting to ground as ourselves, if not a trifle better. It was, however, a rude awakening to the fact that a war was still on, which we had rather forgotten during our stay in the south of France, and in the back areas.

Leaving Candas on March 6th, we marched on a very snowy day, *via* Doullens, to Iverny, moving on the 8th to Maizières, and on the 9th to Acq, where we had to make the best of most uncomfortable billets, the whole village being a seething mass of troops, French and English, and every billet crowded to its utmost limit. On the occasion of this move we marched, in accordance with instructions, in column of three's. This system was tried owing to the narrow roads, but only lasted a few months.

On the following day we moved up into support trenches, just in front of the Route de Béthune, where we stayed for four days cleaning trenches, carrying out general trench repairs, and improving dugouts. There were a certain number of deep dug-outs in this sector— our first experience of them—proof against all but the heaviest shells, though in every other respect a bad invention. Further behind, at Berthonval Farm, were huge caverns hewn out of the chalk, fitted up with wire beds, absolutely shell-proof, and having accommodation for about two companies. The dug-outs in the front line trenches, however, were mere shelters. Later on we were told to make our shelters in this area of a uniform pattern in small saps running back from the trenches, and when men could be spared from other more pressing work, a certain amount of progress was made in this respect.

The French dug-outs possessed one unique quality; they were decorated as only a Frenchman could decorate them, with most wonderful designs in pokerwork, which were always objects of the greatest interest to our visitors.

On March 15th, we were relieved by the 2nd Royal Irish Rifles, and withdrew for four days to rest billets, which consisted of some French huts partly in the wood, and partly in the open, just behind Mont St. Eloy. We are afraid we could not have given our predecessors a "billet clean" certificate in respect of these huts, many of which were a foot or more deep with accumulated rubbish of every description. There were no baths, and we had to rig up home-made ones with ground sheets and other means, using the cookers for providing the necessary hot water. We managed, however, to get clean clothing from time to time from the staff captain, Major Wordsworth, who got together a fascinating crowd of French ladies, and did much useful work as officer commanding laundry, at Mont St. Eloy.

We were at this time called upon to provide a contribution towards the brigade mining section, which was re-formed to help the French miners in the sector, and on March 17th, we had to part temporarily with Lieutenant R. V. Harvey, Corporal Boot and 12 men, who joined the brigade section under Lieutenant Webster, of the Robin Hoods. The arrival of 140 reinforcements the previous day had, however, swelled our numbers considerably, amongst several old friends in the draft being Sergeant G. Powell, who shortly became company sergeant-major of A Company, Seargeants I. B. Bell, S. Foster, Collins and Beniston, and Corporal A. B. North. We thus had a reasonable trench strength when we relieved the 7th Battalion in the left sub-sector on March 19th.

In this area we always kept to the same sub-sector, relieving as on many other occasions with the Robin Hoods. The 5th and 6th Battalions shared the right sub-sector, whilst the 138th Brigade were on our left. Each company, too, had its own section of trench, finding its own supports. From right to left they ran in order: D (Captain Hill), B (Captain Turner), C (Major G. S. Heathcote), A (Captain Vann, who had recently rejoined; during his absence on a course at

3rd Army School, his place was taken by Captain Lawson). Battalion headquarters was in a delightful spot just under the steep side of the Talus des Zouaves, and well nigh out of reach of everything but aeroplane bombs. Second Lieutenant Cox was signalling officer, 2nd Lieutenant Simonet, Lewis gun officer, 2nd Lieutenant Peerless, grenade officer, and 2nd Lieutenant Marshall, intelligence officer. The last-named was the first officer in the battalion to hold that newly created appointment.

The enemy front line was close to ours, in most parts about 70 yards away, but bombing posts in saps were in several cases not more than 10 to 15 yards apart. Talking and movement in the front line could often be heard quite plainly, whilst our bombers in the posts used to indulge sometimes in lobbing practice, and spent their odd moments in erecting or repairing wire netting to catch the Boche "potato mashers."

Our two communication trenches running forward—Boyau Central and Avenue Lassale—though well cared for and kept up by the French, were almost straight, and hardly traversed at all, particularly the former, and movement along them was precarious. The fire and support trenches, bearing such names as Schiller, Grange, Broadmarsh, Duffield, and Bertrand, were in very bad order, and work was at once concentrated in an effort to make a good line of resistance along Guerin Trench, practically the support line. Some work was also done on a reserve trench, known as Blanchetière. We felt this all the more necessary, as just before we took over from the French, the Boche had driven them out of their front line, and it seemed quite within the range of possibility that he might try to make a further advance. Our fears turned out to be correct, for later he did make an onslaught, though luckily not whilst we were there.

Unfortunately the enemy in capturing the trenches, had secured the shafts of all the French mines, and had consequently got a good start at various points along the front before the French could begin again. The result was that practically all the French mines were defensive, and intended merely to try and blow the Germans, before they could get under our lines. No doubt each side knew almost exactly where the other side was working, and at what approximate time any particular mine would go up. These were all shown to us on a plan, and carefully explained by the officer in charge of the French Miners, who were still at work in the sector. Each company had a cut-and-dried scheme for carrying out the instant a mine went up in its own or adjoining sectors. Anticipating the mine, parties were kept available to seize the near lip of the crater formed, with covering parties of Lewis gunners, riflemen, and bombers to go out on each flank, and working parties behind them to begin at once to dig a trench to join up the broken front line across the lip of the crater, wire the front and establish observation posts on the lip. All this work had to be started the instant the mine was exploded, in order to make certain that the Boche did not get possession of our lip of the crater, as well as his own. This entailed constant readiness and considerable anxiety on the part of those holding the front line.

The enemy showed no special activity, though on several occasions our front and support lines were badly knocked about, both by shells and trench mortars, which necessitated a vast amount of repairs, and caused us considerable casualties. In addition to high explosive he now began to send over for the first time *lachrymatory* gas shells, having a sweet smell and doing little harm except to make our eyes water. In the later stages of the war, they became, as we shall see, much more disagreeable.

As it was so difficult in this sector for our gunners to be able to identify our front line, we had to mark it with "artillery boards,"—white boards about 3 ft. by 2 ft., marked with different letters denoting the different sections of the front. These were stuck up by the infantry at night, in such a position that they could be seen by our gunners but be invisible to the enemy. Whether they were any real help or not is doubtful. Later on we were given a smaller portable type of board, coloured brown and marked with a black cross, a number of which were issued to each battalion, and carried with us as part of our equipment. They were intended for use in moving warfare to mark our advanced positions, but were eventually discarded as unsuitable.

We now began seriously to try and harass the enemy with trench mortars, for which purpose Trench Mortar Batteries were formed. The medium batteries fired a fairly heavy shell with a long tail (known as "footballs" or "toffee apples"), and the Stokes batteries a light shell, which could be fired at the rate of 20 or more per minute. We had recently sent 2nd Lieutenant Kebblewhite and five men to a school for a course in this work. It is feared, however, that the first efforts of the trench mortar experts in the trenches were not fully appreciated. A very nervous officer would go to his emplacement, fire off a few shells, and then gracefully, but rapidly retire, leaving the people on the spot to put up with any retaliation. And we well remember Captain Lawson being so annoyed at this going on, that on one occasion the bed plate mysteriously disappeared. On another occasion an emplacement was made one night with much care on D Company's front, ready for a big bombardment, but when completed was found to be in full view of six enemy sniper plates, about 100 yards away!

At sniping we more than held our own, though the enemy were very keen, and used to fire from steel plates fixed round the mine craters. We were unfortunate in losing at this period Sergeant-Drummer Clewes, who went home for discharge. He had done much excellent work in charge of the brigade snipers, his own "bag" being stated to amount to considerably over 100. As some recognition of his good work he was later awarded the D.C.M. His son, Corporal G. W. Clewes, another excellent sniper, left at the same time. Lance-Corporal Hagues took over the duties of N.C.O. in charge of snipers, and with 2nd Lieutenant Marshall, did some splendid work, including the blowing-in of several loophole plates with Colonel Fowler's elephant gun, which was now brought into use again.

Marshall's "pet," however, was the "dummy tree" on the Route de Béthune. This was a hollow tree about 20 feet high, formed of steel casing, and covered with imitation bark. Inside there were ledges to climb up by, and from it a most excellent view for a very long distance around, could be obtained. It had been erected by the enemy before they had been driven back.

Another item in the intelligence department which now came into use, was that extraordinary instrument known as the I-Tok, intended for picking up enemy telegraphic and telephonic messages. We never were supposed to know where its operators performed, and rarely did know, but more often than not they placed themselves near battalion headquarters, and the sheaves of papers they sent to brigade were mostly filled with scraps of our own messages. It is doubtful if much of value was picked up from enemy messages, but they certainly did good in keeping a check on our own conversations over the telephone, and were regularly used from now onwards. The Fullerphone, which was introduced a little later, and largely superseded the ordinary telephone, was reputed to be capable of transmitting messages in such a way that they could not be picked up.

Our firework *artistes*, too, decided that they ought to have a show, and accordingly arranged for us one night to have a display of red rockets in the front line. These rockets had been issued for use for night S.O.S. When the time came for them to be let off, the only visible result to those behind watching, was one feeble rocket which made a short lob, and fell to the earth. Only one other went off at all, and it had a great tussle with John Turner, nearly knocking him through a traverse, and then fizzing itself out in the bottom of the trench.

Another brainy person, one of our German scholars, decided one day to try the result of putting up a placard to give the Boche the news that the L15 had been sunk in the Thames. This was on April 2nd. Two days later a notice was put up opposite B Company's front, which said "Thanks for your news: you are all mad"—showing, we thought, a lack of originality on his part. This was one of the very few occasions upon which we either sent or received a message in this way.

Just about the same time, we had the pleasure of seeing a Hun plane brought down by one of our own, after a short sharp scrap in mid-air. Our man dived at the Hun and opened with Lewis gun fire, killing both the pilot and observer. The plane took charge of itself, and after a brief wild career, crashed near our battalion headquarters. It was no sooner down than it was shelled by the enemy and eventually set on fire. Various useful documents, however, were secured from it including some maps and a signalling code. The bodies of the pilot, Lieutenant Ziemssen, and the observer were buried at Mont St. Eloy by Padre Hales, who a little later received an appreciative letter from the pilot's widow.

With these and sundry other excitements, we got through two six-day tours in the line, and also spent two periods of similar length at our rest huts cleaning, training, and reorganising, for we were continually losing officers and men in various ways, and fresh ones were joining. Amongst the former we lost 2nd Lieutenants G. G. Elliott and Pitt, invalided to England, and the following warrant officers and N.C.O.'s who left us on completion of their term of service: Regimental Quarter-Master Sergeant Tomlin, Company Sergeant-Major Haywood, Company Quarter-Master Sergeant Shelton, and Seargeants Murden, Handford and Kettle. Arrivals included Major Ashwell, Captain H. Kirby, Lieutenant G. Wright, 2nd Lieutenant W. P. Duff, and about 70 men, many of whom were returned casualties, and in some cases anything but fit to resume active service. Company Quarter-Master Sergeant Dench became regimental quarter-master sergeant, Sergeant Bee company quarter-master sergeant of B Company, and Sergeant Hotson company quarter-master sergeant of C Company.

We were able to offer very little in the way of amusement just at this period, entertainers either being more or less non-existent, or somewhat shy. One afternoon, however, we succeeded in rousing sufficient enthusiasm to organise a boxing contest, one of the very few ever carried through by the battalion. In the heavy-weight contest

Regtl. Lance-Sergeant-Major A. Westerman

Company Sergeant-Major J. T. Slater
and N.C.O.'s of 'A' Company, 1917

between those two stalwarts, Sergeant Slater and Corporal Bryan, the latter retired after the third round with an injured hand. The middle-weight competition was won by Sergeant L. Green, and the light-weight by Sergeant Attenborough. The same evening, we managed an impromptu concert in one of the huts.

Our transport lines and quarter-master's stores during this period were back at Acq, and were fairly comfortable. Here for the first time we had the experience of taking rations and stores up to the line on the light railways, already constructed by the French, a system of transport in which both they and the Germans were much ahead of us. Stores were unloaded from the limbers at Ecoivres on to flat trucks, each of which was pulled by three mules. The Decauville track ran past Berthonval Farm, across the Béthune road, branching there right and left for the various battalion dumps, ours being in the Talus des Zouaves, near battalion headquarters. At first, the system did not work well, and there was much confusion, but later it was properly organised so that rations went up first, and Royal Engineers' stores about midnight. When we first took over the sector, the French caused much alarm to our men by carrying their stores to and from the Béthune road by electric trucks, actually the chassis and platforms of trains from Paris Plage, to which the bells used for warning pedestrians were still attached. One brakesman, Alphonse by name, like a wise person, usually went about his own business on arrival at the Béthune road dump, which was often a warm spot. The driver meanwhile got his load to take back, and anxious as all were who ever had a job of work at that particular spot, to get it done and be off, he adopted the practice which seemed to us rather foolish, of vigorously sounding his gong time after time, at the same time shouting "Alphonse, Alphonse," with the result that all our men vanished *tout-de-suite*, leaving him and the errant Alphonse to face any *whizz-bangs* which might result. Truly, the French are a remarkable race!

We must, however, congratulate them on that excellent institution in the Vimy sector, trench coffee shops. Where cooking for the trenches was a matter of some difficulty, as in this sector, it was a great boon to be able to get such excellent supplies of hot tea and other comforts as they provided. They were run by the French for some time after our arrival, but later were taken over by our own brigade, and put under the care of Captain E. M. Hacking, who was attached to brigade headquarters. We feel, however, we must attribute to the somewhat casual sanitary measures adopted by the French, the presence of so many rats in this sector. One often met them in droves in the trenches, and never before or after did we come across such numbers of the beasts, and such colossal specimens as we found during our stay in the Vimy trenches.

On April 12th, after a brief inspection near our huts by Major-General Stuart-Wortley, we went up to the trenches for our last and most eventful tour, which was destined to last eight days. Owing to falls of snow and rain, the trenches were in a deplorable state, and gumboots were in great demand, and our only means of keeping the men at all dry. At this time we had no such luxuries as drying-rooms. Heavy shelling by the enemy during the first three days made things still more uncomfortable. The real business of the tour, however, began on April 16th, on which night the French had arranged to blow one mine on our front, and another on the front of the 6th Battalion. Combined with this we had arranged for a small raid to be carried out by Lieutenant A. Bedford and 12 other ranks, who immediately the mines were exploded were to rush forward round the left edge of our crater, and endeavour to capture any Germans found in a small forward trench they had recently dug there. The mines were to go up at midnight, and at the same time our guns and trench mortars were to put down a barrage on the Boche trenches, which was to be augmented by rifle grenades and showers of grenades thrown from west spring throwers, under the arrangement of our grenade officer. Unfortunately, there had evidently been some bad synchronisation somewhere, for at five minutes before zero two Frenchmen suddenly came rushing towards Bedford, who was waiting in a communication trench with his party, shouting "Tout-de-suite! Tout-de-suite!" and almost at the same instant the mines went up. This was very unfortunate, as it enabled the Boche, who evidently knew all about it, to get their barrage down before our own gunners, who were waiting for zero. Bedford at once pushed on with his party with much dash in face of heavy fire from machine guns, rifles, trench mortars and bombs. He got as far as the advanced trench, which, however, was held in considerable strength, and finding himself bombed on both sides, he had to withdraw without getting a prisoner. His party got back alright, but unfortunately Bedford himself was knocked down by a bomb, and although only slightly wounded had to leave us, and a few days later was invalided to England. Captain Hill meanwhile carried out the consolidation with much success. As soon as the mass of debris, chalk and stones had stopped falling, parties at once got to work digging a new trench across the crater which was something like 30 yards wide by 30 feet deep, to connect the broken front line, establishing observation posts and putting out fresh wire. In spite of intense fire a sufficient trench had been dug by dawn, and the position made good. Great assistance was rendered by Captain Gray and the N.C.O.'s of D Company. Unfortunately Sergeant Markham, after most gallantly controlling the fire of his platoon for nearly two hours, under very heavy fire, was shot through the head and killed instantly. Another excellent piece of work was performed by Private E. Dobb, who leapt out of the trench on seeing a party of Huns trying to get round the crater, and hurled two bombs right amongst them. If they had had any doubts as to the possibility of getting round, this made up their minds, and they retired hurriedly.

The following night at midnight, the enemy sprang a mine on the front of our left company (A), which caused considerable trouble and heavy loss before the position was finally made good. A portion of our front line was blown up, and owing to the heavy state of the ground, which was much water-logged, and to the intense hostile bomb, rifle and machine gun fire, it was impossible to get a trench dug round our lip of the crater. It was not until three nights after that the situation was cleared, and our lip of the crater finally occupied, after some of the most difficult and miserable nights that it was ever our misfortune to experience. During these days there was little rest for anyone, and much excellent work was done by all ranks. Marshall carried out some splendid patrols, ably assisted by Lance-Corporal Hinchley, going out nightly through mud and filth, to ascertain the position around the crater. Duff did almost superhuman work with bombs and rifle grenades, being at it practically the whole night, for three nights in succession, and this was only his second tour in the trenches. The stretcher bearers too, as always, did most notable work, particularly Privates Holbery and Thomas, who fetched in our wounded from the slopes of the crater only a few yards below and in full view of the German sentry post, whilst Seargeants Deverall and Collins, and Lance-Corporal Ostick also did very gallant work, and Lance-Corporal J. T. Templeman throughout carried out his work of repairing telephone wires, with his usual skill and courage. So uncanny was the work of this period, that Lieutenant Peerless was able on one occasion to take deliberate aim, at 30 yards range, at a German digging hard in the bright moonlight, on the top of a crater.

On April 19th, the French sprang another mine, just to the left of our battalion front, as a result of which we got a certain amount of hostile shelling, whilst on the 20th, the enemy put up another, slightly to our left, which also brought its share of shelling on us. This, however, was our last, for much to our relief, and at comparatively short notice, the 10th Cheshires (25th Division) took over our sector on the night of the 20th, and after a weary trudge over that never-ending duck-board track, we got to Ecoivres by 1 a.m. on the 21st. Having done full justice to the excellent tea which the quarter-master and his followers had ready for us, we were taken in 'buses to Tincques, where we arrived about 6 a.m., and found that we were to be billeted partly there, and partly in the neighbouring village of Bethencourt. We fear we did not present a happy sight at that early hour to the ladies just going to church on a lovely Good Friday morning. Dawn is not an ideal time for seeing a battalion at its best, especially after an exceptionally hard eight days in water-logged trenches. Our total casualties in the Vimy sector amounted to 17 killed or died of wounds, 69 wounded and five missing.

It was a matter of great regret to us to hear later that the 25th Division suffered very heavily shortly after we left, when the enemy made a determined attack on the front recently held by us, and recaptured several trenches.

CHAPTER 7

The Battle of Gommecourt
April 22nd, 1916—July 2nd, 1916

At the time of our relief in the Vimy sector, plans at general head-quarters must have been in a forward state for the great offensive, which was to take place later in the year, and the part which the 46th Division was to play in that offensive must also have been fixed, and all our preparations now were for operations on a large scale.

We soon got rid of the mud and filth of the trenches, and were fortunate in finding at Tincques excellent baths run by the 51st Division, of which we made the best possible use, and having got our clothes and boots into respectable order, and everyone generally tidied up, it was not long before we were in very good form and fit for anything. Whilst this and other work connected with the interior economy of the battalion was going on, some of the officers had to spend a rather long day on Easter Monday, April 24th, in making a reconnaissance of the corps line between Maroeuil and Mont St. Eloy.

On April 26th, we were inspected by General Shipley, and felt rather pleased with the result of our efforts at cleaning, for the battalion looked well, and the general expressed his pleasure at the smart turnout.

The weather now was improving fast, and though excellent for training, it seemed too lovely on some of those delightful Spring days, to be spending our time learning how to kill people. Training included the new form of bayonet fighting, expounded by officers and others on their return from the Third Army school, where they had been duly instructed in its art by that expert, Major Campbell, who always succeeded in his inimitable way in so impressing his hearers, that they were not likely to forget for many a long day that "two inches well placed" was ample, and many other similar maxims. Many tips were also given us in bayonet fighting by Sergeant-Major Curly, one of the travelling physical training instructors, who often came to see us, and made a great impression on all who ever came under his instruction by his extraordinary keenness and energy. Eventually we passed on to practise the attack in waves, and were initiated into the art of doing this under the shelter of a smoke screen. In this form of attack, the advance from the moment of leaving the trenches, was carried out behind a smoke barrage, formed by lighting smoke bombs in the front line trench, and heaving them forward over the parapet. If they were good, a dense cloud of smoke was produced, and, provided the wind was in the right direction, it was possible to advance concealed behind the smoke cloud for a considerable distance. This method depended almost entirely for its success on the strength and direction of the wind. Later on, when the method was improved in the light of experience gained, smoke grenades fired from rifles were used, together with smoke shells fired by the artillery, so that a barrage could be put down at any required point, and, except in very strong winds, the smoke made to drift across any desired portion of the front of attack. In many of the later attacks this was done extensively, and was on the whole very successful. We practised at Tincques with hand smoke bombs only, and found it was not very difficult to keep direction through the smoke, whilst at the same time we were screened from the vision of the enemy.

Our period of training at this juncture was not a long one, as we were required nearer the front to begin the many operations necessary to prepare for the big attack. During that short period, however, we had to change our billets, and moved on April 29th, to Averdoignt, a pretty little village near St. Pol, where we were well housed and very comfortable. From there we were called upon to send a detachment for a few weeks' duty at Third Army headquarters, at St. Pol, and a composite company consisting of 60 of B Company, and 100 of C under Major G. S. Heathcote were entrusted with the task. They must have done excellent work and evidently made a good impression, as a letter of special praise on their smartness and good work, was sent to the battalion, on their return by the army commander, General Allenby.

We moved by easy steps from this area, which we left on May 6th, marching that day to Rebreuviette, the following day to Gaudiempré, and on the 10th to Bienvillers. The transport remained behind at Gaudiempré, but moved from there on the 11th to La Bazéque Farm, near Humbercamps. This move brought us into the VII Corps, commanded by Lieutenant-General T. D'O. Snow.

Up to the time of our arrival this part of the line was reputed to be almost the quietest on the whole of the western front. It was said that company commanders slept in pyjamas, even when holding the front line, and certainly the personnel of battalion headquarters at Foncquevillers, which was only about 1000 yards from the enemy line, lived there for all the world, as if in a peaceful country village in England. The dug-outs were made for comfort rather than safety, and were in many cases artistically decorated with pictures, doubtless got from houses in the village, and surrounded with elegant little garden plots, which showed evident signs of careful tending on the part of our predecessors. Together they formed a kind of miniature Garden City. This comparative quietness lasted for a considerable time after our arrival; indeed we often failed to understand why the enemy refrained from shelling, as on many occasions we must have offered exceptionally favourable targets. Day by day work went on often in full view of the Hun, and within a range of between one and two miles, and the roads almost daily were a mass of transport of every kind, moving to and fro in broad daylight, and literally asking for trouble. There can be no question that the chief reason was a great shortage of ammunition at this time amongst the Germans, who were under very strict orders as to its conservation, otherwise no doubt we should have had a very disagreeable time. Doubtless they made careful note of all our doings, and the fact that something big was going to take place must have been perfectly obvious to them. That it was so we found afterwards, when in a successful attack, the diary of the German regiment opposite to us (55th R.I.R.) was captured, and from it we learned that they had been able to foresee exactly where the attack was coming. This diary was most interesting reading, as it noted each day their observations of our doings, and the conclusions they drew from them.

The attack of the 46th Division was to be directed against the German trenches west of Gommecourt, immediately opposite the village of Foncquevillers. The German trench line here, forming the Gommecourt Salient, was the most westerly point that they ever held as a permanent line. The general object of the attack was to cut off this salient. The 56th Division were to attack on the south, and join hands with our division east of the village of Gommecourt, and so establish the left flank of the whole Somme attack.

All the efforts of the troops of our division who were not actually holding the line, were concentrated on preparing the divisional front for the attack. The chief work that we were concerned with, was the digging out of old communication trenches from Foncquevillers to the front line, a distance of about 700 yards. There were something like ten or a dozen of these, several of which were named after our division. The principal were Stafford Avenue, Lincoln Lane, Leicester Street, Nottingham Street, Derby Dyke, Roberts Avenue, Rotten Row, Regent Street, Raymond Avenue, and Crawlboys Lane. All these had to be dug out about two feet below their existing level, making them about seven feet deep, and boarded with trench grids from end to end, which entailed an enormous amount of work. In addition, the front line had to be cleared of the barbed wire, with which the unoccupied portions had been filled, support and reserve trenches had to be prepared for the supporting troops in the attack, forward or "jumping-off" trenches to be dug at the last moment, for the assaulting troops to attack from, "Russian saps" to be dug out into No Man's Land to form communication trenches, by knocking in the thin covering of earth left to hide them, dug-outs to be made for forward battalion headquarters, and several miles of narrow cable trench to be dug about six feet deep for the protection of telephone wires from forward headquarters back to brigade, division and artillery headquarters. In addition to all this navvying work, large quantities of stores had to be carried up to forward dumps in the trenches, ready for taking forward if the attack succeeded, shelters had to be made at various points in side trenches, convenient to get at from communication trenches, for storing large quantities of bombs of all kinds, small arm ammunition, iron rations, water, picks, shovels, sandbags, and other Royal Engineers' material likely to be required to consolidate the ground we hoped to win in the attack. The transport of all these stores, and of all the necessary Royal Engineers' material, and the work entailed in all these preparations was colossal, and our first real experience of anything of the kind. It is probable that at this time the mass and variety of material required in an attack, reached a degree of complication never equalled either before or after. The German comment on this contained in the diary already mentioned is of interest. It states:

> It must be acknowledged that the equipment and preparation of the English attack were magnificent. The assaulting troops were amply provided with numerous machine guns, Lewis guns, trench mortars, and storming-ladders. The officers were provided with excellent maps, which showed every German trench system actually named and gave every detail of our positions. The sketches had been brought up to date with all our

latest work, and the sectors of attack were shown on a very large scale. Special sketches showing the objectives of the different units, also aeroplane photographs were found amongst the captured documents.

During our week at Bienvillers from May 10th to 18th, we were mostly engaged in improving the defences of the village, and the approach trenches behind Foncquevillers, and in work on cable trenches. It was here that one or two civilians roused our suspicions, as they insisted on ploughing and carrying on their cultivations so very near the front, some days working with grey horses, others with brown, and our battalion Scouts were told to keep a special eye on them. Nothing, however, happened so far as we were aware that in any way altered the course of the war, as a result of our or their action.

On May 19th, we relieved the 5th North Staffords in Foncquevillers, being then in reserve to our 5th, 6th, and 7th Battalions, who were holding the front line. Our transport moved the following day to Souastre.

This was a somewhat uneventful period, and after a few days in the front line mostly spent in improving trenches, we were relieved on June 5th, by the 4th Leicesters, and marched back to huts at Humbercamp, preparatory to moving further back for our final training for the "big push." We left there the following night, and arrived in the early hours of June 7th at Le Souich, where we were destined to spend one of the least enjoyable periods out of the line that we ever experienced. We were only there for a week, but into that short time was crammed an immense amount of work both in training, and in cutting wood and making wattle hurdles in Lucheux Forest. The weather was very wet, and our billets were anything but comfortable. In our humble opinion the training here was too strenuous. We had to march out four miles to the training ground, and four miles back in full marching order, practise the attack for two hours through fields of growing corn three or four feet high soaked with rain, and complete six hours training daily (not including the marching) with bayonet fighting, physical exercises, and drill in the fields near our billets. It takes very little of such intensive training to make men stale.

The form of attack practised was that ordered for the general attack, which we now knew was to take place about the end of June: this allowed each battalion a frontage of 250 yards, with three companies in front, and one in support, each company having its four platoons echeloned in depth at distances of about 50 yards, thus forming four waves, the men in each wave being extended to about four paces. In the attack the leading wave was to go through to the final objective, the other waves occupying and mopping up the trenches passed over by the leading wave.

A full size model of the German lines at Gommecourt that we were to attack, was made near Sus-St. Leger, the trenches being dug to a depth of about two feet. Tape lines were laid for the men to form up on, and the whole attack was practised time and again as a drill, until eventually we were able to carry it out without losing direction, with a fair amount of success.

We were now stronger in officers than we had ever been during the campaign, our strength being 38. This was due to the recent arrival of several reinforcements, including Captain Piggford and Lieutenant Hindley, rejoined, and 2nd Lieutenants H. de C. Martelli, J. B. White, C. J. Wells, A. G. T. Lomer, T. G. Day, E. A. Huskinson, H. I. Newton, and A. A. Field. We had, however, lost Captain Lawson, who left for a tour of duty at home, and Major E. H. Heathcote, Captain Gray, and 2nd Lieutenant Hodgson invalided to England, also 2nd Lieutenant Peerless, who unfortunately got badly hurt one day by accidentally kicking a live rifle grenade, which had been left lying on the bombing practice ground. His place as battalion grenade officer was taken by 2nd Lieutenant Duff. Lieutenant Simonet had gone to hospital, and was succeeded as Lewis gun officer by 2nd Lieutenant Tomlinson. Major G. S. Heathcote was attached to headquarters, Third Army, and was succeeded in command of C Company by Captain Piggford, whilst Major Ashwell became second-in-command. We were not particularly strong in other ranks, something less than 500 being available for the attack, though we had recently received over 100 reinforcements, including a very good draft of 61 from the 2nd Sherwood Foresters. Fortunately general headquarters had taken an excellent step in laying down that certain officers and other ranks known as "battle details," were now to be left out of every attack to form a nucleus for carrying on battalions in the event of their suffering heavy casualties. This was a very wise precaution, and was adopted by us for the first time in the attack at Gommecourt.

On June 15th, we marched to Humbercamp, the transport at the same time moving to lines at La Bazéque Farm. Captain H. Kirby was now transport officer, having taken over from Captain Davenport, who, after being attached for some time to XVII Corps Light Railway Company, Royal Engineers, went to brigade headquarters to learn staff work. The transport vehicles had somewhat camouflaged them-

Regt. Lance-Sergeant-Major W. Mounteney, D.C.M.

Company Sergeant-Major W. Stokes, D.C.M.
and sergeants of C Company, 1917

selves, having been decorated on all sides by wonderful and mystic signs, so as to show to the initiated to what unit they belonged. If you enquired you would be told that the dark blue square meant "first line transport," the narrow light green oblong edged with white placed on the left of this square was for the "8th Sherwood Foresters," whilst the square divided diagonally into red and green, and bordered with white, was the sign of the "46th Division." It was not an easy matter to arrange all these coloured patches clear of the odds and ends carried on the different vehicles, and this problem was still exercising the minds of those in authority nearly up to the Armistice—such an important part did it play in the ultimate winning of the war!

We now knew that in our brigade we were to be the battalion in reserve, the 5th and 7th Battalions having to carry out the assault, with the 6th Battalion in immediate support. As a consequence much of the dirty work during the final preparations for the attack fell to our lot. This consisted chiefly in holding the trenches during our preliminary bombardment, and putting up with such retaliation as the Hun might choose to carry out, and in completing the final arrangements in our own trenches. After three days at Humbercamp, during which we found large working parties for digging cable trenches, and putting up screens to conceal the approaches to trenches, we moved to Foncquevillers on June 18th, and took over part of the left sub-sector from the 5th Lincolns. An immense amount of work had been done whilst we had been away; the prospects seemed bright, and our hopes rose. Our headquarters at Foncquevillers became a centre of attraction to all and sundry. At every hour of the day and night we had callers, from the divisional commander downwards. The brigadier and his staff constantly paid us visits. Gunners galore came to sample what we kept, and incidentally to see about finding observation posts. Royal Engineer gentlemen requested our help at every turn and corner, usually wanting working parties rather larger than our total strength, whilst "Tock Emma" officers were on our doorstep day and night. Indeed so great was the crowd that at one time we almost had to put Corporal Cross on to regulate the queue, and all the time our poor stock of victuals and drinks was getting less and less.

All went well until the afternoon of June 23rd, when there was a violent thunderstorm, which practically undid the whole of the work we had carried out in the trenches, filling them in most cases to a depth of two feet or more with mud and water. This area was a difficult one to drain, and it was impossible to get the water away, so that all hands had to be got on as soon as possible to man trench pumps, and endeavour to clear the trenches in that way. This method was extremely laborious, and very little real progress was made, though every available man was put on to the work. Our poor dug-outs were knee deep in water, and the newly constructed bomb and other stores were too weak to stand such a storm, and in most cases collapsed. Our hopes sank, for we realised how much depended on all the careful preparations which had been made, and that the time left before the attack would be all too short for us to get the damage repaired.

It is impossible to give anything like an adequate idea of our plight for the next few days. The artillery scheme, including a six days' bombardment, began on the following day with wire cutting, causing a certain amount of retaliation, which added to our trouble. This got worse on the following days, doubtless owing partly to the fact that we dug a new advanced trench. This was in a deplorable mess, and our men who had to occupy it had a most distressing time. Casualties rose rapidly, especially in B Company, whose front line trench was enfiladed from Adinfer Wood. Our carrying parties, who had to take up Royal Engineer material, ammunition of all sorts, rations and other stores to various points in the line, mostly adopted the very suitable dress of a sandbag kilt and boots. They were objects of much interest, but it was the most workmanlike rig-out for our trenches, which in many cases remained knee deep in mud and water for several days. The carrying had to go on whatever happened, and continued night and day, assistance being got from the 6th and 7th Battalions, from the Machine Gun Company, and from the transport men of all units, parties of whom marched up nightly for the purpose. With trenches in such a state, it is needless to say that it was impossible for men to hold the line for many days, and in order to give us a brief respite, we were relieved by the 5th Battalion on the night of June 27th, and moved back to Pommier.

The nine strenuous days during which we had held the line, had been a severe trial, and where everyone did so well it is difficult to single out any for special mention, but we feel we must say how much we owed to Captains Turner, Vann and Hill, for the excellent way in which they worked to keep up the spirits of their men during those trying times, and to Seargeants Slater and Rawding, for the splendid way they kept their men together during several particularly unpleasant "straffs" by the Boche of our front trenches. During that time, too, much excellent patrolling was done by Marshall, who unfortunately was wounded one day when taking rather too great risks in observing the Boche lines, and Martelli, ably helped by Lance-Corporal Hickman, and Private E. C. Bryan. Our casualties during those nine days included Captain Vann, slightly wounded, Lieutenant Hindley, who got a nasty splinter wound on the nose, 16 other ranks killed, and 44 wounded.

The chief incident during our two days' stay at Pommier, occurred on the afternoon of June 30th, when the Huns began shelling the church. John Turner, Michie and Harvey, were having tea in their mess, which was only a few yards from the church, when a 5.9 blew in the end of the house, practically bursting inside the room where they were sitting. Their escape was little short of a miracle. John Turner, however, as one would expect, came into headquarters smiling and perfectly cool, though covered with dust and blood. Harvey and Michie were a bit shaken, the former having to go to hospital.

The attack, having been postponed owing to the bad weather, was eventually fixed to take place on the morning of July 1st, and we left Pommier again the night before to take up our position at Foncquevillers. Our cookers were taken down to the western edge of the wood behind the village, where we were issued with soup and rum on arrival at about 10 p.m. Each man carried in addition to the following day's ration, his iron ration, and a bacon and bread sandwich. Equipment carried included 200 rounds small arm ammunition, four sandbags, two Mills grenades, two gas helmets, haversack, waterproof sheet, and a supply of wire cutters and gloves. The new pattern tin hat, with which we had by this time all been supplied, formed a by no means unimportant part of our dress. It was not a thing of beauty, and took a little while to get used to, but it proved a good friend to many in the days that were to come.

The attack by the 46th Division was to be carried out with two brigades, Staffords and Sherwood Foresters, with the Lincolns and Leicesters in reserve. The 139th Brigade on the left was to attack between the northern edge of Gommecourt Wood and the Little Z, the 5th Battalion being on the right, and 7th on the left, the 6th Battalion in support, and 8th in Reserve; the German first, second and third lines were to be captured, and in conjunction with the 56th division on the right, our line was to be carried to a point just east of Gommecourt village.

We reached our assembly positions early on the morning of July 1st. Our bombardment opened at 6.25 a.m. and the discharge of smoke from our front line began an hour later. Under cover of this the assaulting battalions moved off from our advanced trenches at 7.30

a.m. A heavy and accurate barrage was immediately put down on our front and support lines by the enemy, who were evidently well aware of the extent of the attack and ready for it. The attack by the 139th Brigade is described in the following extracts from the captured diary of the 55th R.I.R., the times given being German:

G1. sector 7.30 a.m. An extremely violent bombardment began, overwhelming all the trenches and sweeping away the wire.

8.30 a.m. The enemy's fire lifted. The enemy's attack, which was made under cover of gas bombs, was perceived. In consequence of the sharp look-out kept by the commander of the 4th Company, and by a platoon commander holding the most dangerous portion of the line, the shell holes were occupied exactly at the right moment, and the attackers were received with hand grenades. The barrage fire which had been called for began at once.

8.40 a.m. Strong hostile skirmishing lines deployed from Pilier Farm. They were at once met by heavy machine gun and infantry fire. Second Lieutenant—, of the 2nd Company who was holding the 3rd support line of G1, recognised the superior strength of the enemy's attack which was being carried out against No. 4 Company. In spite of the intense bombardment he decided to advance with his platoon over the open, and, crossing the second line, reached the front line of G1 at the decisive moment to reinforce No. 4 Company. The enemy built up his firing line and attempted to press forward with bombers and flame-projectors, but was repulsed everywhere.

10.30 a.m. The fine spirit of the troops of the 2nd and 4th Companies succeeded by their stubborn resistance in annihilating the thick charging waves of the English. The ground was covered with numbers of dead, and in front of our trench lay quantities of English arms and equipment. Gradually the artillery fire recommenced on the front line trenches and rose to a pitch of extreme violence in the course of the afternoon. The fact that all attacks were completely repulsed without the enemy gaining a footing in the front line of G1. at any point is due, next to the bravery of the troops, to the carefully thought-out arrangements of Major—, to the care of the officer commanding No. 4 Company, and to the energy of the platoon commanders.

To resume our own story. At about 8.0 a.m., as the forward trenches were cleared of troops, we began to move forward, but everywhere found the trenches, which were still in many parts deep in mud and water, blown in, or blocked by dead bodies, or wounded men trying to make their way back. Little progress was possible, and there was nothing to be done but to await further developments.

Although little news came through, it soon became evident that the attack on our front had not succeeded. We learnt later that, owing to the difficulty experienced by the supporting waves in getting across our own water-logged trenches, they lost the advantage of the barrage, and that the smoke cleared long before the bulk of the assaulting troops had got across No Man's Land. In spite of our long protracted artillery bombardment comparatively little damage had been done to the German trenches and wire, and our men met with heavy rifle and machine gun fire, not only from their front, but also from the right flank, where the 137th Brigade were unable to gain the German front line owing to uncut wire. A few of both the 5th and 7th Battalions got into the German trenches, but they were soon surrounded and overwhelmed. Some who were wounded before reaching the wire, crawled for shelter into shell holes, where in several instances, they were deliberately bombed or shot by the Boche from their trenches. At 3 p.m. a fresh bombardment was begun by the right brigade, and continued on our front, with a view to an attack being made by two companies of the 6th Battalion, but this was cancelled.

At 5.5 p.m. we were ordered to send out daylight patrols to ascertain the position of affairs in front. Several volunteers, amongst whom were Corporals G. Clay, and C. E. Bryan, Lance-Corporals Moss and Hickman, and Privates Charles, Brett, Adams, and Nightingall, remained out for some time, and brought back useful information. Meanwhile much gallant work was also being done by the stretcher bearers and others. Privates Holbery, Thomas, Nelson, and Shearman worked continuously for nearly 36 hours carrying in wounded, often under heavy fire, whilst Company Sergeant-Major T. Powell, who brought in three wounded men by daylight, and Sergeant Grainger, who controlled his men with great skill during the battle and also rescued a wounded man, are deserving of special mention.

At 6.10 p.m. we received instructions to take over the original front and advanced trenches from the 6th, and remnants of the 5th and 7th Battalions, who were there, and this was done. Later, however, the 5th Lincolns took over the line as they had been ordered to carry out another attack at midnight, in order to try and rescue some of the

5th and 7th Battalions, who it was thought were still in the Boche trenches. This, however, was not pressed, and finally A Company of our battalion were given the melancholy task of scouring No Man's Land to find the dead and wounded. Eventually the 5th Lincolns took over from us on the morning of the 2nd July, and we withdrew the same day to billets at Gaudiempré.

Even as we left Foncquevillers ill-luck pursued us, for a premature burst of a shell from one of our guns took place close to us as we were formed up behind the wood ready to move off, and wounded four, fortunately not seriously. Otherwise our casualties during the actual battle had not been heavy, amounting to three killed, two missing (attached to trench mortar battery) and 37 wounded.

We cannot look back with anything but regret on that awful battle, when so many lives were sacrificed apparently to no purpose. July 1st is not our happiest of days—indeed on two successive occasions it was our most unfortunate day of the year. It must have been quite obvious to the enemy that this was to be the flank of the Somme attack, although some demonstration was made by the 37th Division on our left. The enemy, therefore, were able to bring all their guns from the direction of Adinfer Wood to bear on No Man's Land on our front. Lack of troops had necessitated the employment of the attacking battalions in the most exacting fatigues up to the very eve of the assault. Probably, barely a man had had a full night's sleep for a week prior to the attack, and there had been scarcely a day or night when rain had not fallen consistently and heavily, and working parties had not been soaked through to the skin. Those of us, who eight months later, stood on some of the German concrete machine gun emplacements opposite, commanding a magnificent field of fire from positions proof against the heaviest shells, saw still the lines of dead bodies lying in No Man's Land, a tragic and pitiable witness, if witness were needed, that the failure of the attack was in no measure due to any lack of dash or courage on the part of our indomitable infantry. Practically every officer of the attacking battalions was killed or wounded, and a large proportion of the men, and but an insignificant proportion fell alive into the hands of the enemy.

It was some slight comfort to receive from the corps commander an appreciation of our efforts, which had kept busy a large number of the enemy's best troops, and to know that we had a share in the success of the great Somme attack, and that our terrible losses were not entirely in vain.

CHAPTER 8

Bellacourt
July 2nd, 1916—October 29th, 1916

We spent one night at Gaudiempré, and on July 3rd, moved a few miles north to a delightful camp at Bavincourt, where we made up our minds to have a well-earned rest. The camp was charmingly situated, and we were preparing to have it run on model lines, when alas, in the early hours of July 4th, sudden orders were received to move. We had, however, made the best of our few hours there, most of us going to an excellent entertainment by the Barn Owls, the concert party of the 37th Division, which cheered us immensely.

The fighting on the Somme, which had gone successfully for us in many parts, was causing rapid reorganisation and consequent movement of troops, so that our sudden move was not altogether surprising. We left Bavincourt on the morning of July 4th, and after a little excitement due to the shelling of the road, and a terrific thunderstorm, we eventually got settled once more at Pommier, with the exception of A Company, who went on to Bienvillers. The rest of the battalion joined them there on July 7th, except transport and quarter-master's stores, which moved to La Cauchie. Our most important work there was the somewhat ticklish procedure on two nights of carrying up to the Monchy trenches, about two miles north of Foncquevillers, cylinders of gas to loose off on a suitable occasion. These were drawn at Hannescamp, and for carrying were fastened to poles, each cylinder requiring two men. Special precautions were taken to ensure perfect silence, so as not to give the enemy an idea that gas was being installed. Further, in order to protect the carrying party, in case any of the cylinders got broken by shells or otherwise on the way up, every man wore his smoke helmet rolled up on his head, ready for instantly pulling down over his face. Neither steel helmets nor caps were worn on these occasions. As the cylinders had to be got up to our front line trench, the operation was attended with considerable risk, but fortune favoured us, and it is believed that the battalion never suffered a casualty when engaged on the work, though large parties had to be found on several occasions for a similar purpose.

We moved on July 10th, by route march to Bellacourt, a village about five miles south-west of Arras, and giving its name to a sector which was to prove easily the most peaceful and enjoyable part of the line we ever held. Transport moved to Bailleulval, where they got good lines in a small orchard, and the quarter-master's stores were comfortably fixed up in billets.

It was from this department that we were first to hear of the activities of our new divisional commander, Major-General W. Thwaites, R.A., who made it a practice of frequently visiting transport lines at early morning stables. Torrance with his ready wit at once dubbed him "The Mushroom Picker," an epithet which we were told gave him much pleasure when it reached his ears, but did not have the least effect upon his early morning visits.

Several new officers had recently joined from our 3rd Line, including 2nd Lieutenants C. F. Woodward, F. M. Corry, H. G. Kirby, B. P. Page, W. B. Easterfield, and D. H. Parker. Second Lieutenant A. Bedford also rejoined, and others who arrived shortly afterwards were Lieutenant R. Whitton, who had been adjutant of the 3rd Line, 2nd Lieutenants Skinner and Moore, back for the second time, and 2nd Lieutenants C. H. Hicks, D. F. Ranson, L. E. King-Stephens, G. F. Visser, F. D. Byrne, B. W. Hall, and A. D. Bailey. Company Sergeant-Major Haywood rejoined with a draft of 72 reinforcements, and was appointed company sergeant-major of C Company, where Sergeant Leivers had been carrying on for a short time in place of Company Sergeant-Major J. A. Green, who had been invalided to England.

We were thus fairly well off for numbers, when on July 11th, we relieved the Liverpool Scottish in the left sub-sector of the brigade sector, this being one of the rare occasions on which relief was carried out by daylight. The distribution was as follows: Right—The Willows—A Company (Captain Vann); Centre—The Osiers—B Company (Captain Turner); Left—The Ravine—C Company (Captain Piggford); Reserve—Bretencourt—D Company (Captain Hill). Battalion headquarters was in the sunken road, just in front of Bretencourt, off Engineer Street. Each company had two platoons in the front line and two in support; a system which, besides being more or less in accordance with field service regulations, worked extremely satisfactorily, for whilst the front line posts could be held by comparatively few men, either in the line or at the heads of the various saps running out into No Man's Land, working parties and patrols were found from the support platoons, and were thus able to get back to the support line on completion of their task, and rest in comparative comfort.

The frontage allotted to us was a long one, and the front line was thinly held, some of the posts being as much as 200 yards apart. Frequent visiting patrols were necessary during the night to prevent any daring Boche from getting into our lines. In the communication trenches, blocking posts and gates were fixed at various points to hold up the enemy if they did ever get in and attempt to push forward. To look after the rear portion of these communication trenches the system of trench wardens was instituted during our stay at Bellacourt. These were usually light duty, or warworn men drawn from the various battalions, whose duty it was to repair broken trench grids, relay any that required it, clear falls of earth, and generally look after upkeep.

This sector was reputed to be the quietest on the British front, and though we had one or two lively times, there is no doubt that for the period of three-and-a-half months we were there, it lived up to its reputation. Rumour said that some of our troops had been in the habit of going out and repairing the barbed wire by daylight! Certainly it was normally extremely peaceful. The trenches were from 300 to 400 yards apart, and in the region of the Ransart road on the right, one could indeed go out for some distance without coming in view of the Boche trenches. The weather during most of our stay was of the best, and there could be few things more pleasant than to stroll on a quiet afternoon round some of the communication trenches, e.g., Dyke Street, Couturelle, and La Motte, where masses of wild flowers of every kind and of brilliant colours were in full bloom, and in many parts completely covered the sides of the trenches. Cooking was normally done out of the trenches, and hot meals were carried up in kettles or food containers (something in the nature of large thermos flasks) by the reserve company billeted at Bretencourt.

We had something of a shock during our first tour in the trenches, and began to suspect the reports as to the quietness of the sector, for on our second morning the enemy poured over for nearly an hour, between 4.0 a.m. and 5.0 a.m., showers of heavy trench mortars on to part of the front line held by B Company. Their aim was very good, several bombs falling right into the trench and doing considerable damage, whilst Lieutenant Lomer's platoon, which was holding the part bombarded, had four men killed and nine wounded. One man had to have his foot amputated by Johnstone, the medical officer, in order to be released from a shelter that had been smashed by the bombs. Seargeants Tanner and Yeomans did splendid work in rescuing the wounded, as did also Sergeant Bescoby, Private Axon and other stretcher bearers. This, however, turned out to be the only "hate" of its particular kind that the enemy inflicted on us during our stay. Possibly it was to let us know that he was aware of our recent arrival, and wished to give us a welcome, but most likely it was what we knew as his "Travelling Circus" which he brought up at certain times in order to carry out an organised straff on a particular piece of the line.

For some time after this, and in fact for most of Our sojourn here, life in the trenches was of a somewhat humdrum character. There were a few days of activity now and then, but normally the enemy was very inoffensive so far as we were concerned. He did, however, raid the 6th Battalion one night in the right sub-sector, almost completely levelling one of their communication trenches with heavy trench mortars during the preliminary bombardment, on account of which we had to stand-to, when back at our rest billets at Bailleulval. On another occasion we had a fidgety night owing to a gas alarm having been given. This however, proved but another case of "wind."

The work in the trenches was of a normal character, but we welcomed that new article known as the "A" frame, consisting as its name indicates of framing shaped like the letter A. This was the best form of support for trench revetment that we ever had, and from this time onwards was used almost universally. A suggestion of this exact form of framing had been made by Colonel Blackwall as early as November 1915. and submitted to higher authorities, who turned it down as unsuitable.

A further great advance was made by us here in the provision of deep dug-outs, for which the chalk soil was eminently adapted. Excellent plans were drawn out by Major Zeller, commanding the field company attached to our brigade, for complete systems of these dug-outs to be made in the support line, and a special brigade dug-out company was formed for this purpose, to which we contributed, besides a number of men, 2nd Lieutenants Moore and Powell. Great progress was made with the work, and before we left the sector a large number had been finished, and fitted up with wire beds on wooden framework in two tiers, with rifle racks and other etceteras. The organisation of this work was one of the first tasks of the new brigade major, Captain W. P. Buckley, D.S.O., of the Duke of Cornwall's Light Infantry, who had succeeded Major Neilson, when the latter left to take up a higher appointment. In Major Neilson we lost one who was always ready to help and advise on every possible occasion, and though it was with the greatest regret that we said goodbye to him, it was a great pleasure to know that his hard work had brought its reward.

At this period after doing six days in the front line, we spent six days in brigade reserve at Bellacourt, where three companies were in billets, and usually found large parties for the Royal Engineers for working in trenches and dug-outs, and one company provided garrisons for the four posts in front of the village, Starfish, Boundary, Burnt Farm and Orchard. After a further six days in the front line we went back for six days to Bailleulval, where we were able to have our periodical clean up, do a little training, and generally enjoy life for a brief space. We relieved always with the 7th Battalion, and held the left of the brigade sector, which remained the same as originally taken over, except that we gave up the Willows on the right and took over Epsom on the left.

Our billets at Bailleulval were fairly comfortable, and were constantly improved, under the guiding hand of Major Wordsworth, the staff captain. We had a splendid parade ground on the high land behind the village, a good canteen, a sergeants' mess, a corporals' mess, home-made Russian baths erected with much skill by our own Pioneers, and frequent visits from the *whizz-bangs*, who gave us excellent programmes. We played cricket, football, both soccer and rugger; we had officers' riding classes, which were a source of much interest not to say amusement, to the onlookers, and we got good dinners at the well-known Seven Sisters, in the neighbouring village of Basseux. The weather for the most part was delightful, and life was extremely pleasant.

Major-General Thwaites twice inspected us, and all who were in the battalion during the time he reigned at division will remember what an inspection by him entailed! Our best salute proved very inadequate on the first occasion, and the commanding officer was requested, after putting himself and his horse in front of the centre of the battalion, to do it again! Captain Turner, too, who was acting second-in-command, got a polite enquiry as to what he was doing with his horse! Poor "Strawberry" was apparently rather upset over the fixing of bayonets! As a rule, however, we believe our efforts to make a good show did not pass unnoticed, though a good deal that was uncomplimentary was said. On his second inspection Lieutenant-General Snow, the corps commander, was with him, and appeared to be quite satisfied with the turnout.

Training at this time, so far as the battalion was concerned, consisted only of such general work as could be done in the few days we spent periodically at Bailleulval. The divisional school, however, was in full going order, Regimental Sergeant-Major Mounteney doing duty there for a time, and in addition a brigade school was formed at Basseux, to which Major Ashwell went as commandant and expounded the art of war to young subalterns and others, taking with him 2nd Lieutenant Hopkinson as his adjutant. Whilst Major Ashwell was away, Captain Turner took over the duties of second-in-command, leaving B Company in the capable hands of Lieutenant G. Wright. At an assault competition arranged by the brigade school on October 12th, we almost swept the board, winning five out of eight events—physical drill, bayonet fighting, bombing, relay race, and obstacle race—so we were well satisfied with our efforts, and the training work that was being done. By this time the whole battalion had been fitted out with the short rifle, the last of the old long rifles being handed to ordnance on September 26th.

A new *toy* that was issued in these days was that horrible thing known as the Lewis gun hand cart. Tomlinson had some most entertaining experiences in trying to get mules to pull these handcarts, but the mules usually found it more interesting to try and turn round to see what extraordinary things on wheels they were now being insulted by being asked to pull, or in going off at breakneck speeds to try and get rid of them. These carts were never popular, and never a success, and gradually, by being carefully "left" by the roadside or some other convenient spots, they were eventually disposed of.

The most notable event during this period was undoubtedly Vann's raid, the first really successful raid carried out by the battalion. This took place on the night of September 21/22nd, and was carried out by Captain Vann, with practically the whole of his (A) company. In order to illustrate the thorough manner in which the scheme was devised and carried out, the story is given in some detail.

The point to be raided was a short sap known as Italy Sap, running out from the Boche front line about 300 yards away. The wire protecting the sap was cut during the afternoon of September 21st by our 2-inch trench mortars, and other gaps were cut on another part of the front further north, partly as a "blind" and partly for use in a future operation. In order to verify that the gaps were properly cut, a wire patrol under Lance-Corporal Hickman went out at 8.0 p.m. and reported that the gaps were good, and that the ammonal tubes which the Royal Engineers had in readiness to take out and blow gaps with were not required. Frequent bursts were fired by our machine guns on to the gaps to prevent them being repaired by the enemy

LIEUTENANT-COL. B. W. VANN, V.C

before the raiding party got there. At 11.15 p.m., the wire patrol again went out and laid tapes from the gaps back to Cavendish Sap in our own front line to guide the raiding party across No Man's Land. The party was divided up into several smaller parties, commanded respectively by Lieutenant Martelli, 2nd Lieutenants Duff, White, and Hall, and Company Sergeant-Major G. Powell. In addition there were two teams of brigade machine gunners to guard the flanks, and seven sappers to blow up dug-outs. The total of the party was five officers, and 136 other ranks. All identification marks, badges, letters, etc., had been removed from all members of the raiding party, and faces, hands and bayonets were blackened. Smoke helmets were carried in the pocket, and gas and phosphorus bombs were taken for clearing dug-outs, together with a number of flashlights and torches. At 12.15 am the enemy trenches in the region of the area to be raided were bombarded by 18 pounders, 4.5 and 6-inch howitzers, 2-inch trench mortars, and 3-inch Stokes mortars. The raiding party guided by the tapes, got as close up to the barrage as possible, and as soon as it lifted at 12.28 a.m., went through the gaps and into the enemy trenches. One German who was met was at once bayoneted. Several dug-outs were bombed, and in some cases set on fire, one being blown up by the Royal Engineers with an ammonal tube. An enemy machine gun which opened fire from the right was immediately silenced by our Lewis and machine guns. The time fixed for the return of the party was 12.50 a.m. and it was only in the last minute or so that the main object of the raid, a prisoner, was secured. Most of the dug-outs were empty, but eventually Vann found one which contained some Boches. These he at once ordered to come out. Two came up with bayonets fixed, one of whom was at once shot dead by Vann, and the other wounded. They were followed by four others, including a stretcher bearer, who came out with hands up shouting *"Kamerad!" "Kamerad!"* They were at once hustled out of the trench with the scantiest of ceremony and brought back to our lines. Immediately after this, Vann ordered his bugler to sound the recall signal, and at the same instant the prearranged signal of six red rockets went up at battalion headquarters. During the last ten minutes of the raid the enemy had surrounded the occupied portion of the trenches with red lights and their artillery had begun to shell their front line and Italy Sap, but did the party little harm, and every man got back to our trenches, the only casualties being eight men wounded. The net result of the raid was that five Germans were killed by the raiding party, and five taken prisoners, including one wounded, apart from any casualties inflicted by our bombardments. It is worth noting that a bombardment of the area around the blind gap was also carried out, and that the barrage there "lifted" before that on the gaps where the raid was actually to take place. This was undoubtedly of great assistance to the raiding party in diverting the enemy's attention, and in causing his barrage to come down first in No Man's Land opposite the blind gap, where we had no troops whatever. The number of rounds used to cut the wire was 670, fired by seven 2-inch trench mortars.

Many messages of congratulation were received on the success of the raid, including one from the corps commander. It was a great pleasure to all when it was known shortly afterwards, that Vann, whose gallantry knew no bounds, had been given a bar to his M.C., and that the M.C. had been awarded to Duff, who had already done most admirable work at Vimy, and was one of the pluckiest officers the battalion ever had. Vann was subsequently awarded the French Croix-de-Guerre.

Much of the success of the raid was undoubtedly due to the excellent patrolling which had been done by Martelli and his scouts, Lance-Corporal Hickman, and Privates Bambrook and Haslam, who throughout worked with the greatest skill, and left nothing undone to ensure that all was in order. Many gallant deeds too, were performed in the enemy trenches. Private Chappel, a leading bayonet man successfully showed one Boche the proper way of making the point; Private Walsh wanted to go on to the German second line when he was unable to find any to kill where he was; Drummer Heath showed great bravery and devotion as he had often done on previous occasions, in carrying messages; Drummer A. L. Smith, though wounded, remained at his post to the last to sound the recall signal; while great gallantry was also shown by Lieutenant Martelli, Company Sergeant-Major G. Powell, Sergeant Slater, Corporal Carrier, and Private Needham. The raiding party had a special little dinner of their own a few days after the raid at the canteen at Bailleulval.

There is but little to record of our other doings in the trenches. We recall efforts being made to have daily trench exercises carried out, such as physical jerks, bomb throwing, and rifle practice, but the orders issued on the subject were, we fear, honoured rather in the breach than the observance! We did, however, appreciate the opportunity given us in these days of sending officers from time to time to our gunner friends to learn something of the elements of artillery work, and though these visits were very short, it was certainly not the fault of the gunners if we were not wiser for the instruction they gave us. We on our part were also called upon to do some instructing, having attached to us at various times Lieutenant-Colonel Smeathman of the Hertfordshire Regiment, Lieutenant Haslam (afterwards killed) and 12 men of the Artists' Rifles, and an officer and 14 men of the 1st King's Dragoon Guards, to all of whom we imparted as much of our knowledge of trench warfare as was possible during the short time they were with us.

As time wore on changes took place. Vann, who had once more been slightly wounded during his raid and was not very fit, went to the senior officers' course at Aldershot, and was succeeded in command of A Company by Captain E. M. Hacking. Captain Davenport after a week's tour in the trenches for instruction left to attend the staff course at Cambridge. Hicks, who was afterwards killed, went to the trench mortar battery, E. A. Huskinson to the 138th Brigade to learn staff duties, Easterfield to the Machine Gun Corps, where he won the M.C., Corry (who later died of wounds) and Newton to the Royal Flying Corps, Woodward to the *whizz-bangs*, and Captain A. Hacking (from brigade headquarters), Field, Parker and Wells were invalided to England. Jones, who followed Marshall as intelligence officer, got wounded on patrol, and was succeeded by Martelli. Under the new scheme of sending home as instructors, warrant officers and N.C.O.'s who were feeling the strain of long periods of active service, we lost Company Sergeant-Major Chappell, and Seargeants L. Bell, Shore and Wells. Company Quarter-Master-Sergeant Hotson then became company sergeant-major of B Company, and Sergeant Deverall, company quarter-master-sergeant of C Company. Our casualties during the period amounted to seven killed, and 37 wounded. Against these losses we were joined by two officers, 2nd Lieutenants J. M. Johnston, and E. W. Warner, and about 80 men, including 40 from No. 4 Entrenching Battalion.

All this time the Somme fighting had been going on, more or less successfully, and we wondered time and again when our turn would come to go and take part in it. Divisions around us were moved backwards and forwards, to and from the fighting area, with almost lightning rapidity, and still we were left in this peaceful part with few cares, and almost began to think we had been forgotten, or that the office boy had scratched our name off the list of divisions in France! But it was apparently not so, for on October 20th, we got news of our approaching move to a training area, preparatory, no doubt, to taking a more active part in the fighting. Eventually, on October 29th, we were relieved by the 16th Manchesters and said goodbye to that delightful area where we had such good times, and to which we shall always look back with the greatest possible pleasure.

CHAPTER 9

The Capture of Gommecourt
October 29th, 1916—March 17th, 1917

Having spent the afternoon of October 29th in packing up, we left Bailleulval about dusk, and late the same evening arrived at Warluzel, where we spent the night in indifferent billets. We proceeded the following day to our old quarters at Le Souich, where we rested for 24 hours, continuing the march on November 1st to Neuvillette, and on November 3rd, to our final destination Maison Ponthieu, in the Third Army (St. Riquier) training area, having completed a march of something like 40 miles.

Considering that this area had been used for training for some considerable time, we cannot say that we found the billets of the best or well provided with those comforts, which one might reasonably expect for troops out of the line preparing to take part in an offensive. Our energies at first were therefore concentrated on trying to make ourselves comfortable, and a considerable time was spent in carrying out improvements, making bathing arrangements, cookhouses, canteen and reading rooms. Rightly or wrongly we were inclined to think that we were unlucky with regard to billets, as we so often found ourselves scavenging and cleaning up other people's refuse. Doubtless every other unit thought the same. In the way of entertainments we had little or nothing, and Maison Ponthieu itself boasted nothing more than one or two estaminets. Auxi-le-Château, the home of the Third Army training school, had a few shops and was rather more lively, while, for those who could get there, St. Riquier was quite interesting, and the battlefield of Crécy was not far off. Abbeville some distance away, was patronised only by a few lucky ones.

We stayed in this area for nearly three weeks, and trained hard with a view to taking part in the Somme offensive. The chief points were to make everyone fit, and to practise formations for open warfare. For the former, recreation of every kind and for all ranks was an essential part of the programme, though we were inclined to think that perhaps a little too much compulsion was added to this part of the scheme. Inter-platoon football matches were a prominent part of the recreational training, and created a great deal of genuine interest and amusement. There were also inter-battalion football matches in the division, in which we started well by beating the 7th Battalion, but were hopelessly defeated by the 5th Battalion at Noyelle on November 18th, by eight goals to nil. One of the most entertaining matches was that which took place at Maison Ponthieu, between divisional headquarters and brigade headquarters. When the divisional goal was threatened S.O.S. rockets were sent up and smoke bombs let off, which to the onlookers, seemed rather to baffle the defending goalkeeper, who was none other than the assistant provost marshal, Major Newbold! Preliminary contests held to select representatives for the divisional boxing championship, which unfortunately did not materialise, were won by Sergeant Slater, Sergeant Attenborough, Signaller Gearney, and Private Hall.

For open warfare we practised mostly the attack, beginning with artillery formation. Those who did know something of it had by now grown very rusty, after so many months in trenches, whilst many officers and men in the battalion at this time, had had practically no training at all in this kind of warfare, so that much work was required in the simple practices of shaking out into artillery formation, lines of companies, half-companies, platoons or sections, and eventually extending for the final stages of the attack leading up to the assault. The other main feature of the training, was practice in night marching on a compass bearing and subsequent deployment for attack.

On the whole we must confess we felt that the training was rather overdone. We had to put in many hours daily, and the march to the training ground at Yvrencheux and back, some six miles in all, was to say the least of it somewhat tedious. We were besides, most unfortunate with regard to weather, which was very unpleasant most of the time, and we were hardly sorry when our time came to leave the area. We were not, however, required to take part in the Somme fighting, as this had by now more or less worn itself out. From what we read and heard from troops, who came out of it, of the appalling condition of the ground and the impossibility of making any further progress during the winter, we were not surprised or sorry that there was no need for us in that direction. Our lot was to return once more to our old trenches at Foncquevillers.

Changes in personnel during this period were mostly in officers. Major Ashwell had rejoined and resumed his duties as second-in-command; Major Lane also rejoined after nearly 18 months in England, as a result of his wound at Kemmel, and took over A Company from Captain E. M. Hacking. A further addition was Lieutenant Simonet, who had by some means managed to get the hospital authorities to pass him fit again for general service. We also had a small draft of 32 men. On the other hand we had to part with six officers at extremely short notice to the 12th Rifle Brigade and King's Royal Rifle Corps which had lost very heavily in the Somme fighting, and sent 2nd Lieutenants Ranson, Hall (who later won the M.C.), Visser, H. G. Kirby, Byrne and Bailey (afterwards killed). Second Lieutenant Cox also left us to join the signal company of the 14th Division, his place as signalling officer being taken by Lieutenant Warner. For good work on a subsequent occasion Cox was awarded the M.C. Lieutenant Martelli was still intelligence officer, Lieutenant White, grenade officer, and Lieutenant Tomlinson, Lewis gun officer.

We went by easy stages back to the line, leaving Maison Ponthieu on November 22nd, and proceeding to Bealcourt, and the following day to Neuvillette. The chief item of interest in our two days' stay there, was a revolver shooting match between teams of officers from our own and the 7th Battalion, in which we were badly beaten. On November 25th, we marched to Humbercourt on a pouring wet morning, arriving there about mid-day drenched to the skin. Here we stayed for nearly a fortnight, training and cutting wood in Lucheux Forest. The weather was wet and cold, and as the village lay in a hollow, we got the full benefit of all the rain, and consequent flooded streams. On November 30th, we took part in a divisional cross-country run, a part of the programme left over from the St. Riquier area. The distance was two and three-quarter miles, and we felt quite pleased to finish 6th out of the 13 battalions running, our pleasure knowing no bounds at seeing C. B. Johnstone and F. Torrance finish well within the time limit, happy if breathless.

On December 2nd, a brigade ceremonial parade was held at Sus-St. Leger, where we were inspected by Major-General Thwaites. It was a bitterly cold day, but on the whole the show passed off well. It was perhaps aided a little by the fog, which covered one or two of our more intricate and unconventional movements rather successfully.

On the following day we took part in what was probably one of the most interesting football matches in the battalion's history, when a team of officers played one from the 7th Battalion, and beat them one-nil after a great tussle.

It was at Humbercourt that Sergeant "Sammy" Foster played an important part in trying to make us all "gas proof." With much success he made up a gas chamber in the village out of the shed for the *Pompe à incendie*, where all ranks of the battalion were fitted with the new small box respirator, which had just arrived. This proved to be much the most satisfactory form of gas mask we ever had, and continued in general use up to the end of the war.

We left Humbercourt on December 6th, and the same day went into brigade reserve, in the Foncquevillers sector, the 46th Division having taken over this portion of the line from the 49th Division. The sector was now fairly quiet, everyone having more or less gone into winter quarters. Our rest billets and transport lines were at Souastre, where, considering all things, we were fairly comfortable. There were good baths under the control of one of those celebrated town majors, of whom so much has been heard, a Y.M.C.A. hut, and a new form of entertainment in the shape of a cinema, which our division had recently added to its institutions. The divisional Whizz-Bangs were still showing, but were rather under a cloud, although that great actor subaltern from the battalion, Moffat Johnston, gave them a helping hand for a short time. Being "out to soldier," however, he preferred the front line, and very soon came back to us.

When in divisional reserve all companies were back at Souastre, and carried out a little training in addition to the usual refitting and cleaning. Parties were also generally provided for town major's fatigues. When in brigade reserve two companies were at Souastre, and two at Foncquevillers, the latter finding garrisons for posts on the eastern edge of the village, and at Fort Dick, between Foncquevillers and Hébuterne.

When in the line we held the left sub-sector, relieving with the 7th Battalion, the right company front having its right on the Foncquevillers-Gommecourt road, the centre company being disposed about Lincoln Lane, and the left company front running from Roberts Avenue to the Brayelle road. Companies holding the line, had two or three platoons in the front line, and the remainder in support. The support company occupied the dug-outs in Sniper's Square.

The trenches throughout this period were in an appalling state, though efforts had been made to improve them by the 49th Division, who certainly left Roberts Avenue well revetted, and with a good floor of trench grids. For the most part, however, they were deep in mud, and in a deplorable condition, and "gumboots thigh" were in great demand. Dug-outs were of the poorest, and life in

MAJOR-GENERAL THWAITES OUTSIDE BATTALION HEADQUARTERS,
THE BRASSERIE, FONCQUEVILLERS

the trenches was not pleasant. Efforts were made to improve matters during our stay and the Royal Engineers and Monmouths did a great deal of work, helped by large parties from all battalions, but improvement was very slow.

Fortunately the trenches were no great distance from the village, where company cooks had their cookers, whilst the battalion was in the line, so that hot meals were sent up regularly, and included a hot supper issued generally about midnight, the meals being mostly carried up by the support company. During the latter part of January and beginning of February, we had very hard frosts and much snow, and the carrying parties had a difficult task in walking on the slippery roads and trench grids, but this was overcome to a great extent by the use of sandbags tied over the boots. It was perhaps a somewhat expensive method to employ with sandbags costing something like a shilling each, but they served the purpose very well, and were in great demand in consequence. A drying-room was established at battalion headquarters in the village, in a large cellar, fitted with double-tier wire beds, stoves, and braziers. A supply of blankets was also available, so that the men who had been on patrol, or had got wet through, could come down from the line and get their wet clothes dried and a good rest and sleep in comfort. Inter-Battalion reliefs were carried out every four days, whilst companies were able to relieve their men in the front line every 48 hours, or, when the weather was extremely bad, every 24 hours, by taking up the men from the support line. By this means, the time any particular man was actually in the front line was reduced to the lowest possible limit. During December and January, reliefs were carried out by daylight, usually beginning immediately after breakfast, and being completed by about noon. This system not only enabled the incomers to settle down in the trenches before night, but also gave the relieved battalion four complete nights out, a system which was very much appreciated. At the end of January we changed to night reliefs. The main artery for traffic was the Foncquevillers–Souastre road, and although it was usually fairly quiet, we sometimes astonished ourselves at the pace we made along it on relief nights, and most of us were glad when we got over the crest into Souastre.

Martelli and his Scouts and many others did some very good patrols, but on some nights when the moon was bright, and the ground covered with snow, this work was not easy. Long white nightshirts complete with hoods were tried, but not considered very suitable, as they looked quite dark against the white snow, and on the whole were not a success.

Though normally quiet the sector was occasionally trench mortared and shelled fairly heavily, most attention being paid to the front line about Roberts Avenue and Lincoln Lane, the Gommecourt road, the Orchard in front of the village, where our heavy trench mortars, familiarly known as Flying Pigs, had their quarters, and the village itself. It was in connection with one of these bombardments that the I-Tok machine professed to have some success. By some means a Boche map had been secured showing the areas into which our front was divided for the purpose of "shoots", and if the I-Tok picked up messages from which it was inferred that a shoot over a particular area was likely to take place, the information was at once passed on to the battalion concerned. On one occasion when such information was received, no sooner were the men cleared of the area than it was indeed shelled! It may have been an accident of course, but the I-Tok personnel took the credit, which we hope was deserved.

One night, when the 7th Battalion were in the line, they were raided after a very heavy bombardment, in which they suffered several casualties. The following day the officer commanding that battalion sent us a kind message of appreciation of the prompt way in which Captain Turner and B Company, who were in support in Foncquevillers, had turned out and stood by ready to help. Fortunately their services were not required.

The most unpleasant experience we ourselves had was on February 16th, when we relieved the 7th Battalion for the last time in this sector. The relief itself was carried out under difficulties, owing to a certain amount of gas shelling, but later on the Hun sent over perfect showers of gas bombs, and absolutely deluged the front and support lines, whilst he also fired a considerable number of gas shells into the village. It is estimated that in all between 500 and 600 were put over, mostly filled with *phosgene*. It was our first experience of any real gas shell bombardment, and partly owing to this and partly to the high concentration of the gas used we suffered heavy casualties, four men being killed and 24 wounded.

Christmas Day, 1916, was spent in the line, and passed off very peacefully without anything untoward happening. We were not able to get our Christmas dinners until early in the New Year, when we were back at Souastre, and made the most of all the good things that had been sent out by kind friends at home. Each company enjoyed a most sumptuous dinner, followed by a splendid entertainment provided by local talent, speeches, and so on.

The battalion front remained unchanged until early in February, when we extended northwards to include the Crawlboys Lane area, then held by the 138th Brigade.

About the same time we had companies of the 2/5th, 2/8th, and 2/11th Battalions London Regiment with us for instruction, and a fine lot of men they were. Our difficulty was in knowing where to put them, for whereas we were about 80 per company, they came out with their full complement of 250. One dreaded on occasions what might happen if the enemy suddenly decided to shell the trenches they held, for in some parts they were almost like the proverbial sardines. They came out fully equipped, with mobilisation stores made up to completion. Rumour says that when they had finished their instruction with us they were wiser not only in trench routine, but also in their quarter-master's department!

This period saw several important changes in personnel. With great regret we had to part with Major Ashwell, who left to take up the duties of commandant of the divisional school. This post, however, he only held for a brief space, as his excellent services throughout the war were very soon rewarded by his appointment to command first the 5th, and shortly afterwards the 6th Battalion. He was succeeded as second-in-command by Major Lane. Captain E. M. Hacking, who commanded A Company for a time, was appointed railhead disbursing officer, and handed over his duties to Lieutenant Andrews.

Captain Turner stuck to B Company, but during periods of absence of the commanding officer and Major Lane, acted as second-in-command, leaving Lieutenant G. Wright to look after his company. Captain Piggford, after struggling on for some time, although very unfit, eventually had to go down sick, and shortly afterwards was appointed divisional claims officer, to which he later added the duties of divisional burials officer. When he left, C Company was handed over to Lieutenant Abrams. Captain Hill, after a long and successful period in command of D Company, also had to leave owing to sickness, and was succeeded by Lieutenant Simonet. In 2nd Lieutenant King-Stephens we lost a very gallant officer, and a great favourite. He was killed one morning when returning from wiring. The fog which had been so helpful for the purpose, cleared rather suddenly and a Boche sniper picked him off just as he was getting back to the trench. Reinforcement officers who joined during the period were 2nd Lieutenants C. H. S. Stephenson, A. E. Geary, and J. E. Mitchell. So far as other ranks were concerned there were now no discharges as the Military Service Act, which was in force, gave to very few the opportunity of getting home. We lost, however, two excellent company sergeant-majors, G. Powell and Hotson, who went to England to train for commissions, and were shortly followed by Company Sergeant-Major T. Powell. George Powell was destined one day to be awarded the D.S.O., whilst Hotson unfortunately met his fate in Italy. Seargeants Slater and Rawding, and Company Quarter-Master Sergeant Deverall, then became company sergeant-majors of A, B, and D Companies respectively. Our casualties in the line during this period were not heavy, amounting to seven killed and 47 wounded. Reinforcements who joined totalled 243, and included several men from the Sherwood Rangers Yeomanry.

On February 19th, after handing over our portion of the front line to battalions of the 138th Brigade, we marched back to St. Amand.

We now entered upon what turned out to be one of the most interesting periods in the history of the battalion. The idea at the moment was that the 46th Division should take part in an early offensive against Beaurains, just south of Arras, and the immediate purpose of our relief was to withdraw to the Sus-St. Leger area and dig a model of the front to be attacked, ready for one of the other brigades of the division to practise over. With this object we moved back on February 20th, to Ivergny, where we spent the first few days refitting and reorganising. The latter was now becoming of great moment, for important changes were taking place. To begin with the battalion grenade platoon, that picked body of specially trained bombers, to which it was everyone's ambition to belong, ceased to exist, and the personnel rejoined their companies, in which from this time onward each platoon had its own section of bombers. This was only a preliminary to the absolute reorganisation of the platoon, which was now rightly coming into its own, and regarded as the most important tactical fighting unit. We had already been lectured at Souastre by Lieutenant-General Sir Ivor Maxse, our corps commander, and later director general of training, also by Major-General Thwaites, on the new organisation of the platoon, which was now to consist of four specialist sections: (1) riflemen, (2) bombers, (3) rifle grenadiers, (4) Lewis gunners. We now began the preliminaries of this new organisation, which was to remain practically unchanged for the rest of the war. The signallers were also reorganised under Lieutenant Warner, and divided into battalion and company signallers.

After only a few days training in Lucheux Wood, and digging model trenches near by, we were ordered to move to Simencourt, preparatory to taking over the line near Beaurains. Just about the same time, however, the Boche began his great Somme retirement, and on February 27th, the news came through that he was evacuating the Gommecourt salient. This of course entailed a complete change in our plans, and instead of moving north, we marched back towards Foncquevillers, reaching Grenas on February 28th. There we stayed for one night, proceeding the following morning to St. Amand, where hurried preparations were made to relieve the 138th Brigade, who were busy following up the retreating enemy. We left St. Amand early on the morning of March 3rd, for Gommecourt, where we took over the old Boche lines from the 5th Leicesters. The enemy were still in the northern and eastern outskirts of the village, and the line was in a more or less fluid state. The enemy's retirement continued slowly during the day, and our troops kept moving on in close touch. The 7th Battalion were working in conjunction with us on the left, and the 31st Division on our right. On March 4th, the withdrawal was more rapid, and it became somewhat difficult to keep touch. The few dug-outs that were not set on fire or otherwise destroyed, were found to contain quantities of stores and rations, and showed evident signs of having been evacuated very hurriedly. A neat souvenir in the shape of a Boche bugle was got from one of these dug-outs, and is now treasured with the battalion plate at Newark. One was rather nervous of booby-traps in some of them, but so far as our experience went at this time there were none. Pigeon

Wood was captured during the afternoon, after some fighting and an unpleasant sort of game of hide and seek, and we also occupied Rettemoy Farm, and The Z.

Evidently thinking that we were too close on his heels, the enemy delivered a determined counter-attack about 6 p.m. against C Company, who were holding the trench line in front of La Brayelle Farm, forcing them to withdraw slightly. During this attack Lieutenant Duff did magnificent work in holding off a bombing attack, and Lance-Sergeant Sansom gallantly held on to a bombing post which was cut off, until he was rescued by a party ably led by Corporal Street, who went forward under heavy fire, and opening fire on the attacking enemy, enabled the post to withdraw. Sergeant Henley also did splendid work in holding his post against a strong bombing attack, until he was eventually wounded in the head, dying the next day.

The battalion suffered a great loss the same day by the death of Lieutenant Abrams, who was killed during the afternoon whilst reconnoitring near La Brayelle Farm. Thinking, apparently, that the coast was clear, he was walking across the open with his batman when a Boche machine gun suddenly opened fire on them at close range, killing them both instantaneously. C Company then came under the command of Lieutenant A. Bedford. The casualties that day in other ranks, were seven killed and 17 wounded.

Very little happened on March 5th, except a certain number of bombing encounters, and at night the 5th Battalion took over the right portion of our front from Rettemoy Farm to Brayelle Graben. On March 6th, we were relieved by the 6th Battalion, commanded by Major Ashwell, and moved back to dug-outs in and around Gommecourt. It was with much regret that we heard on the 9th that Major Ashwell had been badly wounded the previous night in an attack on Kite Copse.

The line had not altered appreciably when we relieved the 6th Battalion again on March 10th. The weather was cold, and the trenches were deep in mud and water, and movement was extremely exhausting. The object now was to force the enemy to retire more rapidly, and orders were received that we were to seize Hedge Trench and Kite Copse as soon as possible, and form a line across to Rettemoy Graben on the right, which was to be captured by the 5th Battalion. As a preliminary during the night of March 11/12th, a party from C Company under Corporal Kirk successfully cut gaps in the wire in front of Hedge Trench.

At 1.10 a.m. on March 13th—a wet, pitch dark night—the 5th

Battalion attempted to seize Rettemoy Graben in conjunction with a hastily planned attack by the Staffords on their right. In spite of the most gallant efforts, these attacks were dismal failures, and attended with a large number of casualties. At the same time strong parties of A, C and D Companies made demonstrations along communication trenches towards Hedge Trench. At 7 a.m. on the same day Captain A. Hacking, who had now rejoined the battalion and taken command of A Company, ordered Lieutenant A. H. Michie with his platoon to seize Kite Copse. Michie made a rapid reconnaissance, and in a very short time found himself in possession of this important point, the enemy garrison having nearly all left to fetch their rations. The water was boiling in the dug-outs, and a supply of coffee was found, which enabled Michie's platoon to get breakfast as soon as the position was consolidated. During the evening the enemy made two determined counter-attacks against the position, but these were both driven off with heavy loss by the excellent work of Private Teare with his Lewis gun, Sergeant King and Corporal Scrimshaw.

In the afternoon of the same day Lieutenant Hopkinson attempted to push through the Burg Graben to Hedge Trench, but was met by strong opposition. He, however, withdrew his party without casualties, after inflicting several on the enemy. For his gallantry here and splendid work on other occasions "Hoppy" was awarded the M.C. On this occasion Corporal Kirk again did splendid work. Many other gallant deeds were performed during these strenuous days, special credit being due to Sergeant Edis for good work in charge of a platoon, Corporal J. Wilson, who worked unceasingly for 36 hours, when in charge of an advanced bombing post, Corporals Blythe and Marvill for good patrol work, and Lance-Corporals Fern, Martin and Leonard, and Privates Simpson, Crane, Peplow, W. Barwise, and Bacon. Invaluable work was also done by the transport section, who had a very hard time in getting supplies up to Gommecourt. The roads were in an appalling state, and every night were thronged with horses and vehicles, whilst the enemy had ample ammunition to loose off before retiring, both high explosive and gas, most of which he sent over to Foncquevillers or Gommecourt, or the road in between. It was on one of these nights that Private Chapman did excellent work in clearing a block in the road, in the midst of heavy shell fire, and enabling the masses of transport to pass.

In this miniature moving warfare, the signallers found their task more entertaining than it had hitherto been. Warner one day went so far as to try flag-wagging, until he found that his performance was in

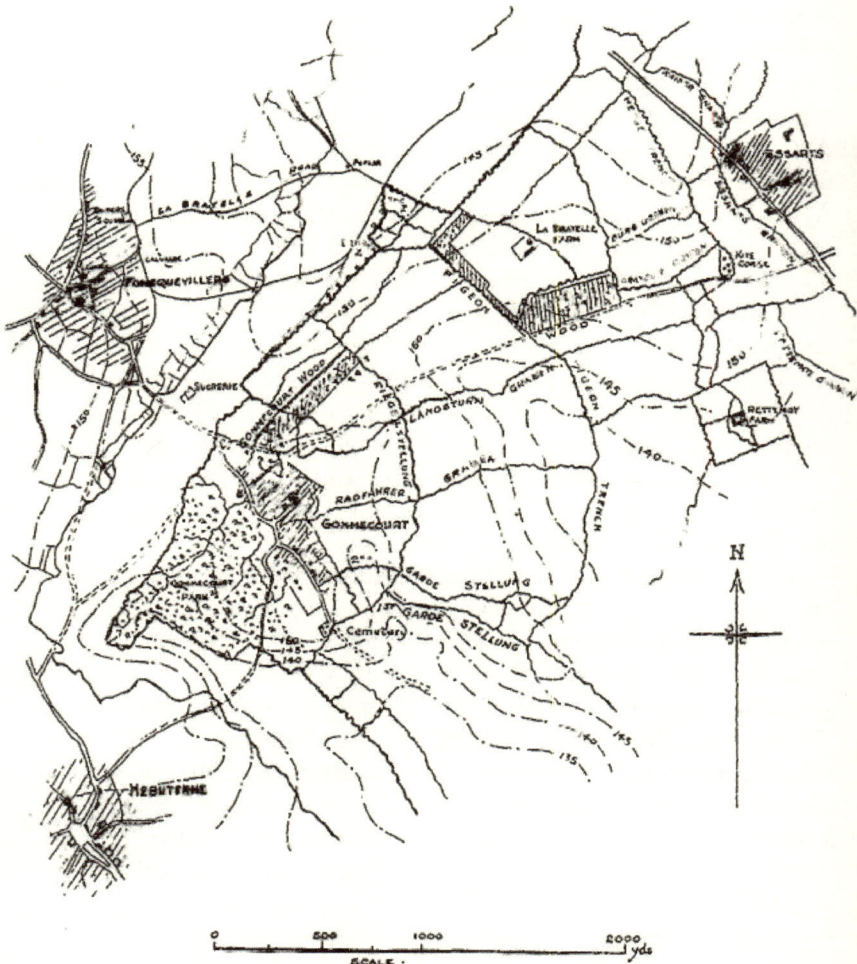

MAP TO ILLUSTRATE CHAPTERS 7 & 9

full view of the enemy. On another occasion he established a trench wireless set to brigade, which he maintained successfully for an hour, but at the end of that period the whole apparatus was dissipated in the explosion of a German shell. A second effort with new apparatus met with a precisely similar fate.

As evidence of the closeness with which we had followed up the retreating enemy it is interesting to note that at one time Captain Hacking reported that from his front line, he could hear perfectly plainly both our own gunners and those of the Boche giving their fire orders.

An incident in the quarter-master's department that was not without interest, was a great ride by our great quarter-master. In his anxiety to see that all our wants were provided for (or was it for a heavy wager?), long before horses were allowed so far forward "Harry" Torrance arrived one night at Pigeon Wood mounted on "Buster," having defied the military police and all other traffic controls. Another unique experience was that of Lieutenant Whitton, who for a brief space held the appointment of town major of Gommecourt, and was we believe, the one and only person ever to occupy that post of honour. As officer commanding 300 dozen Boche mineral waters found in the village, he was a very useful person to know.

On March 14th, we moved back to Gommecourt, where we were finally relieved by the 4th Leicesters three days later. The enemy were retiring very rapidly, and on the same day evacuated Essarts and Bucquoy. Being squeezed out owing to the shortening of the line, the 46th Division began to follow several other divisions to the back areas, preparatory to taking part in operations in other spheres. Never again did we go to Gommecourt, which we believe is being retained by the French untouched. It will thus ever remain a type of a completely destroyed village, for it is probably one of the worst treated in the whole of France. There were certainly one or two spots where the remains of buildings were still standing, but practically every sign of a once prosperous village had been obliterated. As a type of German fortification it was probably one of the best, containing the deepest and best constructed trenches we ever saw. The wire in front was almost impossible to break through; each line of trenches was protected in much the same way; the dug-outs were deep and proof against all except the very heaviest of shells, and there was a long subterranean passage built by the Boche from behind Gommecourt Wood to his second line, along which reinforcements could be brought in safety to counter-attack any troops that might have gained a footing in the front line. It was sad to find magnificent tapestries and valuable pieces of furniture, evidently taken from the *château*, which once existed there, adorning the German dug-outs or ruthlessly cut and knocked about, but sadder still to find the bodies of our own officers and men lying unburied exactly as they had fallen on that fated 1st of July, 1916. It is pleasing, however, to record that the grave of an officer of the brigade was found in Essarts with the inscription in English on the cross: *To the memory of a very gallant British officer and gentleman, killed July 1st, 1916.*

CHAPTER 10

Lens

March 17th, 1917—July 4th, 1917

After relief at Gommecourt we spent two days at Souastre, and then marched *via* Bayencourt and Courcelles-au-Bois to Contay, where we arrived on March 23rd. The roads for much of this journey were in an appalling mess, partly as a result of constant shelling, and partly through being cut up by the masses of transport which had passed over them during the recent wet weather either in following up the retreating enemy or in withdrawing to back areas. Vehicles were often up to the axle in mud, whilst bicycles gave an immense amount of trouble, and this was not the only occasion on which we found it far preferable to foot-slog, even with heavy packs, than to be signallers with bicycles, which practically had to be carried. Loaded with pack and other paraphernalia, the heavy army pattern bicycle is not a lovable companion, except on a more or less perfect road. A really first-class exhibition of bicycle manoeuvring was given during the move by Private Bunce, who always seemed to be in trouble, and was a source of much amusement to his fellow signallers. We stayed one night at Contay, moving the following day to Bertangles, and on March 25th to Revelles, a delightful village about seven miles west of Amiens. We were taken through Amiens itself in motor 'buses, which picked us up just north of the town, and deposited us on the other side, leaving us to finish the journey on foot.

On passing through one village during this backward march we saw some men wearing Sherwood Forester badges. They turned out to be men of the 2/8th Battalion, and proved the correctness of rumours we had recently heard that that battalion was actually in France. One of the 2/8th men accosted a fellow man of our battalion, as he passed, with the remark "Who are you?"

"1/8th" was the reply, "Who are you?"

"Right", said our friend—we believe a signaller—"You can tell your mother you've seen some real soldiers now!"

We were supposed to entrain for the north almost at once, but as five or six other divisions were being moved besides ourselves it was not surprising that trains were running a day or two late, so we were able to have a short rest at Revelles, which was much enjoyed, especially as we were able to make trips to Amiens, which at that time had only been slightly damaged by bombs, and was full of life. The chief centres of attraction were the Hotel Godbert, the Savoy, Charlie's Bar, and the Café du Cathédral.

Eventually we entrained at Bacouel station in the afternoon of March 28th, the entrainment being one of the most expeditious ever carried out by the battalion. Not so, however, the journey! Times without number we came to a stop with a succession of jerks, not on account of signals—indeed it would appear that few, if any, existed—but because other trains were in front. During a tedious night of such progress, we passed through Abbeville, Boulogne, Calais and St. Omer, and arrived about 9.0 a.m. on March 29th, at Hazebrouck. Being told there by a French railway official that the train would stop for 15 minutes, most of the officers dashed for the buffet on the opposite platform and ordered *omelettes et café*. As one might have imagined, the train began to move without warning just as breakfast was started. There was a wild dash, but all to no purpose, for the train was well under way. By the best of good luck, however, a supply train was found, which apparently was going in the same direction, though the guard and driver appeared to have different views on the subject, which led to a decidedly heated argument between them. At any rate our party boarded the train and fortunately found it brought them very shortly to Berguette station, where the rest of the battalion were just detraining.

The adjutant's duty of seeing the battalion safely across the railway, near the station, was indeed a pleasant one, and less fortunate members of the battalion have accused him of carrying on in an unseemly manner with the fair keeper of the level crossing. We have his assurance, however, that though he felt proud indeed at having such a charming young lady by his side, his behaviour was beyond reproach! A few hours' march brought us to Westrehem, where we found most comfortable billets, and were welcomed and treated in the most cordial manner by all.

This move brought us into the First Army (General Horne), of which we were now to form part for many months, and into the II Corps, and though we only remained in this corps for a few days the commander, Lieutenant-General Sir C. Jacob, lost no time in coming to make our acquaintance, having all the officers paraded to meet him at the school at Westrehem, two days after our arrival.

We spent about a fortnight there refitting and training, the most important part of the latter being practice in the new company and platoon formations for attack, in which much attention was paid to the question of the numbers and positions of the personnel attached to company and platoon headquarters. Practice advances were also carried out with these formations behind a creeping barrage represented by flags and drums. Outposts and advance guards were practised, as well as tactical open warfare schemes, with officers and N.C.O.'s, and firing was carried out on a range near the village. One day was devoted to a divisional route march, in which every unit in the division took part. It was carried out as a tactical scheme, the division supposed to be pursuing a retreating enemy, and the 8th Battalion forming part of the advance guard.

On the recreational side, football was the chief feature, and several very interesting matches were played, in one of which the 7th Battalion officers got their revenge by beating us three—nil at Nédonchelle. Westrehem was also the venue of a Rugby football match, between a team from the 6th and 8th Battalions, and one from the 5th and Machine Gun Company, which ended after a hard fight in a draw. Padre Uthwatt, who had recently joined us, did his best to try and organise amusements, and the divisional cinema came over and gave one or two shows. There was small attraction in the village except one or two shops and estaminets, but you could get anything from chewing gum upwards at Lane's Emporium, and the inhabitants were so extremely kind that we lacked little. The chief drawback during our stay at Westrehem was the weather, which at times was very cold, and on several days there were heavy falls of snow.

On April 13th, we began to move towards the line once more, spending that night at Vendin-les-Béthune, and proceeding the following day to Houchin. There we went under canvas, sharing a camp with the 7th Battalion, and had a comfortable if chilly stay of three days.

Changes which took place about this time included the departure of our medical officer, Captain C. B. Johnstone, who was replaced for a brief period by Captain Walsh, and later by Captain W. C. Gavin; Captain E. M. Hacking, and Lieutenant Moore were invalided to England, and "Weetie", who had been our adjutant for over 18 months, handed over his duties to Lieutenant Whitton on being attached to brigade headquarters. A little later he succeeded "Peter" Wordsworth, who left to take up a higher appointment after being staff captain for over three years, during which we were grateful for his kind help on many occasions. Regimental Quarter-Master Sergeant Dench went home to train for a commission, but we met him again in the later stages of the war, when he did excellent work with the 5th Battalion, gaining the M.C. and two bars. His place was taken by Company Quarter-Master Sergeant Pritchard, who was succeeded in D Company by Sergeant Gammon; Armourer Quarter-Master Sergeant Loughman went to hospital, and from that time onwards no official armourer was allowed.

We left Houchin on April 18th, and soon found familiar signs of our proximity to the front. In Noeux-les-Mines, a not exactly encouraging notice said "*These cross-roads are registered.*" Needless to say we did not loiter there, especially as it had been shelled several times during the preceding few days. Passing Petit Sains and Aix Noulette—the latter mostly in ruins—another notice warned us that "*Small box respirators must be worn in the alert position east of this point.*" A little further on we found parties of men at work making good the roads, and laying temporary corduroy tracks across what had recently been No Man's Land. Passing over this waste we descended to Angres—known later as Angry Corner—and entered Liévin, where we took over billets from the 13th Middlesex.

Liévin had only been evacuated by the enemy and occupied by the 24th Division two days before our arrival. This evacuation was not part of his general scheme of withdrawing from some of his salients and shortening his line, which we had experienced at Gommecourt, but had been forced on him by the capture by the Canadians early in April of Vimy Ridge.

Included in the line now held by the enemy west of Lens were the strong positions of Fosse 3 and Hill 65, opposite the south of the front taken over by the 46th Division, and Hill 70 on the north. His outpost line ran through the Cité-de-Riaumont and eastern outskirts of Liévin, across the Lens-Liévin road, through Cité-St. Laurent to Hill 70. Lens itself was one of the most important centres in the mining district and the whole area was a mass of mining villages or *cités*, with their rows of cottages and neat gardens, pits or *puits*, slag-heaps, and other usual features of a colliery district.

The town of Liévin lay astride the Souchez river, about three miles west of Lens. Previously a thriving mining centre, it had now been badly knocked about by shelling, though large numbers of

CITÉ ST. AUGUSTE

CITÉ ST. LAURENT

LENS

CITÉ ST. PIERRE

VENDIN

LOOS

DOUBLE CRASSIER

AIR PHOTOGRAPH OF LENS–LOOS AREA, 1917

houses were still more or less intact. The Boche had done much work in strengthening the cellars of the houses by covering them with concrete, paving setts torn up from the road, bricks and other material, the only drawback being that much of the extra strengthening had been put on the side facing the old front line, so that we now got little advantage from it, and felt we should like to turn the houses round, as the side towards the enemy was often none too strong. The evacuation had been so hurried that the enemy had not had time to destroy or remove much of the furniture and clothing from the houses, in many of which we found all the available beds collected in the cellars, which were also well furnished with chairs, tables, cupboards, cutlery and much other civilian property and made very comfortable billets. Sappers made an inspection of all these cellars, and of the dug-outs recently evacuated by the enemy before we occupied them, in order to ensure the absence of booby-traps, and in this respect we had no excitement.

Information from prisoners indicated that a further retreat behind Lens was imminent, and the impression of the higher command was that only slight pressure was necessary to push the enemy outposts out of Cité-de-Riaumont and Hill 65, and to establish a line east of that town. Unfortunately this information was true only up to a point. It has transpired since that for a day or two before the 46th Division came into the line there really was something approaching a panic in the German command in this sector, and that all preparations had been made to evacuate Lens. By the time of our arrival, however, the panic was at an end, and the enemy were undoubtedly holding the southern portion of Cité-de-Riaumont and the strong defences of Hill 65 in considerable strength. Corps and army intelligence refused, however, to believe this to be more than a show, and the general trend of orders was that attacks by small numbers should be made at once to clear the enemy out of Cité-de-Riaumont and finally from Hill 65. The loss of this last covering position should, it was thought, necessitate their withdrawal from Lens.

The flexibility of the position is indicated by the fact that a divisional commander, in making a reconnaissance in Riaumont Wood, had run against an enemy patrol. History does not relate which was the more surprised, but both escaped without casualties.

On April 19th we took over the left sub-sector of the brigade sector from the 7th Northamptons, commanded by that gallant sportsman, Colonel Mobbs. The main defence just established was on the eastern edge of the Bois de Riaumont. The northern two rows of houses in the village of Riaumont were occupied by our outposts, and the enemy were reported to be holding the remainder in force. A Company (Captain A. Hacking) took over the outpost line; B Company (Lieutenant G. Wright, during the absence on leave of Captain Turner) were in support in the Bois de Riaumont and Cité des-Bureaux, whilst C Company (Captain A. Bedford) and D Company (Captain Simonet) were in billets in the River Line, not far from battalion headquarters, which were at the White Château.

It was clear that no attempt to capture Hill 65 would be possible until the whole of Riaumont village was in our hands, and instructions to this effect were given to Captain A. Hacking, operations to secure which were carried out on the night after relief in conjunction with the 6th Battalion on our right. The advance took place quietly in pitch darkness. Several parties of the enemy were encountered, some being killed and one captured. By midnight the battalion's objective had been secured, and posts established in the railway cutting along the company front. In this difficult and rather uncanny work of clearing and searching the houses and cellars of the village, Lieutenant Geary, Sergeant Stokes and Corporal Brett did splendid work, for which the first-named—who was the last officer of the battalion to be killed, a fortnight before armistice—was awarded the Military Cross. Later in the night the enemy opened a sudden and very heavy bombardment, and parties were seen advancing down one of the streets, but were driven off with loss. We had no casualties during this operation.

Meanwhile the 6th Battalion were not able to make good the remainder of the village south of the cross roads, which the enemy were holding in greater strength, and it was apparent that he intended to hold the trench on the south side as part of his Lens outposts.

The work put into the cellars of the colliery houses here was quite extraordinary. In several cases, fifteen feet under the cellars, were found subterranean passages with large dormitories and rooms capable of accommodating large numbers of men. These were well furnished, but owing to their depth and the proximity of the enemy, we were unable to use them as much as we should have liked.

Further fighting and a good deal of shelling took place during the night of April 21/22, causing us several casualties, but not any material alteration in the situation. Particularly good work was done during that time by Sergeant Bolton.

It was in these circumstances, and rather to the surprise of those who were acquainted with the position, that orders were received that we were to attack and capture Hill 65 in conjunction with the 6th Battalion, who were at the same time to attack Fosse 3, and make good the remainder of the village and the enemy trench to the south. The attack was to be carried out by C Company, starting from the railway cutting, so far as this had been established by A Company. There was little time to make any preparations. A hasty reconnaissance was made from an old Boche reinforced observation post east of the railway cutting, just off Absalom Trench, kindly placed at our disposal by a gunner officer, from which an excellent view was obtained of Hill 65, a bare hill with a row or two of colliery cottages on the top, later found to contain the inevitable deep cellars. The rest of the details were fixed at hurriedly summoned conferences of officers and N.C.O.'s. The final objective was Advance Trench, just beyond the Hill. The 137th Brigade on the left were to send patrols to gain touch with us at Abode Trench, and the 6th Battalion on the right were to meet our parties in Admiral Trench. Their attack was not in line with ours but was more or less echeloned in rear.

As soon as it was dark the company moved up from their quarters in the River Line to Cité-de-Riaumont, where the men were safely got into the cellars of the houses, relieving part of A Company. Private Bradshaw, a most excellent company cook, having decided that a company mess in Advance Trench would be a dreary place for his officers without whisky, slung on his back a bottle which the mess president had thought of leaving behind for the incoming mess. Unfortunately it proved to be a case of *Love's Labour Lost*, for the man, and it is feared the bottle too, fell into the hands of the Boche!

D Company, who were to mop up, took over the rest of A Company's area, the latter company returning to Liévin, and two platoons of B Company occupied Absalom Trench. The imminence of our attack was evidently known to the enemy, whose artillery during the night liberally shelled Absalom Trench, Riaumont Château, the eastern edge of the village, and the approaches from Liévin. Trench mortars were also very active on the village, in fact, at one time it was thought that the Boche himself might be attacking, and shortly after midnight C Company were got out of the cellars and ordered to stand to. During that time Company Sergeant-Major Haywood was slightly wounded and had to go back. Nothing further happened, however, and the company eventually took up their final position in the railway cutting about 4.0 a.m. on April 23rd (after waiting for the rum and tea which were delayed by the shelling and arrived too late). Several casualties were caused now by our own artillery firing short, one shell, which luckily was a dud, burying itself in the side of the embankment amongst a group of men. Leaving a right flanking party to deal with the enemy in the railway cutting, the remainder of the company, deploying from the cutting at zero, 4.45 a.m., changed direction half-right and moved forward under a barrage of artillery and trench mortars. The preliminary bombardment had more or less destroyed the houses on the hill and cut good gaps in the wire, which the party had little difficulty in getting through. The right leading platoon under Lieutenant Skinner got into one of the numerous trenches and at first met with little opposition, but being separated from the rest of the company, were rapidly surrounded by large numbers of the enemy, and practically all were killed or captured. The left platoon, under 2nd Lieutenant Hopkinson, reinforced by the remainder of the company, were held up by machine gun fire, which caused many casualties, until Corporal Fletcher managed to get a direct hit on one of the guns with a No. 23 grenade. A message was meanwhile taken by C Company runner, the redoubtable "Mungo" Marsh, to D Company, asking them to try and work a party round to the north side of the houses. Further attempts made to rush another gun which was doing much damage, were met now with bombs thrown from a trench just in front of the houses. The folly of attempting the attack with the southern half of the cutting still in the hands of the enemy, now became apparent, for at this moment large parties of the enemy appeared on the right rear, with which the flanking party had apparently been quite unable to deal. Then from the cellars of the houses on top of the hill also emerged many of the enemy, and the now small remains of the company were in imminent danger of being completely surrounded. Orders were given to withdraw, but few returned to tell the tale. Duff, one of the most heroic and stout-hearted officers the battalion ever possessed, was last seen firing his revolver amid a horde of the enemy. Hopkinson was never heard of again. Sergeant Cox died of wounds and Seargeants Curtis, Sansom and Chalk were amongst the 70 missing, whilst the wounded numbered 34. The highest praise is due to all ranks of C Company for their magnificent efforts and especially to Captain A. Bedford, who throughout worked incessantly and led the attack with the utmost gallantry. It was only through a hard fate that his endeavours did not meet with the success they so well deserved. Very good work was also done by the mopping-up platoon of D Company, under Sergeant Painter, which helped to cover the withdrawal of the remnants of C Company.

147

The 6th Battalion fared no better, and the attack produced, what was suspected by those who knew the ground, exactly nothing except a total of casualties which are felt to have been sacrificed on the altar of faulty intelligence.

It is easy, perhaps, to be wise after the event. All information received by corps intelligence indicated an imminent retreat by the enemy. On no other premises could an attack by so small a force on so strong a position have been justified. One further principle of warfare, by no means new, was justified to the hilt—no frontal attack should ever be attempted unless all counter attack from a flank is impossible, or unless sufficient forces are available to render such an attack an impracticability. The ultimate capture of the hill necessitated nearly two months' artillery preparation and the employment at intervals of two brigades. Perhaps there is one further illustration of the uncertainty of modern warfare in the history of Hill 65. With that Hill in our hands, and later on the dominating position of Hill 70, all the tenets of war would conclude that Lens would be completely untenable, and yet it was not until more than a year afterwards that the enemy, in the last stages of the war, evacuated a town which will, in the history of the battalion and of the 46th Division, be for ever associated with the fortunes of Hill 65.

On April 24th we went back into brigade support with battalion headquarters at the Red Mill, and companies billeted in cellars. Some readjustments had to be made the following day, when battalion headquarters moved to cellars on the Lens road. This spot seemed to be a favourite target for a *whizz-bang*, which fired straight down the road, and was responsible for many sprints and much language at different times on the part of various members of battalion headquarters.

Three days later the brigade was relieved by the 137th Brigade and moved into divisional reserve, the battalion proceeding to a delightful little spot known as Marqueffles Farm, nestling under the wooded slopes of the Lorette Ridge. Here we were extremely comfortable, and on this and a future occasion spent a most agreeable time, being especially fortunate in the matter of weather. It was a stiff climb to the top of the ridge, at the eastern edge of which were the remains of Notre Dame de Lorette. This was the favourite spot of the Gipsy bomber, whose story was told in *Punch* a few years ago:

> But most he loved to lie upon Lorette
> And, couched on cornflowers, gaze across the lines
> On Vimy Ridge—we had not Vimy yet—
> Pale Souchez's bones, and Lens among the mines.

Till, eagle-like, with hoarse indignant shrieks.
Gunners arose from some deep-delved lair.
To chase the intruder from their sacred peaks
And cast him down to Ablain-St. Nazaire.

Torrance on one occasion climbed the ridge with Colonel Black-wall, and can testify that the view from the top was worth the walk! It formed a perfectly ideal observation post, and we now understood why the Hun had fought so strenuously to maintain a footing on the ridge.

The chief item whilst at rest was the reorganisation of C Company, which was practically non-existent. Each of the other three companies contributed a quota, the transfers including Sergeant Stokes, from A Company, who was appointed company sergeant-major. A little later Sergeant H. J. Wilson, who for a long period had ably superintended the battalion cooking arrangements, was appointed company quarter-master-sergeant, and was succeeded as sergeant-cook by Corporal Bateman. In addition to other casualties we had lost Lieutenant G. Wright, who injured his knee up in the Riaumont sector and was now invalided to England, whilst 2nd Lieutenant White went to England for temporary duty as a bombing instructor, and 2nd Lieutenant Mitchell was appointed adjutant of I Corps school. Our strength was thus considerably reduced, whilst reinforcements at the moment were exactly nil.

On May 6th we relieved the 5th Lincolns in the left sub-sector of the left brigade sector, with battalion headquarters in the remnants of some mine galleries at the back of Hart's Crater, just in front of Loos. There were only two brigades of the division in the line at this period, and each brigade went to each sector in turn. We always went into the left sub-sector of each sector, relieving with the 7th Battalion. The trenches here were very bad, so shallow that it was almost impossible to get round by day, and considerably overlooked by the enemy, particularly from the tower of Fosse 14. Their names began with the letter N, the best known being Nero, Novel, Netley, and Nash. They were old Boche trenches taken in the recent advance. The whole sector had a very desolate appearance and life was not pleasant there. The discomfort was increased by the enormous number of wing bombs and rifle grenades and occasional deluges of gas bombs and shells fired by the enemy, which in our first six-day tour there, caused us 39 casualties. This was followed by six days in support, when we lived in dug-outs in some trenches between Loos and the famous Colliery slag heap, known as the Double Crassier. Battalion headquarters were at an exceptionally fine dug-out known as Elvaston Castle, which had been dug by the 2nd Sherwood Foresters. Here, in addition to ordinary work, we amused ourselves at times by cutting the vetches which were thriving on some parts of the area, and sending them back for the transport animals. It was here also that a certain Padre was overheard one day by the I-Tok, arranging for a funeral at Maroc, with the result that he was requested to attend at brigade headquarters to explain his indiscretions.

After a short rest at Noeux-les-Mines, we went back to the Liévin sector again on May 25th and took over the line from Fosse 9 and Cité-St. Théodore to just south of the Liévin-Lens road. Battalion headquarters were at the corner house near the Marble Arch in Liévin. Here the monotony of trench life was varied by long distance patrols, and an enemy raid on the night of May 29/30th on our post at the junction of Crocodile Trench and the railway cutting, when we lost two men captured, three killed and seven wounded. Casualties during the whole of this period unfortunately were heavy and reinforcements few, one officer, 2nd Lieutenant H. C. Orton and 36 men who joined in May, being our sole additions. We also lost Sergeant Burton, who had done much excellent work as signalling-sergeant. He went for a commission, and was succeeded by Corporal J. T. Templeman. Our strength at this period was so small that for some time companies had to be organised in three platoons instead of four. About the same time, much to the regret of all those who had been privileged to serve under him at any time, during the long period in which he so successfully commanded the brigade, both in England and France, General Shipley left for a tour of duty at home, and was succeeded by Brigadier-General G. G. S. Carey, C.B., R.A.

The first six days of June were spent in brigade support in Liévin, at the end of which time we went back into the line in front of Cité-St. Théodore, where the only excitements were the pushing forward of advanced posts to help to protect the left flank of the 138th Brigade in an attack on Fosse 3, and a number of long distance patrols in which Lieutenant Martelli and his scouts always played a prominent part. After another short rest at Marqueffles Farm, where on June 12th we won first prize for the best transport turnout at the brigade horse show, we went back for a short tour in brigade support in front of Loos on June 15th.

We had now fairly sampled most of the area and found little of it to our liking. Hart's Crater sector was the most monotonous for both front line and support work, there being nothing but trenches to live in. In Liévin sector, though the front line work was more interesting and we had fairly comfortable billets when in support, the enemy shelled the town itself so incessantly both with high explosive and gas, that one had to take more than ordinary precautions. Apart from the fact that our own division and the Canadians on the right were carrying out stunts of one kind or other almost every day, provoking considerable retaliation, we had an immense number of batteries tucked away amongst the houses in Liévin, and under almost every bank round about it, besides many more or less in the open. The Boche located these batteries with considerable accuracy, and from time to time literally rained shells (principally 5.9's) on to them, and almost every day knocked out numbers of guns.

Many of the gardens in the area close behind the front line were now in full bearing and provided a very welcome addition to our rations, and more than one has pleasant recollections of the excellent dishes of early asparagus and stewed gooseberries gathered from the garden of Riaumont Château. Strawberries, currants, gooseberries and rhubarb were also plentiful in Cité-St. Pierre. Indeed the attractions of the first were too much for one greedy German, who was so much occupied in filling his helmet with this luscious fruit that he walked into one of the outposts of the 6th Battalion. It is doubtful if he was allowed to reap the fruits of his labour, at any rate when he eventually arrived at battalion headquarters both the helmet and the strawberries were conspicuous by their absence!

The transport and quarter-master's stores were back in a very nice spot at Sains-en-Gohelle, but their journeys to the line with rations and stores were almost as unpleasant as they could be. In going to Liévin they usually got shelled with high explosive and at Loos with gas, and it says much for the excellent way in which Captain H. Kirby and Sergeant Blunt handled the transport on these occasions that they never failed to deliver the stores and had scarcely a single casualty. For a short period in the Liévin sector, stores were sent up by light railway from Bully Grenay or Aix Noulette.

The higher command all this time had the fixed idea that the enemy could be driven out of Lens, and all the efforts of the 46th Division and of the Canadians on the right were concentrated to bring this about. The idea was probably strengthened by the fact that fires and explosions were observed almost daily in Lens itself, evidently due to the enemy's desire to leave as little as possible in the event of his having to withdraw. Numerous small enterprises carried out from time to time enabled some slight advance to be made, but towards the end of June operations took place more frequently and on a larger scale.

The Canadians having just captured the generating station and the high ground around it, south of the Souchez River, which overlooked the Boche positions about Fosse 3, the 138th Brigade were ordered to attack the Fosse again on June 19th, and this time succeeded in taking it, and on the night June 21/22nd, we relieved the 5th Leicesters in their new outpost line in Boot and Brick trenches, having spent the last three days at Calonne, to which place we had moved from the Loos area on June 18th. The two days spent there were two of the most unpleasant in the history of the battalion. All four companies were in the line, there was little accommodation or shelter, the enemy shelling and trench-mortaring were intense, and there was the constant fear of a counter-attack from the right—altogether rather a nightmare. We were lucky in not getting more casualties than we did; as it was we lost ten killed and 31 wounded in the two days, during which we were attached in turn to the 138th and 137th Brigades. We were relieved on the night June 23/24th and went back to Calonne. A Company had a particularly unpleasant relief, as the enemy chose that time to send over a number of gas shells and trench mortars, most of which fell amongst that company, causing them several casualties.

On June 25th the 137th Brigade, with little or no trouble, at last occupied Hill 65, and the same night we were again attached to that brigade, and moved into Liévin, with headquarters at the Red Mill.

Here we got orders for working parties required for carrying and digging assembly trenches at Cité-de-Riaumont for the 137th and 138th Brigades, who were to carry out further operations. company commanders assembled at the Red Mill to get their orders for this work at the same moment that the Boche had planned to shell a battery of our guns almost adjacent to it. Heavies arrived in salvoes for some time; several direct hits were obtained on the guns, the ammunition dump just behind it was hit and explosions continued for days. It caused considerable inconvenience to company commanders and further entailed the hasty exit of Lieutenant Tomlinson from the delightful bathing pool which had been made in the stream adjoining the Mill. It was whilst out with one of these working parties at Riaumont that Moffat Johnston, temporarily in command of B Company, got badly knocked about by a shell and had to leave, the company then being taken over by 2nd Lieutenant Day, Captain Turner being away with the 46th Division Depot Battalion. On the night of June 27/28th we moved back to billets in Maroc. The following evening the 137th and 138th Brigades made further progress in another successful attack, the Canadians also pushing on south of

152

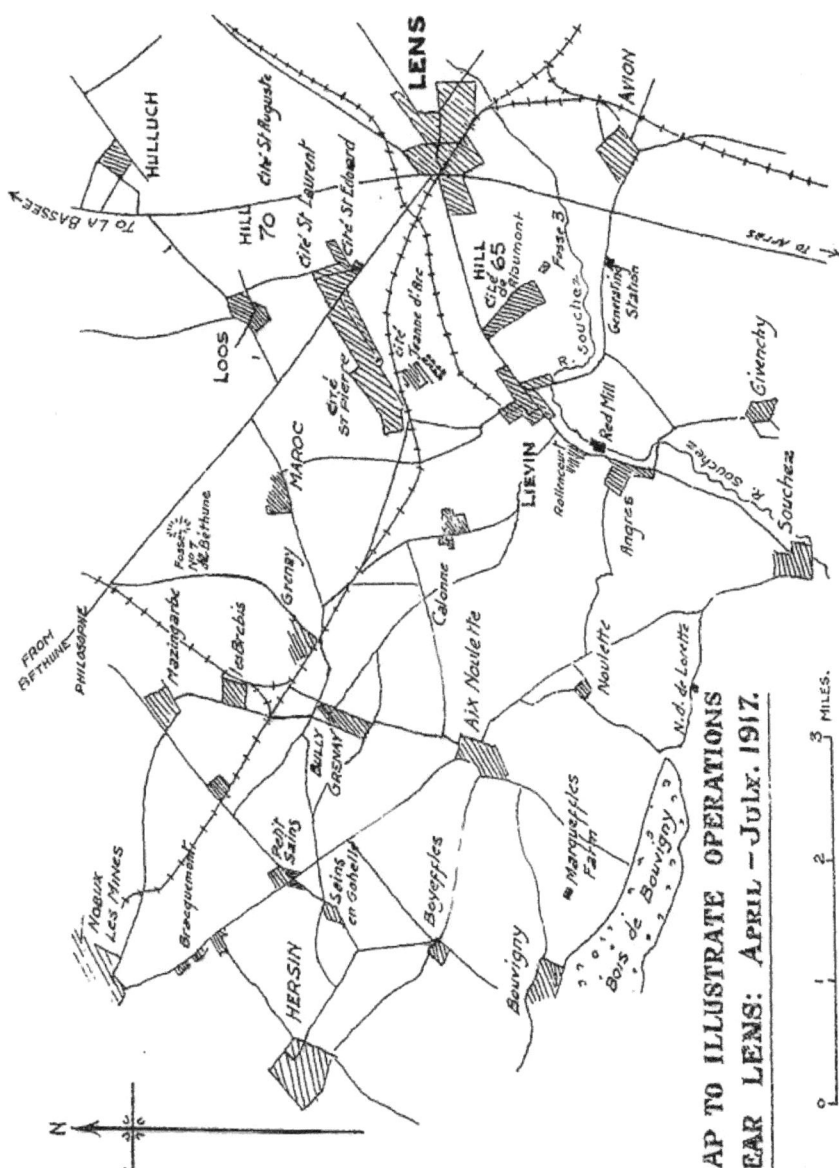

MAP TO ILLUSTRATE OPERATIONS
NEAR LENS: APRIL — JULY. 1917.

the River Souchez, practically into the outskirts of Lens itself. At the same time the 6th and 7th Battalions cooperated with considerable success north of the Lens-Liévin road.

The higher authorities were now more convinced than ever that the Germans opposite us were completely demoralised, and that with a small push we should capture Lens itself. Hasty plans were accordingly devised, and, although we were now lamentably weak in numbers, it was resolved to put the whole division into a final effort on the morning of July 1st. The 137th and 138th Brigades were to attack south of the Lens-Liévin road and the 139th Brigade north of it. For this attack the 2nd Sherwood Foresters and the 9th Norfolks from the 6th Division on our left were attached to our brigade. The assaulting battalions were the 2nd, 5th and 6th Sherwood Foresters. We were in support and late on June 30th moved into St. Pierre. A and D Companies were attached to the 6th Battalion, A being now commanded by Captain Andrews, who had recently succeeded Captain A. Hacking on the latter's appointment as second-in-command of the 5th Battalion. This company held the 6th Battalion left company front, whilst D Company remained in support. B Company were attached to the 2nd Battalion, but were not required until the following afternoon, when they were taken up to Crook Redoubt. Owing to casualties this company came under the command of Sergeant Cobb, who carried out his duties and looked after the company during a rather trying time in a most excellent manner. C Company were attached to the 5th Battalion and were in support in Cowden Trench.

The attack was launched at dawn on July 1st and part of the objective taken, but an enemy-counter attack found our men too weak to hold the position, and apart from a small portion in the neighbourhood of Crocodile Trench, the ground gained had to be evacuated. The 137th and 138th Brigades on the right met with no greater success and Lens remained in the hands of the enemy. July 1st is not a lucky day in the history of the 46th Division.

We remained in St. Pierre, with some companies still detached, until the night of July 3/4th, when we were relieved by the 23rd and 27th Canadian Battalions, and went back to the Square at Bully Grenay, where 'buses picked us up soon after dawn on July 4th, and took us back to the delightful little village of Chelers. In spite of considerable shelling our casualties during the last few days had only been two officers (Day and Hammond) and four men wounded. Our total casualties during the Lens operations amounted to five officers wounded, three missing, 42 other ranks killed, 180 wounded, and 72 missing.

The whole history of the Lens operations proves, if proof were needed, how important a part intelligence plays in modern operations. Intelligence is gained by reconnaissance by land or from the air, and from information from prisoners and captured documents. The responsibility of the officer, who must judge the truth from what must often be conflicting reports from these sources, is serious indeed. On his appreciation of the position depends to an extent not always recognised the success or failure of active operations. The infantry in the line unfortunately take the hard consequences of faulty information or false appreciation.

In reviewing the short history of these operations we are inclined to forget other occasions in which the credit of successes was due not only to the dash and courage of the infantry but to the information sifted from one source or another, weighed in the balance, and finally put forward as the premises on which operations have been based. In our humble judgment the army of the future should take care that this branch of technical training receives a greater measure of attention than it had received up to the commencement of the Great War.

CHAPTER 11

St. Elie and Hill 70
July 4th, 1917—January 21st, 1918

After nearly three months' strenuous fighting, it was a great relief to us to find ourselves back once more in the quiet regions, and the change was thoroughly appreciated by all. The weather was delightful and the country was looking its best, and altogether the 18 days spent at Chelers were extremely enjoyable. There was not much in the way of amusement, as there was little opportunity for it, and we were so far in the heart of the country that visits to towns were impossible, except for the few lucky ones with horses, for whom the journey to St. Pol and back was a pleasant afternoon's ride. Billets were quite comfortable, and battalion headquarters were certainly in clover at the *château*, where it was one of their pleasures to bask in the delightful garden and regale themselves on peaches brought by the small daughter of the house. Otherwise there was little attraction in the village, though in "Lizzie Five-Nine," it possessed a pearl of great price. Major Lane was in command for part of the time, as Colonel Blackwall was on leave. The latter on his return, not being fortunate enough to be met at Boulogne by a car—battalion commanders only got cars when they were not wanted by the gilded staff—found, as so often happened, that railway transport officers knew nothing of our movements, and sent him off to quite the wrong place, about 30 miles from Chelers, to which he had to get as best he could. On a hot summer day this was not a nice experience to pile on to that "end of leave feeling" that most of us had at getting back. and to make matters still worse he found on his arrival that the supply of lime-juice at the headquarters mess had run out! The truth of course was that not being in demand during his absence, it had not been replenished!

In training special stress was laid on bayonet fighting, taken by Company Sergeant-Major Lowe of the Canadian army gymnastic staff, musketry, and firing practice on the Rocourt range, where a two days' divisional rifle meeting was held on July 19th and 20th, at which our representatives shot remarkably well, and carried off amongst other prizes two silver bugles, which now repose with the battalion plate at Newark. A large marquee was erected on the ground, where refreshments could be obtained, and a band was in attendance each day. All the arrangements were admirable, and the programme was carried out without a hitch. Teams from B Company won the inter-company snap-shooting and rapid-firing competition, and the Lewis gun competition, whilst a knock-out competition for officers was won by our team composed of Lieutenant-Colonel Blackwall, Captain A. Bedford and 2nd Lieutenants Tomlinson and Martelli. In the final round this team beat the one from divisional headquarters, which included Major-General Thwaites. In the General Officer Commanding's Cup competition for revolver shooting for officers, our team won second prize. On the whole the results from this competition and the practice leading up to it, were extremely good, and had a marked effect on the shooting all round, both with rifle and Lewis gun. Two ceremonial inspections were carried out, one by the brigadier on July 11th, and another by the divisional commander on July 17th, both of which went off successfully.

Our stay at Chelers came to an end on July 23rd, when we started back once more to the forward area, marching that day to Verquin, where we billeted for the night. The next night we relieved the 1st Leicesters (6th Division) in the St. Elie Left sub-sector trenches. We were not very strong at this time, about 650 all told. Four new subalterns who had just joined, were 2nd Lieutenants J. H. Hofmeyr, C. J. Elly, W. H. Sutton, and R. W. Clarke. Second Lieutenant White rejoined from duty in England, and further officer reinforcements who came up shortly afterwards, included 2nd Lieutenants H. G. Kirby, F. C. Tucker, C. J. Wells, D. Tanner, and J. A. Pearce.

We now entered on what was to be the longest continuous period of trench warfare that it was ever our lot to take part in, for we were destined to remain in the forward area, holding trenches with but short reliefs, for a whole six months, and there was little to break the monotony except one or two changes of trench areas and the interspersal, now and then of raids carried out either by ourselves or the enemy. Raids had now become part and parcel almost of trench warfare routine. The divisional commander's wishes were that they should be carried out frequently, and he was strongly supported by General Carey, who insisted on each battalion preparing a scheme for a raid, either large or small, as soon as it took over the line, so that no time should be wasted in preliminary arrangements after the order was given for a raid to be carried out. The drawback, perhaps, was that raids were apt to be of much the same type, for it was not easy to introduce variations. In the normal raid there was always the cutting of gaps in the enemy wire, which was almost bound to give them the intimation that something was going to happen, the bombardment about "zero" of the area to be raided, and the forming of a "box barrage" round it, to prevent the enemy bringing up reinforcements, whilst our men dealt with any enemy found within the barrage.

This sub-sector of trenches, St. Elie Left, was named after the village of St. Elie, the remains of which were in the enemy lines opposite. This sector was just south-east of the Hohenzollern Redoubt, and was entirely overlooked by that old enemy of former days The Dump, which had now for some reason changed its name to Slag Heap. It was difficult at first to recognise the front lines, so changed was their appearance. Instead of a more or less level tract between the front line trenches, No Man's Land consisted of a chain of whitish chalk peaks, the sides of huge mine craters, which had entirely changed the aspect of the area. There were not so many, perhaps, in the sector in which we were immediately interested, as there were opposite Hohenzollern itself, but the general appearance of the so-called front line was much the same in both. All this part of the front had remained practically unmoved since the finish of the fighting in the Autumn of 1915. The withdrawal of the enemy further south early in 1917, and our attacks later at Messines and other parts to the north, had not affected this portion. Mining had been begun and carried on pretty regularly by both sides so long as that kind of warfare was thought worth while,—a method in which the Boche, who was a nervous miner, had been completely beaten—but for some time before our arrival it had lapsed, and the only visible signs of it were the craters, on each lip of which sentry posts had been established by ourselves and the enemy respectively. A certain amount of excavation was still going on underground, under the supervision of Australian tunnellers, but this was mainly connected with the somewhat complicated system of "listening" in vogue. Apparatus was fitted up, and men were always on duty so as to notify at once any indication of mining operations being started by the enemy. Nothing more as a matter of fact did happen in the way of mining, which had already had its day.

Behind the chain of craters all along this area was another feature peculiar to this part of the line, an extraordinary system of tunnels. It

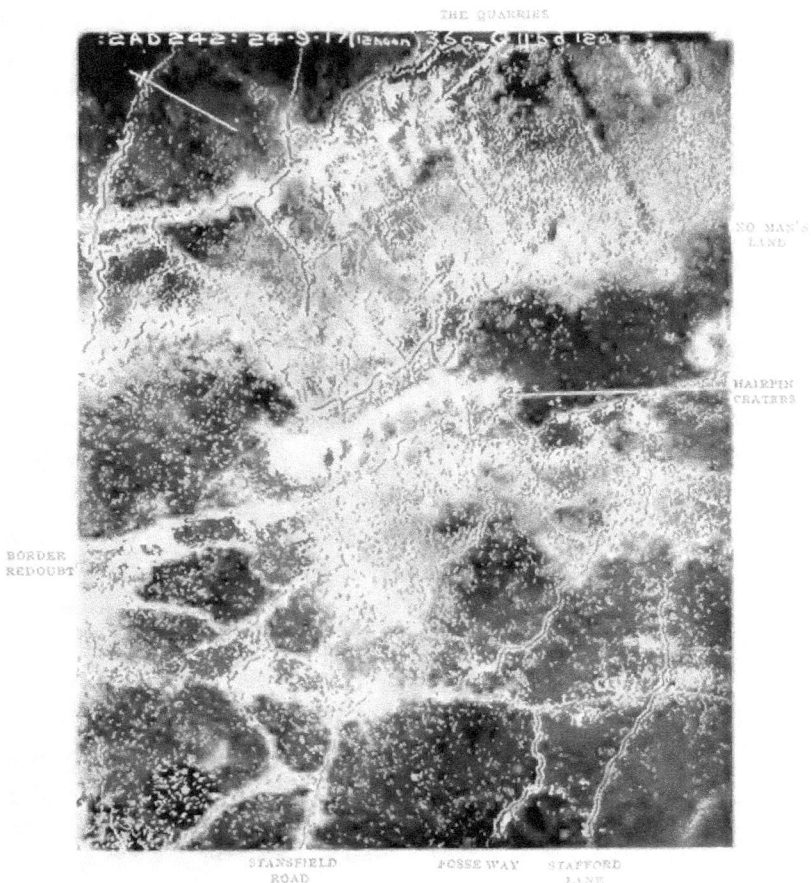

AIR PHOTOGRAPH OF PART OF ST. ELIE SECTOR, 1917

is believed that these first originated owing to the necessity for finding ways up to the front line by day, without using the communication trenches, which were mostly overlooked from the Slag Heap,
and other prominent points, from which the enemy could get an
excellent view over most of our forward area. Behind the trench system attempts had been made to obviate this drawback by the erection of long lengths of camouflage screens, which were a great feature of this part of the front. In the trench system itself underground
passages were dug some 15 to 25 feet deep, from about the reserve
line up to the front. These in due course got connected with the
mine levels and shafts, and eventually rooms were excavated off the
passages, timber and wire beds put up, electric light plant installed,
cook houses and cooking apparatus fixed, wells sunk, and in fact a

sort of underground barracks was formed, and all within 100 to 400 yards of the Boche front line. It was a remarkable development.

The posts in the so-called front line were arranged almost entirely round about the craters, and were reached by flights of steps from the tunnels. These posts were some distance apart, the system of holding these trenches being a thin front line of posts well wired in, with No Man's Land protected by active patrolling, and a strong, well-built, and well-wired support line or "line of resistance," where every effort would be made to hold up any big attack which might develop. An elaborate arrangement of doors and gas blankets fixed at entrances, and at various intermediate points in the tunnels, was made to protect them in case of gas attack, and a carefully arranged system of electric bells was fitted up from the sentry posts to the garrison living in the tunnels, so that warning could be given immediately in case of an enemy attack. These tunnels served an excellent purpose, but there is no question that had they been in use to any extent they might easily have become a great source of weakness, as they undoubtedly had a very demoralising effect on the troops who had to live in them.

The battalion sector extended from Fosse and Stansfield Posts on the right, through Hairpin Craters, North and South Craters, Border Redoubt and Rat Creek to Hulluch Alley and Russian Sap on the left. Communication trenches in this sector were the best we ever met, floorboarded and revetted practically throughout their entire length. The support trench was also fairly good, and the front posts not too bad, though they frequently got knocked in with heavy trench mortars, and required constant repairing. Work in the trenches, therefore, normally consisted more of general upkeep, than of any extensive new work. Three companies were in the line, with the fourth in support, living mostly in Stansfield Tunnel. Battalion headquarters was in a dug-out in Stansfield Road. Company commanders were:—(A) Captain Andrews, (B) Lieutenants Tomlinson, Lomer and Day in succession, followed a little later by Captain Turner, (C) Captain A. Bedford, (D) Captain Simonet. We only had two tours in these trenches at this time, one of six days, and one of four, during which the enemy were active mainly with trench mortars, including a large number of "wing bombs" or "pineapples." A raid which we were ordered to carry out during this period was left in the capable hands of Captain Simonet, and fixed to take place at 11.30 p.m. on August 4th. It was all carefully rehearsed beforehand, on ground near the support billets at Philosophe. In addition to his own company, Simonet had the help of B Company under Lieutenant Tomlinson. The raid was made against the enemy's first and second line trenches nearly opposite North Crater, and was intended in addition to inflicting casualties to obtain identification, and destroy suspected trench mortar emplacements and dug-outs. Unfortunately success did not attend their efforts on this occasion, for, though B Company reached the enemy trenches, and a few men got as far as the second line, they had to be recalled, as D Company were unable to make any headway owing to heavy machine gun fire from the flanks. Both companies suffered a few casualties in withdrawing.

It was on the following day, August 5th, when the battalion was in brigade support in Philosophe, that we got what was probably the heaviest shelling of billets that we ever experienced, for the Boche deliberately shelled the village without a break from 6 to 10 p.m. with 4.2's and 5.9's. As soon as the bombardment began, everyone withdrew to the open fields behind the village, and remained there until it was over. We were fortunate in escaping without a single casualty. Some of the billets were badly knocked about, but we saved our skins, which after all was the main thing. We must confess to having felt on this occasion almost a suspicion of satisfaction in seeing brigade headquarters get a full share of this shelling. Their mess was so shaken and upset that the brigadier had to dine at a much later hour than usual off cold bully beef. It is perhaps difficult to understand exactly the reason, but there is no shadow of doubt that in every formation there was a feeling almost of delight when a unit saw the headquarters of the next higher unit being straffed!

On the night August 10/11th, we moved back into support with battalion headquarters, A and C Companies at Noyelles, and B and D Companies in support trenches. On August 14th, the half battalion at Noyelles handed over to the 5th Leicesters, and moved back to billets at Fouquières, and on the 16th to Verquin, where they were joined by B and D Companies.

By a brilliant attack on the previous day, August 15th, the Canadians finally captured Hill 70, which had so often been a bone of contention, but was now to remain always in our hands.

We now had ten very enjoyable days in comfortable and homely billets at Verquin. Some of the officers were fortunate enough to be invited to play tennis at the *château*, both there and at Fouquières, and owe a great debt of gratitude to the kind ladies at both those places, for many acts of kindness and hospitality. It was almost like being at home to be playing "mixed doubles," and after dinner to have music in the drawing room. The men, too, had a very nice time in the min-

161

ers' cottages in Verquin, and other mining villages. Shops and village life always had their attraction, and we felt very much at home in this part of France, which in the end we came to know almost by heart. The French miner was always particularly kind to us all. It may be that many of our miners, by exchanging views on their calling, enlisted the sympathies of the Frenchmen in the battalion as a whole. Whether this is so or not, in no part of France did the inhabitants behave to officers and men with such invariable kindness and courtesy, as that exhibited in the various French colliery districts, in which we were so fortunate as to be billeted at this time. In addition to the village attractions, we were getting splendid shows given by the Whizz-Bangs, who were now in good form once more, and did much to liven things up, whilst Béthune with its many attractions, was within easy walking distance, and always a popular resort for all ranks.

There were several training grounds within easy reach, and pleasantly situated. Training consisted mainly of musketry and attack practice, whilst the usual ceremonial was introduced in the shape of a brigade parade, at Vaudricourt Park on August 18th, when the general officer commanding distributed medal ribbons. On August 24th, Regimental sports were held in a field at Drouvin, in conjunction with the 139th Machine Gun Company, and 139th Trench Mortar Battery. Perhaps the most entertaining and amusing feature of a most successful day, was the winning of the Victoria Cross race on a pack pony by "Doc" Johnstone, whom we found stationed at Verquin.

We now entered on the second phase of this long trench warfare period, relieving the 23rd Battalion Royal Fusiliers (2nd Division) in Cambrin Left sub-sector on August 26th. There we remained until September 13th, with the exception of a short interval in brigade support, when battalion headquarters were in billets in Annequin, and companies in dug-outs in the reserve trenches in front of Cambrin. It was here that we first came across our Portugese allies, who were holding the trenches north of the La Bassée canal.

This sector extended from just north-west of the Hohenzollern Redoubt, nearly to the Béthune-La Bassée road, and was of a similar nature to the St. Elie sector we had recently held, except that it was not so much overlooked by the enemy. Familiar names in the front line, are Railway Craters, Twin Sap, Minehead Sap, and Fusilier Sap. The support trench was named Old Boots. There were two main tunnels, Munster on the right, and Wilson on the left. The main communication trenches were Railway Alley, Lewis Alley, Munster Parade, and Dundee Walk. After a little rearrangement on first taking over, all companies were in the line, finding their own supports, battalion headquarters being in dug-outs just off Railway Alley. The first tour was very quiet, but was marred by the unfortunate loss on patrol of 2nd Lieutenant D. Tanner, and Corporal Wright on August 30th. Tanner very gallantly undertook to reconnoitre a Boche post, and took out with him Corporal Wright and two men. The two men got back safely, but Tanner and the N.C.O. were missing, and were reported later to have either been killed or to have died of wounds. Another misfortune occurred in our next trench tour on September 11th, when a raid was attempted by Captain Martelli, in command of a party consisting of C Company and half A Company. The raid was to be carried out against enemy trenches opposite Railway Craters, at 11.45 p.m. It was carefully practised beforehand over a taped model. Unfortunately, the enemy were evidently aware of our intentions, probably divining that a raid was in prospect from the fact of our having cut gaps in the wire, and whilst our men were forming up in No Man's Land, they suddenly opened an intense bombardment, mostly of gas bombs, which fell right amongst them. Our men immediately put on their box respirators, but in the dark it was quite impossible to advance with them on, and seeing that progress was impossible, Martelli, who was himself wounded, withdrew his party, suffering in casualties during the whole operation, three other ranks killed, and 30 wounded. C Company were again unfortunate the following night, when they were bombarded with heavy trench mortars, and suffered nine more casualties.

On September 13th, we left this sector on being relieved by the 7th Battalion, and moved back to Fouquières, where we spent a very enjoyable week training and refitting. Leaving there on September 20th, we marched to Mazingarbe, where we spent a night in huts, and the following day took over the support trenches in the Hill 70 sector, just north of Loos. Shortly after its capture by the Canadians, Hill 70 had been handed over to the 6th Division to consolidate, and it now fell to the lot of the 46th Division to complete the consolidation.

Just before the change, we had been joined by a new medical officer, Lieutenant St. G. L. M. Homan, who replaced Captain Gavin, and three new subalterns, Lieutenant C. Cursham, and 2nd Lieutenants S. Bridden and E. W. Hartle; but on the other hand, we lost Lieutenant Michie, and 2nd Lieutenant Orton, invalided to England, and 2nd Lieutenant Pearce, who joined the 139th Trench Mortar Battery. Company Sergeant Major Haywood had also gone home to train for a commission, only to be killed later when serving with another battalion.

It was an agreeable change for us to occupy such a position as Hill 70, as observation could be got from there over the enemy country for many miles, and it was pleasant after having almost invariably been overlooked, to be able now to see something of the other side of the picture. The enemy, however, had good observation from Hulluch and Wingles, over our approaches through Loos, in the valley, and movement was mainly by that never-ending communication trench Railway Alley, running from the top of the ridge behind Loos, through the outskirts of that village up to Hill 70, where it joined up to Humbug Alley, the main communication trench of the left sector. The front line which was in none too good order, was known mainly as to its position with regard to the remnants of woods in its neighbourhood, Bois de Dix-huit opposite the right, Bois Rasé in the centre, and Bois Hugo on the left. All the forward trenches bore names beginning with H, two of which were Heaven and Hell, but the former was not quite the Paradise one might expect from its name. Such dug-outs as were usable, were deep, but small. Many had been blown in, and practically all the entrances faced the wrong way, which was a distinct drawback.

For seven weeks, probably the most monotonous in the history of the battalion's trench warfare, we helped to hold Hill 70, relieving in the line with the 7th Battalion. When in brigade support, we lived in dug-outs in the old British and German front line trenches in front of and behind the Loos-Hulluch road, with battalion headquarters in Tosh Alley. When in divisional reserve, we lived in the Mazingarbe huts, which were fairly comfortable, but capable of much improvement. Battalion headquarters occupying a house in the aristocratic street known as Snobs' Alley. Tours in the trenches, in support and reserve were each of six days. Life in the trenches was of a most humdrum nature. There was not even a raid of any kind, so far as our battalion was concerned. We simply slogged on week after week at real trench work, making fire-bays and fire-steps, thickening the barbed wire in front, improving dug-outs, and making good the communication trenches and reserve line, by revetting and trench gridding. The latter was probably the most important work carried out, and many were the "A" frames that were fixed, and trench grids that were placed in position during those tedious times, to say nothing of the tons of earth that were dug out in order that this might be done, for the trenches had mostly been flattened out by our bombardment before the hill was captured, and needed the expenditure of untold energy and hard work to get them in good order. Great keenness in connection with this work was shown by Captain E. J. Grinling, M.C., of the Lincolns, who had recently succeeded that most energetic officer Captain Buckley, as brigade major, when the latter left to take up a higher appointment.

The weather during the early part of October was fine, hot and dry, but with the inevitable rain which set in later, the trenches, where not cleaned and floorboarded, soon became in an almost impassable state, for the mud and chalk together made a sort of paste, two or three feet deep, of an extraordinarily sticky nature, almost impossible to get through, so that the carrying of all kinds of stores was extremely exhausting work. Fortunately we got some slight assistance by the use of tump lines—a leather arrangement by which the load was carried on the back, but the weight taken by a broad leather across the forehead—and Yukon packs—a kind of wooden framework covered with canvas, on which the material was fastened with thin rope, and the whole carried on the back, and held in position by straps round the shoulders. Constant practice in their use was carried out when back at the Mazingarbe huts, and in the end a number of men became quite expert, and could carry big loads with either of these devices, with much less fatigue, and in a much shorter time than was possible in any other way.

Water was supplied here, as in the Cambrin sector, by a system of pipes. These were the only two instances we met with where this system of supply was in vogue. To supply the Hill 70 sector, Australian engineers had tapped the water from the mine at the end of the Loos *crassier*, and pumped it up to tanks fixed at different points in the trenches. The chief drawback of course was that the pipes were apt to get broken by shells. It was a drawback to be short of water for more reasons than one, as an essential part of trench discipline was to shave regularly, and the visitor to battalion headquarters must have noticed on more than one occasion a petrol tin labelled "shaving water," put in a prominent position so as to catch the eye (of the brigadier!) Two of General Carey's pet orders in connection with trench routine, were that all ranks as far as reasonably possible should shave every day, and that tea leaves should not be deposited in or on the sides of the trenches.

Rations and supplies were mainly brought up by pack mules, the only sector in which this method was used regularly. The mules were taken from the transport lines at Sailly-Labourse by road to Fosse 3, thence over a cross-country track past brigade headquarters at Prèvite Castle, to the battalion dumps at Tosh Alley, and the old British front

Centre Coy

Advanced Plateon H.Q^{rs}

Right Coy.

Power Buzzer Station

Left Coy

Report Centre & Exchange

Right Coy

POWER BUZZER

Support Coy

Right Flank Bn. H.Q^{rs}

Trench Mortars

Amplifier Station

Left Flank Bn. H.Q^{rs}

Battalion Headquarters

Machine Guns

Support Battalion Headquarters

Left Flank Brigade Headquarters

Infantry Brigade Headquarters

18 Pounder Battery

Artillery Group

Artillery Exchange

= VISUAL STATION.

= PIGEONS.

Wireless Station.

Divisional Headquarters

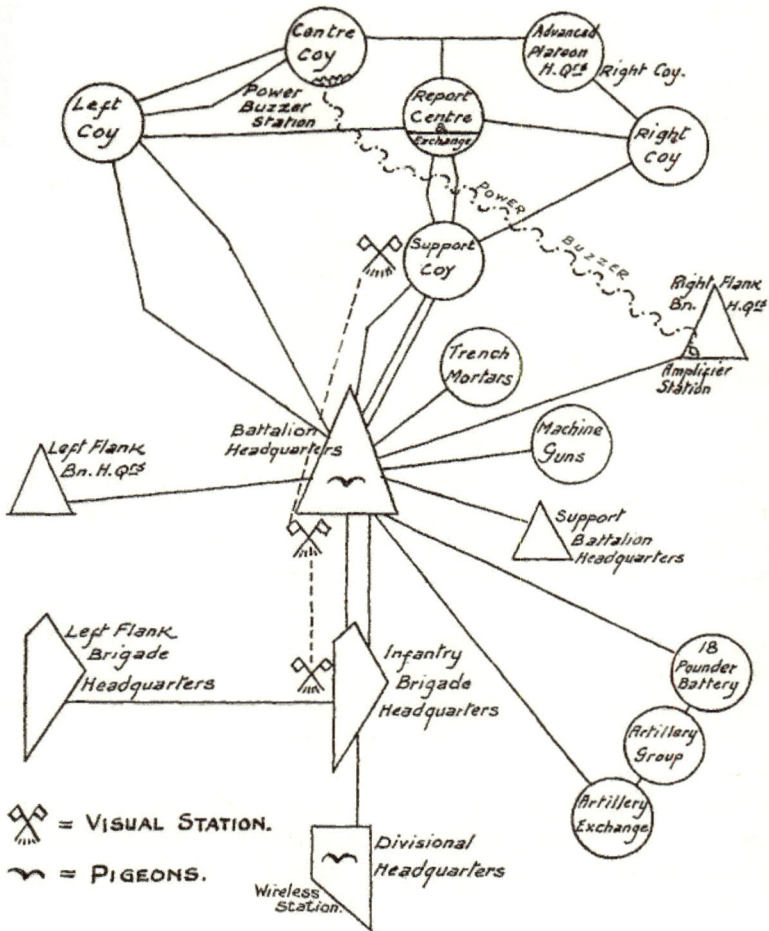

STRAIGHT LINE DIAGRAM OF TRENCH COMMUNICATIONS AT HILL 70. NOVEMBER. 1917.

line. This was a perfectly silent method, and one which, with little practice, soon became a very expeditious one. During our stay, work was begun on the laying of tramlines up to Hill 70, but whilst we were there they were not used to any great extent.

There was a normal amount of shelling in the area, and an uncomfortable amount of heavy trench mortaring, particularly of the left-company front, whilst machine gun bullets along the front line, and about the Tosh Alley dump, which was enfiladed from Hulluch, often took much dodging. Otherwise the sector so far as we were concerned was fairly quiet. Our most unpleasant experience undoubtedly was on October 4th, when we got caught in the bombardment connected with an attempted Boche raid on the 7th Battalion, whom we were relieving. They had been very heavily shelled and trench mortared, and suffered numerous casualties, the clearing of which caused the relief to be a long and difficult business. Several dug-out entrances were blown in, and the front line in many parts was almost unrecognisable. B Company unfortunately got mixed up with some of the shelling, and lost several men, including Sergeant Drabble, who was killed. Private Frank Green did very good work on this occasion, in rescuing buried men, working for five hours on end, though severely shaken as a result of the trench mortaring, and Lance-Corporal Stewart did excellent work in repairing broken telephone wires.

A very good daylight patrol was carried out on November 11th, by 2nd Lieutenant A. C. Fairbrother, a newly joined subaltern, who managed to get into the enemy trenches, shoot a Boche, and return with the two men who were with him without casualty. For this he was awarded the M.C. A decoration of a different kind ought to have been awarded to another officer, who on a perfectly quiet night in the line, when we had nothing to disturb our peace of mind, boldly sent off the cryptic message "G.A.S."—only to be used in case of cloud gas attack, and likely to cause every officer and man, horse and mule, back almost to general headquarters to have their box respirators or gas masks put on! Not content with that, he turned on a Strombos horn, which was also to be used only on occasions of cloud gas, but fortunately it could not rise to anything more than a painful kind of wheeze. The cause of all his excitement apparently was that he imagined he heard another Strombos horn some miles away!

Whilst we were in the Hill 70 sector, the 59th Division (our second line territorials) took over a portion of the line about Avion, just south of Lens, and it was a great pleasure to welcome some old friends who came over to see us, including A. C. Clarke commanding the 2/6th Battalion, M. C. Martyn commanding the 2/7th Battalion, and F. W. Johnson, commanding a field ambulance in the 59th Division. Over an excellent little dinner, at Béthune, arranged by our good friend Colonel Barron of the 1/1st North Midland Field Ambulance, we were able to compare notes, and go over many items of interest.

We were not sorry when news came that the divisional general had decided that, as the Hill 70 sector was the most unpleasant one of the three held by the division, an inter-brigade relief should be carried out with a view to giving another brigade a chance of "doing its bit" there as well. The lot fell on the 138th Brigade, and on November 15th, we were relieved by the 5th Leicesters, and moved back once more to support in the St. Elie sector, with battalion headquarters and two companies at Philosophe, and two companies in trenches, one in support to each of the two battalions holding the line. This was the beginning of the last phase of this trench warfare period.

Much to the regret of all ranks we now lost Major Lane, who left us for a tour of duty at home, and was succeeded as second-in-command by Major E. M. Gingell, of the Wiltshires. Captain A. Bedford also went to England for a rest at the beginning of November, and Captain Geary then took command of C Company. Lieutenant Lomer went to brigade headquarters, where he later became intelligence officer. Second Lieutenant Hofmeyr unfortunately had been killed whilst we were at Hill 70, and Captain Vann after holding various appointments during the summer, had finally left to take command of the 6th Battalion at the end of September. Several reinforcement officers, however, had arrived, including 2nd Lieutenants T. Saunders, W. B. Newton, A. D. Sims, N. Martin and C. M. Bedford, and our strength in officers was consistently kept up to something over 30, and in other ranks to about 650.

Our second period in the St. Elie Left sub-sector lasted until the middle of January, 1918. We continued the old system of six days in the line, six days in brigade support at Philosophe, and after a further six days in the line the same period in divisional reserve at Verquin. The weather was now getting very bad, and as few troops as possible were kept on duty in the front line, which as usual was held by posts at considerable intervals, the defence of the line being assured by the activity of patrols which were out in No Man's Land much of the night, and did some excellent work, on several occasions getting right inside the enemy lines.

We were lucky in being out of the line for Christmas, which was spent at Verquin with much feasting and merriment. There seemed to be no shortage of good things, and we feel sure that the inhabitants of Verquin will not think that at any rate at Christmas time we take our pleasures seriously. Of course tales of all kinds are told of our doings, and though perhaps some of them may have been exaggerated, there is no doubt we did ourselves proud. It was a memorable sight to see the four company commanders slogging back to the trenches on December 28th, to relieve the 7th Battalion in the line. Jack White in temporary command of A, John Turner of B, Geary of C, and "Simmy" of D. Passing brigade headquarters at Philosophe they wore a look that seemed to say "another little drink wouldn't do us any harm," and after a refresher there, they went on looking as if they didn't care two straws if the Boche attacked or not. As a matter of fact on January 2nd, 1918, the enemy did actually attempt a raid on our front, but thanks mainly to much careful planning by Simonet, and supervision by Major Hacking, who was in temporary command of the battalion, the raid was successfully beaten off. The first intimation of anything of the kind being likely to happen, was a message received from Colonel Vann of the 6th Battalion, on our right, at 3.30 p.m. on that day stating that an obvious gap had been cut by the enemy in their wire opposite Breslau Sap, on the 6th Battalion front, and asking for co-operation in the event of a raid at that point. Steps were accordingly taken to cover the front between Breslau and Hairpin Craters with Lewis gun fire, whilst trench mortar co-operation was also arranged, and all companies warned to be particularly alert. The raid was attempted as anticipated, the intention apparently being to surround Hairpin Crater post. The barrage began at 9.30 p.m. with heavy trench mortars and *whizz-bangs*, opening south of Breslau and gradually extending north. A barrage was also put down on the front of the battalion on our left. The heaviest bombardment was on Hairpin Craters. Lewis gun fire was at once opened by us along the whole of the front, from Breslau to Border Redoubt. Various groups of the enemy attempted to push through to our posts when their barrage lifted, but it was evident that they had lost direction, and got very disorganised, and we had no difficulty in driving them off with rifle and Lewis gun fire and bombs, and eventually things quietened down. Our casualties were only one officer, and seven other ranks wounded, all slight, whilst we captured two unwounded prisoners, and a third was brought in dead. For his excellent preliminary arrangements, and for his wise judgment and control of the situation during the attack, Captain Simonet was awarded the M.C. Great gallantry was shown on the same occasion by Sergeant W. H. Martin, Lance-Sergeant Turner, and Private Wildsmith, and good work was also done by Lance-Corporal Rowley, and Private Crouch.

During our stay in the St. Elie sector, much more use was made than on any previous occasion of trench light railway and tram systems. At first rations and stores were brought up nightly by our own transport to the mansion house at Vermelles, and there transferred to small trench trams, which were taken up to forward dumps by pushing parties found by the battalion. As we were so short of men, however, mules were requisitioned for this purpose. Later on, stores were brought up all the way from Sailly-Labourse on the light railway. The larger trucks on this railway were also available on one or two occasions to take the battalion on relief to Sailly, a ride which was much appreciated, and saved some part, at any rate, of the weary tramp back to billets.

The chief recreation in these days was as usual football. A league was formed, including practically every unit in the division. So that the notices of matches might not give direct evidence of our identity, each unit was allotted a code name. We rejoiced in the name of County, whilst teams we played included those having such aristocratic names as Dragons, Miners, Tigers, Wyverns, and Maconochies. We were not very fortunate and occupied a somewhat humble position in the final league table.

Our losses in personnel during the last two months of this period included Captain Turner, who after a wonderfully successful and lengthy period in command of B Company, left to take a commission in the Indian Army. He was succeeded by Lieutenant Day. Second Lieutenants Tucker, Bridden, Sims, Wells, and E. A. Palmer (a newly joined subaltern) were wounded, and Lieutenant Cursham went to the Machine Gun Corps. We were also constantly losing N.C.O.'s on transfer to England to train for commissions. Fresh subalterns who joined were 2nd Lieutenants C. P. O. Bradish, T. R. Christian, H. L. Kennett, A. S. Judd, A. Spinney, J. S. Whitelegge, A. B. Miners, C. G. Druce, A. Jewell, E. H. Seymour, J. Bloor, M.M., V. L. Morris and L. Bromham.

On January 17th, we were relieved in the St. Elie sector and moved to billets at Verquin, where we spent a few days cleaning, and were lectured on the all-absorbing topic of "war savings." Leaving there on January 21st, we marched to Burbure preparatory to a long period of training, the 46th Division having been relieved in the line by the 11th Division.

CHAPTER 12

Spring, 1918
January 22nd, 1918—April 20th, 1918

What the ultimate object of our training was to have been is somewhat uncertain. Our withdrawal from the forward area after six months may have been merely to give us a thorough rest, but with affairs in the state they then were, we can hardly imagine that the intention was to fit us for anything of an offensive character for some time to come, for as a result of the withdrawal of Russia from the war, and the consequent release of German troops from the Russian front, everything pointed to the allies on the western front being on the defensive for some considerable time. That the I Corps knew this had been clear for some time before we left the St. Elie sector. Their headquarters had remained in the same billets at Labuissière since the beginning of the war, and they were taking all precautions not to have them disturbed—in fact sometimes we used to think that they intended to end their days there! There was no doubt a genuine fear that the Boche might try to break through and capture the rest of the mining district round about Béthune and Bruay, and this caused them to take early steps to prevent such a catastrophe, and for some time before we left the St. Elie sector, they had all available labour and material disposed strengthening the defences behind the line as far back as Béthune. This mainly consisted of putting up row upon row of "double-apron" barbed wire entanglements every few hundred yards, which was looked upon, rightly we think, as the best kind of obstacle to hold up an attack. With machine guns skilfully placed at intervals, so as to enfilade these entanglements, it was thought that the best form of defence had been attained. Work on trenches in the division and corps reserve lines was also pushed on, and the machine gun emplacements were made ready for occupation in case of need, and provided with supplies of ammunition and water. We were called upon to help in this work shortly after we were relieved, and on January 30th, sent a party of 460 of all ranks by motor lorry to Mazingarbe for this purpose. They stayed there with Colonel Blackwall himself in charge until February 7th, and during that time worked hard in digging reserve trenches, constructing anti-tank trenches, and wiring localities under Royal Engineer supervision, near Vermelles. These localities were points in the different reserve lines most suitable for, and capable of, all-round defence; they were selected mainly as having a good field of fire on all sides, and so as to command approaches by which the enemy might advance in case of a break through.

The detailing of such a large party naturally left us with very few men for training at Burbure, so that we were able to do little in that respect. Such refitting as was possible was done, and bathing after a good deal of trouble was arranged at Lillers, but as was the case in many of the back areas "billet comforts" were not good. Just at this time, too, we suffered from a scarcity of clean clothes, and later on the scarcity became worse. The supply was extremely short, and more often than not the clothes were rather dirtier on their return from the Abbeville laundry, than when they were sent off. This was not our experience in the I Corps, which we had just left, and whatever we may have thought or said about some of the doings of that corps, it must be confessed that many of their "Q" matters were very well worked, and in the whole of their area, which included the entire region round about and in front of Béthune, in which we spent many months, we were seldom short of anything in the nature of supplies which one might reasonably require, though there may have been some battalion commanders who considered that there should have been a much more liberal allowance of motor lorries, which they were certainly very chary about letting us have.

Economy in all things was now the order of the day, and in order to make the most of our diminishing forces, and to reduce the number of units, it was decided to reorganise the Army on the basis of three instead of four battalions to a brigade. This was begun whilst we were at Burbure, the 46th Division being one of the earliest to undergo the change. In the 139th Brigade the 7th Battalion was the one selected to be temporarily broken up. The change was carried out with lightning rapidity, and within about three days of first getting the order that they were to be so treated, our old friends the 7th, were scattered almost to the four winds. We were very glad to be allotted of their number six officers, Lieutenants R. B. Gamble, S. E. Cairns, S. Sanders, who was attached to the 139th Trench Mortar

Battery, and B. W. Dale, and 2nd Lieutenants W. S. Peach and O.S. Kent, also 151 other ranks, who joined us and were absorbed into our battalion on January 29th. On the 30th we said "goodbye" with much regret to their commander Colonel Toller, who left that day with the bulk of his headquarter staff, to join their corresponding unit in the 59th Division. From the 2/8th Battalion, which was the Sherwood Forester Battalion of the 59th Division to be broken up, we also got a quota of five officers, Major F. G. Cursham, Captain C. P. Elliott, M.C., Lieutenants G. G. Elliott, M.C., and G. Thomas, and 2nd Lieutenant E. R. Elphick, and 85 other ranks, who joined us on January 31. Frank Cursham, who later met such a sad fate in England, was known to some of the older members of the battalion, and G. G. Elliott too, had already served with us. This large influx sent up our strength with a bound, and at the end of January, we were probably the strongest we ever touched, viz., 53 officers and 987 other ranks. The old nomenclature "1/8th" and "2/8th," used to designate the 1st and 2nd lines of the battalion, was no longer necessary, and we were henceforth known simply as the "8th Sherwood Foresters."

On February 9th, the division moved back by route march to the First Army training area, known officially as the "bomy area." This move was carried out as a sort of scheme, the idea being that the division was following up a retreating enemy, and that at the end of the day's move we should billet just as though we were actually pursuing in a hostile country, without so much prearrangement as was generally possible. This did not tend, perhaps, to billeting in as great comfort as one might have wished, and we were inclined to think it was unnecessary. Be that as it may, we found ourselves at the end of the day with headquarters and two companies at Laires, and two companies at Livossart, all somewhat crowded. This in the nature of things was unsatisfactory, and steps were at once taken to try and bring about a change, with the result that on February 13th, we moved to a very nice little mining village, Enquin-les-Mines, which we had to ourselves. The headquarters mess was at the *maire*'s house, where we were particularly comfortable, and received much kindness from the *maire* and his family. There we had rather more callers than on some other occasions, but none of them seemed disappointed if we were not at home, so long as they could leave a message with the *maire*'s charming daughter, and officers of the battalion positively vied with each other in gallantry!

Musketry played the most important part in our training, and ranges were in great demand. An A.R.A. platoon competition was carried out in the division and roused considerable interest. The winning platoon in the battalion was No. 15 (D Company), but unfortunately in the brigade competition, they were beaten by the platoon from the 5th Battalion. Much open warfare and trench-to-trench attack practice was also carried out, a very ominous sign being that this consisted mainly of counter-attacks to regain portions of trenches lost! The training culminated in a fairly successful brigade field day, near Coyecque.

Recreation of course figured largely in the training. In a brigade inter-company football competition, B Company's team reached the semi-final, in which they were knocked out by a team from the 5th Battalion. For amusements we were not well off, as we were somewhat isolated. We did, however, manage to get the divisional cinema for the last week of our stay, a very acceptable acquisition.

Whilst we were at Enquin our tin hats which had recently been shorn of their questionably ornamental or useful sandbags, with which we had been ordered to keep them covered, were painted a dull green, with, for some curious reason, the transport sign (dark blue square), and narrow light green stripe on the left (denoting 8th Battalion) painted on the side. The change was doubtless due to the pressing need for economy.

By the first week in March, it was realised on all hands that the great Boche offensive could not long be delayed. The enemy had brought division after division from the Russian front across to the western, and, during the winter, had got together an enormous concentration of troops in France and Belgium, including at least three Austrian divisions, and it was now only a question of knowing exactly when and where the onslaught would come. In these circumstances our training was cut short, and on March 5th, we began to retrace our steps once more towards the forward area, marching that day to Westrehem, where we had been so comfortably billeted nearly a year before, and were now enthusiastically greeted by our old friends. Only one night was spent there, and the next day we were taken in 'buses to Béthune, and billeted once more at the Orphanage, this being our third time to be quartered there. We were now back again in the I Corps.

Then began a period of about seven weeks activity, during which we had a considerable amount of excitement, some of it of not too pleasant a nature, and one was never quite certain what a day might bring forth. The first week, however, was spent in absolute peace at Béthune in most delightful summer-like weather, and was thoroughly enjoyed by all. During that time the 46th Division took over the

Cambrin sector again, and on March 14th, we relieved the support battalion in that sector, the 5th Lincolns, who were holding the Annequin locality, including the whole of Annequin Fosse and its colliery cottages, which was being put in a state of defence, and was to be held to the last in the event of the enemy breaking through the front line system of trenches.

With the greatest regret we had now to say goodbye to Colonel Blackwall, who left us for a tour of duty at home. He had been in command of the battalion without a break since October 15th, 1915, and during the whole time had never been off duty, except when on leave or attending courses. We feel sure no one felt more than he did what bad luck it was that he should go just at this important juncture, but he left with the best wishes of everyone for a well-earned rest at home. At the same time we welcomed to the command of the battalion Lieutenant-Colonel R. W. Currin, D.S.O., of the York and Lancaster Regiment, who was destined to remain with us, with only a short break, until the conclusion of the war.

Several other changes had recently taken place. Hugh Kirby had left to take up a commission in the Indian Cavalry, and the transport was now under the charge of Captain Tomlinson. We had also lost Lieutenants White, Day, and Cairns, who had gone to England for a rest, and were followed shortly afterwards by Lieutenant H. G. Kirby. Lieutenant Gamble, and 2nd Lieutenants Sutton, Peach and Saunders were unfit and were struck off strength, and 2nd Lieutenant Clarke went to the Machine Gun Corps. Major Cursham had taken over C Company from Captain Geary, and Captain C. P. Elliott had succeeded Lieutenant Day in command of B Company. We had been given a new Padre, W. N. Kempe, who made himself very popular during his few months' stay with us. Sergeant J. Eggleston, after a long period of excellent work as pioneer sergeant, was appointed company quarter-master sergeant of D Company, in place of Gammon, who went home for a commission.

Transport was lucky in being put in lines at Le Quesnoy, probably the best constructed and best equipped that we ever struck during the whole war. Units which had been there before had evidently worked hard on them to carry out improvements, and for once we were really lucky in finding a good spot. The stables were strongly built, well roofed, floored, and provided with harness and fodder rooms, and to a certain extent protected from bomb splinters by earth revetments.

On March 20th, we relieved the 5th Battalion in the Cambrin left sub-sector, with which we were already well acquainted. On the follow-

THE BEUVRY-LA BASSÉE ROAD, NEAR CAMBRIN

ing day there took place in the south the first onslaught of the Boche, in his great spring offensive of 1918. There was no actual attack anywhere near us, the only offensive action on our front being a "demonstration" in the shape of a heavy bombardment with gas shells, which was decidedly unpleasant, though not causing us any casualties.

During the night of March 21st/22nd, we did experience a real touch of the offensive in the shape of a big raid on the right company, the most vulnerable portion of the line on the whole brigade front. This front, which was held by A Company was of enormous length, extending from Railway Craters on the right to Munster Parade on the left, a distance of about 600 yards. Three platoons (about 60 all told) held the outpost line in small posts of four or five men, each under a N.C.O., the fourth platoon being held in support as a counter-attacking platoon in Old Boots Trench at the west end of Munster Tunnel. The latter was about 400 yards behind the outpost line, and was also occupied by the support company, and contained the right company headquarters. The orders laid down were that in case of attack the platoon detailed for the task was to counter-attack either through the tunnel (quite impossible if the enemy obtained a footing in the trench at the tunnel mouth) or over the top.

Shortly after midnight, the enemy put down an intense barrage of trench mortars, wing bombs, and shells of all calibres, along the whole of the brigade front and support lines, forward communication trenches, battalion headquarters, the Village Line, and extending even to roads, villages, and batteries far behind the line. Telephone wires were broken immediately, but the "S.O.S." was sent by signal rocket and power buzzer, and our artillery and machine guns replied at once. There had been no preliminary bombardment or warning of any kind. The enemy entered our trenches directly behind his barrage from the cover of the craters on the right, between our right post and the left company of the 138th Brigade, who were on our right, also near Dundee Walk in the centre, and just north of Munster Tunnel on the left. Such wire as had been put up by the few men who were usually available was swept away by the hurricane bombardment, which prevented movement of any kind, either to or from the front or support lines. Two runners were wounded whilst attempting to take messages between company headquarters and Munster Tunnel, a distance of 50 yards. The posts in the front line were unable, owing to their small numbers, to offer any prolonged resistance, or on account of the distance between them, to assist neighbouring posts.

The front line entrance to Munster Tunnel was held by us the whole time, and an attempt to blow it in, which was one of the main objects of the raid, was frustrated, 2nd Lieutenant Hartle being wounded by a hand grenade. That the garrison of the outpost line withstood the onslaught to their utmost there is no doubt, and to this the pools of blood and reeking bayonets of some of the rifles found afterwards in the trench, bore convincing testimony. After the enemy's withdrawal, one unwounded and one seriously wounded German were left in our hands, the former having apparently become detached from his party, and being discovered later in front of our trench with a sheet of newspaper fluttering from his rifle.

The thoroughness with which the Boche trained for this raid was proved from the prisoners' statements and documents, which afterwards came into our hands. For six weeks the raiding party, consisting of about 250 men, had been training over an exact replica of our trenches, constructed with the help of an aeroplane photograph. The training had also included the teaching of several words of English. The work of the raiders was extraordinary, and our own men in the front line testified to the remarkable dexterity with which they removed their casualties. This is the more wonderful inasmuch as they had to penetrate our barrages, in order to regain their trench, and there is no doubt that in doing so they lost heavily. Our casualties amounted to three other ranks killed, including a very gallant N.C.O.,

Corporal Tyne, 26 other ranks missing, and one officer (Hartle), and ten other ranks wounded. We should like to pay tribute to the excellent work done by the signallers, who as usual worked their hardest, to try and keep their lines in order, in spite of the heavy shelling. Lance-Corporal Parry's efforts to repair the broken lines back from one of the front companies, were especially praiseworthy.

Though there was an element of surprise in the raid, there is no doubt that its success was due to the fact that the defence was designed for an attack on a large scale, and led inevitably to a weakening of our outpost line, making it peculiarly vulnerable to a raid or attack with a limited objective.

The following night, the whole battalion was ordered to wire as hard as possible, and hundreds of reels of barbed wire were put out. Even battalion headquarters shared in the work, the whole staff being out in an endeavour to wire themselves in.

On March 24th, we were relieved by the 6th Battalion, headquarters and two companies proceeding to Beuvry, and two companies remaining in the trenches in close support. "Wind" at this time was very "high," and our intelligence reported that we must be prepared for any eventuality. The enemy had made enormous progress in their attack in the south, and everything pointed to the possibility of a general attack along the whole front. As a matter of fact no such attempt was ever made on the Cambrin-St. Elie sector, but we had to take every precaution, and for the next two or three nights, we marched up to our battle positions in front of Cambrin, in case the expected attack should mature. We even made arrangements for a possible retreat, and worse than that, all leave was stopped.

It was at this juncture that our brigade commander, General Carey left us to take command of the 20th Division, with everyone's good wishes and congratulations. He arrived near Amiens in time to assume command of a composite Army, known as Carey's Force, and to assist materially in finally stopping the great German onslaught. He was succeeded by General Wood.

The "wind" in this quarter, dropped for the moment, but we heard that things just north of Arras were not looking too bright. The enemy were expected to attack at Vimy, and the Canadians who were holding the sector opposite Lens, were to be moved to that part to help the defence. As a result, we got orders on March 25th, to move back once more to the Lens region, to relieve the Canadians. Hasty plans were made by which the 11th Division took over from us, and on March 27th, we marched to Calonne and relieved the

72nd Canadian Battalion there in reserve, moving up the following night to the St. Emile sector, in front of St. Pierre, where we took over the right sub-sector front line from the 78th Canadian Battalion. The completion of the relief had to be rather hurried, as the enemy attacked at Oppy on March 28th, and the Canadians were hastily sent there to help. Transport and quarter-master's stores had meanwhile gone to Fosse 10.

The front line in this sector was now of course much further forward, than when we were last there, as the Canadians in connection with their attack on Hill 70, had forced the enemy out of the whole of St. Pierre, St. Laurent, and St. Emile Cités, back to the outskirts of Lens itself. These *cités* were now to all intents and purposes destroyed, and presented nothing but a mass of streets heaped up with broken tiles, brick and other debris, interspersed here and there with trenches, the remains of houses, and a few shattered trees. Amongst the ruins the Canadians had laid a splendid system of tramways, and the transport of stores and rations to the line was carried out every night by this means, in a most expeditious manner. Canadian engineers continued to run the lines during our stay, and we must confess that we did not envy the drivers their job, for the lines went up uncomfortably close to the front line, and a good deal of noise accompanied the arrival and departure of the trains, unloading of stores, and loading of empties for the return journey, the guard or man in charge usually helping matters with a few shrill blasts of his whistle, quite in approved Canadian fashion.

After a quiet tour of four days, we were relieved in the early morning of April 1st, by the 6th Battalion, and went back to brigade support at St. Pierre, where we lived in the cellars of the otherwise destroyed houses. Our stay there was rendered less pleasant than it might have been, by the fact that practically the whole of the village was under observation from Lens, so that during the day hardly any movement was possible, and most of our exercise had to be taken by night, when we were kept pretty busy with carrying and working parties. The nightly gas shelling of the village made this work anything but pleasant. Bathing parades too, were held at night, and took place in the weirdest bathing establishment we ever met, which was in the crypt of the church. It was well protected by the ruins of the church, and had been fitted up with a spray bath.

On April 3rd, we relieved the 5th Battalion in the line, and had a somewhat thin six days, owing to the enemy being extremely active, particularly with heavy trench mortars, with which he did a lot of damage to our front line, being particularly obnoxious on the night of April 5/6th, in retaliation for one of our gas projector shows. Lance-Corporal Beech did especially commendable work during these days in charge of a Lewis gun post.

One morning during a tour in the front line in this sector. Colonel Currin very nearly lost his runner. It was a rather foggy morning, and the commanding officer sent him to find an officer in an adjoining company. Unfortunately the runner made a mistake at a trench junction, and gaily followed an old communication trench, running straight to the enemy's lines. It was doubtful which party was the more surprised when he suddenly found himself confronted by a Boche sentry post behind a barricade. At any rate the latter were too amazed to shoot, whilst true to his calling the runner ran, and never stopped until he nearly crashed into the arms of the colonel, who was wondering what on earth had happened.

On April 9th, the 6th Battalion relieved us again, and we went back to St. Pierre. On the same day there happened an event which was to have an enormous effect on the future of the war, at any rate so far as the fighting on the northern portion of the front was concerned, *viz.*, the attack on the British line immediately north of the La Bassée canal, and on the Portuguese in the Neuve Chapelle area. The result was that whilst the 55th Division put up a magnificent defence on the canal, and completely beat off all the enemy attacks, the Portuguese gave way, and the enemy were able to push on west for a considerable distance, until brought to a halt by the British, who were later helped by reinforcements rapidly sent up by the French. This had an almost immediate effect on us, for on the night of April 11th/12th, we were taken out of the line, being relieved once more by the Canadians (13th Battalion) who were hurried up from the area north of Arras, where things seemed to be quiet once more. After a great scramble, relief was completed by 5.30 a.m. when it was practically daylight. Some got rides on the trains which brought up the Canadians, but the rest had to walk, and eventually we all got to Noeux-les-Mines, where we had breakfast and dinner, and proceeded in the afternoon to Vaudricourt. The whole division had been relieved—one of the quickest reliefs known—and we now found ourselves in army reserve, to be sent to any spot where we might be required.

Things once more were in a very nervy state, as it was felt that ere long the enemy would make another desperate attempt to capture the rest of the mining area, either by direct frontal attack from the east towards Béthune, or by continuing his enveloping movement from the north, and attacking it from that direction across the La Bassée canal. A large part of this area now formed a prominent salient, with the enemy on the east and north, and the consequence was a rapid evacuation of the French inhabitants from many of the mining towns and villages in that district, including Béthune, Beuvry, Annequin, Sailly-Labourse, Noeux-les-Mines, and Bully Grenay—all of which we knew well. For several days we watched the wretched inhabitants toiling along the roads, taking with them by whatever means they could, the few belongings they most treasured or required. Some had carts loaded with bedding and furniture, some their little dog carts full to overflowing, others footed it burdened with loads almost beyond human strength to carry. Ever the throng kept passing back from the forward regions, having left everything that they could not carry just as it was in their houses, with no other protection than locked doors. Their cattle and horses too, were driven back, and taken to pounds in villages in safer regions. Several more mines had to cease work, and the French miners thus thrown out of employment were mostly set to work in digging line upon line of additional trenches about Fouquières and Drouvin, for us to fall back on in case of a break through, as it was determined to contest every bit of the ground to the very utmost. Right well they worked, and in an incredibly short time, they had dug miles of trenches, and well wired them in front with substantial entanglements. Our only fear was that if the enemy got through, we should not have sufficient men to garrison these trenches so excellently dug!

This was probably the darkest period of the war. The inspiring message from the commander-in-chief was read to all ranks, and all indeed realised that we had our backs to the wall and were fighting for our very existence, and that it was touch and go whether the Hun would not, after all, break through the whole line and sweep through to the coast, and ultimately to England.

It was in these circumstances, after a few days quiet training about Vaudricourt, that we got word at 2.30 a.m. on the morning of April 18th, that a German prisoner had been captured, and had given information to the effect that the enemy were going to make another desperate attack that morning along the La Bassée canal. We were accordingly ordered at once to man part of the Sailly-Labourse locality, known as the Tuning Fork line, just in front of that village, so-called because it formed part of a system of trenches and breastworks shaped like a tuning fork. There was some slight delay in getting the orders passed on, and it was 4.30 a.m. before we marched off. This was unfortunate, for we were not able to reach our battle position before dawn, when the enemy's barrage began. This as usual included heavy shelling of the rear roads and villages through which we had to pass, particularly Verquigneul and Sailly, where we suffered several casualties, and lost Corporal Caudwell, who had done such good work with the transport, and two men killed and several others wounded. One of the cookers was also badly blown about by a shell in Verquigneul. We got to our position at 6.30 a.m. where we were comparatively comfortable. The enemy had actually attacked at Givenchy, but once again, thanks to the 1st and 55th Divisions, he was completely defeated, and never again did he try to get through on this part of the front. We were kept in our positions here for two days, by which time things had become normal once more, and in the afternoon of April 20th, we marched back to our billets at Vaudricourt.

CHAPTER 13

Gorre and Essars
April 21st, 1918—September 6th, 1918

Two days after our return to Vaudricourt, the 46th Division was called upon to relieve the 3rd Division in the area north of the La Bassée canal, afterwards known as Gorre and Essars sectors, where they had recently held up the German attack. This front extended from the 55th Division boundary on the right, near Givenchy, where the line bent now almost at a right angle, to Mesplaux Farm on the Lawe canal, on the left, this line being more or less parallel with the La Bassée canal, and at the nearest point about two and-a-half miles from Béthune.

Leaving Vaudricourt on the evening of April 23rd, we marched the short journey to Béthune, where after some rearrangement, we were eventually allotted billets in one of the French barracks. How changed was our favourite old town of Béthune! From the earliest days of the war a resting place for the traveller, the chief shopping centre for a very wide area, probably the most popular and best known town to British troops on the whole of the Western Front, full of life, and to a certain extent gaiety, although within such a short distance of the line, she had now been deserted by all her inhabitants, and was like a city of the dead. Previously only hit by a few stray shells on odd occasions, she was now being bombarded regularly, as the enemy had brought up his guns much closer, and they had already made their presence known in no uncertain manner. Everywhere notices had been put up warning troops against the crime of looting, but is it not more than human nature can stand to see houses, as they were here, often open for anyone to walk straight into, filled with all kinds of valuables, many quite easy to carry away, and all liable at any instant to be destroyed by shell or fire?

At the moment, however, we had little time to trouble about the town ourselves, as on April 24th, we moved out again. After a novel and amusing cricket match—if such it could be called—in the barrack square in the afternoon, we relieved at night the 2nd Royal Scots in the right sub-sector of the Essars sector, with two companies in the front line and two in support, battalion headquarters being at Le Hamel, in the cellar of a farmhouse. Company commanders at this time were: (A) Captain Andrews; (B) Captain C. P. Elliott; (C) 2nd Lieutenant Kent, who had taken over command when Major Cursham went to hospital; (D) Captain Simonet. It was fortunate that they had been up to reconnoitre the day before, for when platoons reached the appointed rendezvous, the guides were not there. We had had sufficient experience by this time to know that, although all possible precautions were taken, it was a most difficult problem to make certain that every guide was a picked man, knew exactly where he was to meet his party, what that party was, and where it was to be guided to, and to be able to do all this by night without a hitch. Ian Hay has classified guides in two grades (a) the guide who doesn't know the way and tells you so; (b) the guide who doesn't know the way and doesn't tell you so until he has lost both you and himself. We might add to this (c) the guide who doesn't turn up! In this case however, nothing desperate happened, and in due course the relief was carried out.

The conditions here were indeed novel, and more like those of open warfare than any we had yet experienced. It might almost be said that we had now bidden farewell to real trenches, for, though the line in the Gorre and Essars sectors, remained stationary for nearly four months and trenches certainly were dug, from now onwards we never had quite the same type of front line as we had hitherto been accustomed to. The German rush had been brought to a halt, not many days before we took over, so that there were practically no defences of any kind. The outpost line consisted of a few shell-holes, and small slits dug in the ground at intervals with a very small amount of barbed wire in front. The support line, known as the Liverpool Line, consisted mainly of a few slits, but was protected for a great portion of its length by the Beuvry River, and a fair barbed wire entanglement. A few shelters had already been made in both lines, by putting sheets of corrugated iron over some of the small trenches which had been dug, and camouflaging them with earth. Some distance behind the Liverpool Line there were some old breastworks, forming part of a reserve line, which some of us remembered seeing the French constructing in the autumn of 1915, when we were in the Vieille Chapelle area, just north of this. In some of these there were small concrete shelters very much like old-fashioned pigsties, which on the left of the Essars sector, were used for battalion headquarters. There were of course no communication trenches whatever, all communication to the front posts being over the top, mostly by tracks through the growing crops.

The whole area was perfectly flat, and almost entirely under observation, so that by day no movement was possible, and no work could be done, and as the nights were now getting shorter and shorter, very few hours in every 24 could be utilised for doing the work we were so anxious to get on with. There was nothing to be done by day, apart from ordinary sentry duty, except to keep out of sight and make ourselves as comfortable as very cramped quarters would allow.

A further disadvantage was that the water level in the ground was very near the surface, so that dug-outs were impossible, and the most we could do was to put up small corrugated iron shelters, mainly in T-shaped saps running back from the trenches. These we pushed on with as rapidly as possible, in order to afford some protection in case of bad weather. In this respect we were extremely lucky, and for a very great part of our stay the weather was delightful, days and sometimes weeks together passing without a single drop of rain.

The first tour of four days was quiet, except for some gas shelling, which the Boche was doing much more extensively now, especially about sunrise and sunset, when he was particularly fond of dosing battalion headquarters at Le Hamel, and Essars and Gorre. At the latter place the *château* and the wood were the favourite targets, and on several occasions were absolutely drenched with gas. At this time it was mainly "yellow cross" or mustard gas that was used, a very deadly gas, affecting any part of the body exposed to it, and particularly dangerous when the sun was up. A certain amount of "green cross" or *phosgene* which was decidedly dangerous, was also used, as well as a little "blue cross," which apart from making one sneeze had no very ill effect, unless inhaled in large quantities. During this tour we did little except get used to the new conditions, and try to find our way about. It was the simplest thing in the world to get in front of the outpost line without knowing you were there, and on occasions people were even discovered in No Man's Land asking for the support line! Visiting the posts in the front line was also at first more or less a matter of conjecture, but in course of time most of them were joined up by a continuous trench. At first the novelty of it all amused us, and after all it was a very welcome change from ordinary trench life.

It was during the first tour that we had the great misfortune to lose a very gallant officer and sportsman—H. K. Simonet. He had moved his company headquarters from an unprotected shell-hole to a cottage at Les Façons, in the outpost line itself, only to get a direct hit on it almost immediately which resulted in Simonet and his runner, Private Garratt, one of the most reliable and gallant men in the battalion, being badly wounded. Neither recovered, and they were buried near each other in the Cemetery at Lapugnoy. A most capable officer, of fine leadership and magnificent character, "Simmy" was liked by all and his loss was felt most keenly throughout the battalion. He was succeeded in command of D Company by Lieutenant Warner, whose place as signalling officer was taken by 2nd Lieutenant Stephenson.

On April 28th, we were relieved by the 5th Leicesters, and moved back into divisional reserve at Fouquières, where we stayed four days, during which the chief excitement was that we had to stand to in the early hours of May 1st, as there were rumours of another German attack, which fortunately did not mature.

We took over from the 6th south Staffords in support in the Gorre sector, on May 2nd, and had something of a shock on finding that they had lost nearly 50 per cent. of their numbers during their tour by mustard gas poisoning, with which the Boche had literally drenched the whole of Gorre Wood and *château*, and most of the village. It was not a comfortable introduction to the sector! Fortunately most of the casualties proved to be slight, and the greater part were able to rejoin a few days later.

There was nothing fresh about the kind of work required of us in support. It was as ever, and was for several more months, the carrying of Royal Engineers' and other material to front line battalions, and the provision of working parties for Royal Engineers. How we blessed them and their working parties! It would fill a book much larger than the present one to attempt to put down half what one thought, and what one heard and said about them, but this shall be our last uncivil remark! They had a splendid dump at Le Quesnoy, known as Kantara. Situated next door to the station and canal, almost adjoining the road, and having a branch from the tramline running into it, this dump could not very well have been in a more suitable position, though the same advantages made it a most convenient target for the Hun gunners. Almost next door to it was Gorre Brewery, also very well situated, and having the additional attraction of a tall chimney which gave the Boche the line of the bridge over the canal a few yards behind it. Though they did some quite good shooting at these targets and damaged the canal bridge, the chimney in the end

GORRE BREWERY AND BRIDGE, 1918

was blown up by our own Sappers. In view of these facts it seemed at first rather curious that this spot should have been chosen for the headquarters of the support battalion and the aid post. Perhaps the first people went there to find the beer; if so they certainly took it all, for there was none left when we got there!

On May 4th, we relieved the 6th Battalion in the right or Route A keep sub-sector, undoubtedly the unhealthiest part of the whole divisional front. The so-called keep was merely the highest ground in the locality, overlooking the Boche to a certain extent, and so an important tactical feature, though having nothing in the way of defences to warrant the term keep. There had been considerable fighting over its possession during the time the 55th Division held this area, and counter-attacks were made time and again by the enemy to get them out. Eventually they got tired, and in the end, after its capture by the Stafford Brigade on April 29th, they made no further efforts to retake it. Corpses lay on all sides, both of our own troops and of the enemy, and made the place distinctly offensive. Life was made still more unpleasant by constant trench mortaring and shelling, whilst protection was of the scantiest. We tried to improve this during our first tour by digging an advanced trench well in front of the outpost line, and so as to conform with the front lines of flank battalions. Though the trench was dug with little interruption on the part of the enemy, we did not exactly look upon it as a masterpiece, nor by any means our best piece of work in France, but it served its purpose very well, and in time was considerably improved.

On May 10th, we went back to bivouacs in Vaudricourt Park, in divisional reserve. These bivouacs and the villages of Fouquières and Verquin, were from now onwards allotted in rotation to the three battalions of the brigade out at rest.

The atmosphere during the greater part of May was again very "breezy." From various sources, including prisoners' statements, our intelligence department were led to believe that another big attack was going to be made, and might begin at any moment, with the object of getting Béthune, and the rest of the coalfield. In fact, so great was the general anxiety on the occasion of our relief on May 10th, that we had to remain in the Béthune locality all night. The attack passed off without happening, as did several others! The bridges over the La Bassée canal were mined and guarded by Sapper and infantry sentries, with instructions as to blowing them up in case a further withdrawal became necessary. We felt quite certain that they would be blown up alright should the occasion arise, but had grave doubts as to what might befall those who happened to be on the wrong side of the canal! That well-known landmark, Béthune church tower, which commanded views for miles in all directions, had also had a powerful charge laid at its base, so that it might be blown up in the event of our retirement. Ultimately it was blown up, not on account of any retirement on our part, but by the enemy shelling the town. Having brought up numbers of guns into the newly-formed Merville Salient, they shelled Béthune daily, until on May 17th, a shell landed near enough to the base of the church tower to explode the charge, and the remnants of the tower disappeared with the most appalling explosion, followed by an enormous cloud of dust and debris, bricks and stones being thrown for hundreds of yards. Numerous incendiary shells were also fired into the town, and with the delightful weather we were then having it did not take long to set fire to the whole of the central congested part, which blazed away for days. It was a glorious sight to watch the flames and the smoke rolling away, but sad to see so much useless destruction.

The constant fear of further enemy attacks, coupled with the absolute impossibility of our thinking of any offensive action for some considerable time, decided the authorities that a really strong line of resistance was of first importance. Work of battalions holding the line was, therefore, concentrated on strengthening the Liverpool Line, whilst divisional troops, Royal Engineers, Monmouths, and special working parties found by the brigade in reserve, were engaged in building lines behind, known as the Manchester and Newcastle lines. To build a double line of breastworks protected by barbed wire entanglements along the whole divisional front was a colossal task. The wire was put up, and long sections of breastwork were more or less completed, but by that time things had fortunately so altered that no further defensive work was necessary. The other important work was the improvement of billets in the forward area, which was destitute of buildings, except for a few farm houses and cottages, mostly knocked about by shell fire. With the possible prospect of having to winter here, efforts were made to improve these buildings, by putting inside them "elephant" shelters, covered with concrete. The Royal Engineers made considerable progress with this work, and before we left, several comfortable billets had been thus improvised.

Another work in which all could help—no matter what their rank—and which took a prominent part in our daily life in these days, was salvage. Undoubtedly there was apt to be great waste by allowing material to be left lying about, and at this time there was a pressing need to retrieve everything that could possibly be found. We did our best and endeavoured to rescue such articles as 18-pounder guns and limbers, which we thought might come in useful, but judging from the screeds that were received as to "the true spirit of salvage" we were wrong, and found that the returns of salvage that got the most marks were those containing such items as "socks 200" (got generally from derelict quarter-master's stores found in the forward area, and packed into a limber in about half-a-minute), but the work entailed in hauling 18-pounders and limbers out of dangerous parts of the front, apparently counted for little. Towards the end of our stay, when we moved into the XIII Corps (Lieutenant-General Morland) and Fifth Army (General Birdwood), even greater attention was paid to salvage, and every scrap of paper had to be returned to the paper dump, bottles to the bottle dump, tins to special incinerators, to have the solder melted out and collected, and so on, all no doubt of vital necessity, though seeming at the time rather a bore to carry out.

By the end of May several changes had taken place in the personnel of the battalion, not the least important being that of the quarter-master. Torrance, who had not been well for some time, went to England for a tour of home duty at the end of April. Lieutenant Dale, who acted in his place for a few days, managed to get wounded, and then Regimental Quarter-Master Sergeant Pritchard carried on until

May 26th, when Lieutenant J. Brewer from the "pool" of quarter-masters at the base joined for duty. Kent, in command of C Company, had a very brief period in which to enjoy the company commander's well-earned privilege of being granted the rank and pay of captain, for he got badly wounded by a machine gun bullet on May 31st, in the Gorre sector, and was succeeded by Captain Miners. We also lost 2nd Lieutenants Christian, Judd, Jewel, and Fairbrother—all wounded— and 2nd Lieutenant Russell, sick. Reinforcement officers who joined were 2nd Lieutenants A. D. H. Dunkin and H. Hallam.

Trench reliefs continued more or less according to schedule, 12 days being spent in the line to six out at rest, and though there were minor excitements now and then, nothing exceptional happened on our part of the front for many weeks, although on May 27th, the enemy renewed his attacks near Rheims in the south, and Locre in the north, and made some further progress. Of the brigade sectors, Essars was looked upon as the more preferable, if only on account of the excellent vegetables which grew there in large quantities, and need-less to say, found their way to the messes of officers and men alike, where they were a most welcome addition to rations. There were also numbers of livestock left behind by the French, which owing to the rapid onrush of the Boche they had been unable to take with them. It is reported that two pigs found at "tank" or "Portuguese" farm, by a certain company commander were not unconnected with a notice-able improvement in the rations the next time we were out at rest! A cow which was kept at battalion headquarters for a few days, came to an unfortunate end by dying of gas poisoning!

In order that the men might do a little cooking for themselves in the trenches, as it was impossible to take hot meals up to them by day, special issues of "Tommies' cookers" were made, with which they were able to make hot drinks, and warm their savoury maconochies, meat and vegetables, pork and beans, and other delicacies, whilst dur-ing the night hot porridge and tea were made at battalion headquar-ters, and sent round in food containers.

Rations were taken up each night in the early days by our own transport, which had been provided with lines in a rather low lying field at Fouquières, but later moved to the back of divisional head-quarters at Gosnay, where timber and corrugated iron brought back from derelict horse lines in the forward area, made useful huts and shelters. There was little to choose between the sectors so far as trans-port was concerned, for the shelling of roads was a regular feature of the enemy's offensive action, particularly during the night. It seemed of little use trying to avoid it by going earlier or later, for at whatever time transport was about, there were sure to be shells, mostly gas. The most lively spots were Gorre and Le Quesnoy villages on the right, and the road between Béthune Cemetery Corner and Le Hamel on the left, and it was always advisable to get a move on at night along these particular roads. Later on the trench tramway system, which already existed on the right, was improved and extended to the Essars sector, and eventually stores of all kinds were taken up each night to both sectors in that way, the trains being loaded up at Speedwell Spur, near Fouquières. The engine was taken off at Essars on the left, and at Le Quesnoy on the right, and from there the trucks were man-handled forward to battalion headquarters, or other points.

During the first three and a half months of this period we were not called upon to carry out a raid or attack of any kind. Gunners and trench mortar people carried out shoots on various occasions, and our machine gunners, who were now formed into one battalion for the division, made the most horrible noise every night with their barrages, but we were let off with nothing more serious than patrolling. The country was admirably adapted to this form of reconnaissance, and patrols were out by day almost as much as by night. The corn crops which covered much of the area, were of course left untouched (except just in front of our lines, where they were cut so as to afford a field of fire), and provided excellent cover, as did also the hedges and ditches, which were fairly frequent, and by these means it was possible to get right up to the German outpost line by daylight, and at times even past it. The enemy, of course, played the same game, and unfortunately on one occasion managed to snaffle the N.C.O. and two men from one of our posts. Sometimes patrols went out just before dawn, and remained out the whole of the day, observing from some ditch or other place of concealment, returning to our lines again when darkness fell. Of the many splendid patrols carried out, probably the most daring were those by Captain Andrews, who had previously got a good "chit" from the corps and divisional commanders, for an excellent daylight patrol at Hairpin Craters, in the St. Elie sector. It is reported that on one occasion, when trying to get back to our line he was mistaken for an enemy patrol, and fired on by his own Lewis gunners, and that when he did eventually get safely back, the No. 1 of the team got severely straffed for his poor shooting! Others who did most excellent work in connection with patrolling were Lieutenants Elphick and G. G. Elliott; 2nd Lieutenants Spinney, C. M. Bedford, Hallam, Seymour, Sellis, and Fairbrother; Company Sergeant-Major

Rawding; Seargeants Brett, Teece and Sharrock; Corporals T. H. Johnson, Foster, Brooks and Hurt; Lance-Corporal Beech, and Privates Stanley and Hinton (A Company), Curley, Walker and Elliott (B Company), Green (a stretcher bearer), and Miller (C Company), and Huckerby, Wildsmith and Stubbings (D Company).

So far as training was concerned, an important change was made during this period by the formation of the battle details, into what became known as the divisional wing. As the periods out of the line, were too short for any satisfactory battalion training, to be carried out, a number of officers and men selected from each battalion were left out of the line at regular intervals, to undergo a short course of general training. These courses usually lasted for twelve days. The first assembly was at Bruay, but later more permanent quarters were found at the aerodrome at Hesdigneul. Each brigade had its own wing, and each battalion had a senior officer on the spot to supervise the training. Lieutenant C. H. Powell of our battalion was for some time a most efficient adjutant of the 139th Brigade wing. Lewis gun training and instruction in the meaning of chain of command were at this time perhaps the most important points. Every man in the battalion had to be taught to load and fire the Lewis gun, and to know not only who his commanders were, but how the command might descend to him in case of casualties. Fresh issues of Lewis guns, which were made from time to time, allowed each company to have eight. Their transport was provided by the allotment of two limbered wagons per company, which carried, in addition to the guns, their ammunition drums, spare parts, some boxed ammunition, and other paraphernalia. Lieutenant Bradish, a most conscientious Lewis gun officer, both in and out of the line, was responsible for the Lewis gun work, in which he was ably helped by Seargeants King, Teece, and Milne.

There were two brigade ceremonial parades during this period, both of which were held at Gosnay. On May 28th, the divisional commander inspected us and presented medals, and on June 10th, General Horne, commanding the First Army, honoured us in a similar way. Both inspections went off well, and without any adverse criticisms.

For entertainments we had the Whizz-Bangs, who seldom gave better shows than we got almost every night in the hut in Vaudricourt Wood, and the cinema at divisional headquarters at Gosnay. There were the additional attractions of *estaminets* and shops in the neighbouring villages, especially Verquin, where we had many a good dinner, and drank many bottles of Veuve Cliquot at the *estaminet* of a great favourite of the battalion, Mlle. Bertha.

THE CLOCK TOWER, BÉTHUNE, 1918

On July 18th, a whole day was given up to battalion Sports, on the aerodrome at Hesdigneul. Beginning at 9 a.m. they were not over until 7.30 p.m., after a most successful day, which was mainly due to the excellent arrangements made by Major Gingell, and Sergeant Major Mounteney. At the brigade horse show and sports held two days later, we won first prize for a good type of officer's charger, a chestnut, at one time ridden by Captain Whitton, and later by the second-in-command (this horse won again a little later at the divisional show), whilst the first three places in the cross-country run also fell to the battalion, and firsts in the 100 yards and quarter mile races. Whilst we were not quite so successful at these shows with transport turnouts, their smartness reflected great credit on the transport officer, Lieutenant Tomlinson, and that veteran N.C.O. Sergeant Blunt. As they had got the transport satisfactorily through one of Major-General Thwaites's critical inspections early in June, we felt sure there could be little cause for complaint.

What was, perhaps, from a rather selfish point of view, a drawback to the long spells of fine weather and brilliant moonlight nights that we had during this period, was that it enabled the enemy to make frequent night bombing raids. Our own bombing squadrons of course, did precisely the same thing, but it was not pleasant to be disturbed at night when out at rest, by aeroplanes, cruising around and dropping bombs. Fortunately we escaped with little harm, but the billets and transport lines of many units suffered severely. For our better protection in this respect, a regular system of anti-aircraft defence was devised, and a special allotment of Lewis guns made for the purpose. These were mounted on poles, fixed at various points in the trenches, at the transport lines, and in the vicinity of the more important villages behind the line. Though perhaps in a general way they added to our protection against aeroplanes, for which we had hitherto relied almost entirely on our anti-aircraft guns, known as Archies, we seldom saw them bring anything down, and were inclined to look upon them as likely to give away the positions they were supposed to be protecting.

As the months went by several changes took place in personnel. We lost Captain Whitton, who after being adjutant for 14 months, went for duty to the First Army rest camp at the end of June, and was succeeded by 2nd Lieutenant Martin. Captain Warner went to the divisional signal company early in July, and D Company was then taken over by Captain White. Second Lieutenants Bromham and Russell went down sick, and 2nd Lieutenant Elphick to the Machine Gun Corps. New officers who joined were 2nd Lieutenants E. J. Taylor, James Howard Smith, T. J. Sellis, H. M. Toyne, F. L. Harrap, J. F. Shackleton, F. T. W. Saunders, W. Pennington, S. A. Tebbutt, and S. Bradwell, D.C.M., and we were given a new padre in the person of D. E. Sturt. Sergeant Bescoby, who had done excellent work in charge of the stretcher bearers, became company quarter-master sergeant of A Company, in place of Godfrey, who left to train for a commission. Our strength was kept fairly level by drafts, and we averaged throughout this period about 40 officers, and 920 other ranks.

Our somewhat humdrum existence eventually came to an end about the middle of August. By this time the German offensive had finally ceased, having received its knock-out blow in the fruitless attack made against the French near Rheims on July 15th. On this occasion the French had received ample warning of the attack, and were consequently able to dispose their forces in such a manner as to inflict appalling casualties on the enemy with insignificant losses to themselves. This was followed up by a series of attacks by French, Americans, British, and Italians, which began on July 18th and finally drove the enemy out of the Marne Valley. Even before that time it had been realised that the Germans were not likely to make any further attacks on our part of the front, and about the middle of July we had gone so far as to contemplate an offensive in the Merville Salient. Preliminary plans were actually made for the attack to be made on July 15th, by the Canadians and our own division, but eventually the scheme was cancelled.

The offensive in the south met with extraordinary success at all points, and soon extended to the Third Army area, nearly as far north as Lens, with the result that in the end the Boche decided that he must take steps to withdraw from the Merville Salient. His offensive on this front was, undoubtedly, from the first a serious strategic error. The unexpected ease with which the enemy had advanced on the Portugese front had induced him to push forward further than had been the first intention. Consequently, in holding the inner portion of a most pronounced salient on flat ground, overlooked from the high land south of the La Bassée canal, he had at last experienced some of those difficulties and losses which had been for so long our experience in the Ypres Salient. The many destroyed guns which we ultimately found on our subsequent advance bore witness, not only to the remarkable accuracy and efficiency of our own artillery, but to the folly of attempting to hold the salient when once the possibility of capturing Béthune and the area south of the canal had disappeared. Owing to this mistake of tactics and strategy there is no question that the enemy's losses had been extremely heavy since his advance in April.

During the second week in August, whilst we were in the Gorre sector, we heard that the enemy were carrying out extensive demolitions behind the line, and our patrols were constantly out, so as to ensure keeping touch, should he begin to move back. He had already begun to do so on our left, but we were not actually affected until August 19th, by which time we had moved across to the Essars right sub-sector. About noon on that day, our left company reported that the enemy had evacuated several of the front line posts astride the Rue-du-Bois. A and D Companies, which were in the front line, accordingly sent out strong patrols to keep touch, the remainder moving forward to the old German front line. Some 600 yards in front of our old line, lay the hamlet of Le Touret. This was cleared by the leading companies with little opposition, except for a few snipers left to harass our advance, and by evening the line ran east of that place, a total advance of about 1,000 yards. The same night we handed over to the 6th North Staffords. On August 26th, the battalion moved up to support in the Gorre sector, and was disposed about the Tuning Fork breastworks, with battalion headquarters by the canal side, near Le Préol. Lieutenant G. G. Elliott was badly wounded here during a bombardment of the position held by A Company, of which he was then in command. A battery of guns had been put in the orchard adjoining his headquarters, in spite of many protests, and naturally drew a considerable amount of shelling. Several men were wounded at the same time. "G.G." had succeeded Captain Andrews, who had recently been appointed second-in-command on Major Gingell's departure for a tour of duty at home, and the command of A Company now passed to Lieutenant Thomas.

Readjustments of the divisional front became necessary, owing to the continued withdrawal of the enemy, and on September 1st, we crossed over to relieve our 6th Battalion in the left brigade sector. Here the withdrawal had been fairly rapid, Lacouture and Vieille Chapelle both having been evacuated, and the enemy were now holding a line roughly running from Richebourg St. Vaast through Windy Corner to Richebourg L'Avoué, the general direction of our advance being north-east. At the time we relieved them, the 6th Battalion were engaged in sharp encounters trying to dislodge the enemy from a number of posts just west of Windy Corner. We continued this hole and corner fighting, and on September 3rd, C Company occupied Hens Post, Windy Corner, and Edward's Post, after some sharp scrapping, taking one wounded prisoner, whilst B Company occupied Dogs Post without opposition.

Very gallant work was done during this fighting by Corporal Mosgrove, who in spite of heavy fire established liaison with the company on his right which was held up, thereby enabling the advance to continue; by Private Stamford, a stretcher bearer, who on two separate occasions went forward into the open, in full view of enemy snipers at close range to help wounded comrades, and by Lance-Corporal Beech, who did exceptionally good work in charge of a Lewis gun team.

Those who had been with the battalion in the autumn of 1915, were now on familiar ground, as the fighting was taking place on what was then the area just behind the line that we held in the Richebourg sector. The capture of the posts about Windy Corner straightened out the line, and enabled us to obtain suitable jumping-off positions for an attack which was to take place the following day, as it had been decided to speed up the enemy's retreat in this part, and drive him back far enough to enable us to retake the old British front line near Neuve Chapelle, the enemy being at this moment about 2,000 yards west of that line.

Instructions for the attack were issued somewhat hurriedly during the night. B and C were to be the leading companies, with A and D in support. The 5th Leicesters were attacking on our right, and the

19th Division on the left. There was little or no time to make any reconnaissance. zero was 5.15 a.m. on September 4th, and the barrage came down on the stroke 200 yards east of a line through Haystack, Orchard, Albert, Dogs and Edward's Posts. Having remained on this line four minutes it moved forward at the rate of 100 yards in two minutes, closely followed by the leading troops. The enemy made little resistance, and had evidently decided not to offer any serious defence to operations on a large scale, but to get out of the way as quickly as possible. The result was that within a couple of hours we had regained possession of the old British front line, and the "contact aeroplane" which cruised round a little later, saw our ground flares burning in the identical trenches we held in November, 1915. The 5th Leicesters met with equal success, and were abreast of us on the same line. The 19th Division on our left had met with considerable resistance at Neuve Chapelle, and did not get the whole of their objective until later in the day. The enemy had decided for the moment to stand on his old line running through the Bois-du-Biez, a strong position, from which it would be difficult to dislodge him. The troops on our left suffered several casualties in a fruitless endeavour to push platoons forward into the wood. Our casualties were negligible owing to the feeble resistance offered, and the weak counter-barrage put down. Battalion headquarters moved immediately after the attack to Lansdowne Post.

Communication had been well maintained during this and other recent advances, and we were seldom out of touch by telephone, either with advanced companies or with brigade headquarters. In fact, on the advance into Le Touret, there was so much cover available, on or near the Rue du Bois that a forward Signalling station, supplied by a south and a north line, was established only a few hundred yards behind the front line, within a few minutes of that line being consolidated, and of these two lines the north line was not a mere ground line, but a poled cable. We owed it to the untiring efforts of the signal section, under Lieutenant Stephenson, ably backed by Sergeant Templeman, Corporal Osborne and others, that communications were kept up so well.

The peace that we enjoyed for the rest of the day, was unfortunately not maintained, for on September 5th, the Boche made things unpleasant by shelling the various posts we were holding, which were nothing but isolated shallow trenches with a few corrugated iron shelters covered with earth. One of these, which was used as battalion headquarters, got a direct hit with a 4.2 whilst the whole of the headquarters' staff, except the medical officer were in it. The result was disastrous. Every officer in it was wounded, though "Andy" escaped with nothing worse than a few scratches. Colonel Currin got a leg damaged, Martin the adjutant, and Elly, intelligence officer, both got broken legs, and several other wounds. Stephenson and Taylor (works officer) were also wounded in the leg, whilst Spinney (assistant adjutant) and Salmon (artillery liaison officer), sustained serious head and face wounds. Elly died the following day at the casualty clearing station, at Pernes.

Owing to the continuance of the shelling, battalion headquarters moved to Hens Post near Windy Corner, but again were not left alone, as the enemy put over some eight-inch and gas shells in the vicinity. Altogether it was a decidedly unpleasant day, and we were not sorry to hear that the 19th Division were to relieve us the same night. The relieving battalion, the 9th Cheshires, fortunately for them did not arrive until things had quietened down, and the relief, if somewhat lengthy, was carried out more or less in peace. The lucky ones got a ride from Le Touret on the light railway, but the trains for the rest failed to turn up, and they had to foot it back to Beuvry, where the battalion was billeted, with Major Andrews in temporary command.

CHAPTER 14

Auchel to Pontruet
September 7th, 1918—September 26th, 1918

We left Beuvry on the morning of September 7th and were taken back on the light railway to Ferfay. On this occasion, much to our surprise, the trains moved off at the scheduled time. From Ferfay it was but a short march to Auchel, another mining village, where we found very good billets, and were welcomed in their usual hospitable way by the French miners and their families. Thanks to a most generous town major we got all sorts of little billet comforts, of which he seemed to have an unlimited supply, whilst opposite the headquarters mess was a very comfortable little restaurant, bearing the sign, Cosy Corner, where we found helping to run the show, an old friend known to us in earlier days at Béthune as Lily.

On the day after our arrival Lieutenant-Colonel J. F. Dempster, D.S.O., 2nd Manchesters, took over command of the battalion, Major Andrews resuming the duties of second-in-command, and Lieutenant C. H. Powell temporarily acting as adjutant. Changes had also taken place in the higher commands in the division. Brigadier-General John Harington, D.S.O., from the 46th Machine Gun Battalion, had succeeded General Wood in command of the 139th Brigade, and Major-General Thwaites, who had laboured so assiduously to keep the division up to the highest pitch of perfection in every respect, had gone to England to take up the duties of director of military intelligence at the War Office, and we now had the pleasure of meeting his successor, Major-General G. F. Boyd, C.B., C.M.G., D.S.O., D.C.M., who was to command the division for the rest of the war. He came to see us at Auchel, and we soon realised that under his leadership, given ordinary luck, we could not help doing well. Fresh from the battles of the south, he had much to tell us about the latest forms of attack, particularly those carried out in conjunction with tanks, and we were not long in finding out that what he could not tell us about the kind of fighting that was going on was not worth knowing. He introduced to us the system of advancing in the early stages of the attack in the "blob" formation, that is, with companies on wide frontages, echeloned in depth, with each platoon in a line of sections in "blobs," or small and somewhat open groups. With this formation there was less likelihood of severe casualties from shelling or machine guns, whilst it was a most simple formation from which extensions could be carried out, and at the same time it allowed the section commander to retain control of his men up to the last possible moment. This system we at once set about practising, and later on used it in all the battles in which we took part. Very little training was possible during the few days spent at Auchel owing to the bad weather.

It was, of course, general knowledge that we were shortly to take an active part in the fighting in the south, and therefore no surprise when we received orders to entrain. This was carried out in the early hours of September 12th, at Calonne-Ricouart station, and was rendered extremely uncomfortable by a torrential downpour, which made it specially difficult to get the transport vehicles up the steep ramps on to the trucks. C Company had to do the loading for the whole brigade, and were at the station for nearly twenty-four hours, working in shifts. They left by the last train at 12.40 p.m., the main body having left at 3.16 a.m. This was our farewell to a district of which we had got to know practically every inch, and of which we shall always retain most happy recollections. We had been there for seventeen months without a break.

Slowly but surely we wended our way southwards, until we reached Amiens. At one period the town had been emptied of all civilians, but they were just beginning to come back and the streets were now showing slight signs of life again. A certain amount of damage had been done by shell-fire, and as we moved eastward from Amiens, signs of the one-time proximity of the front line became more marked. Eventually we came to a stop at Corbie station, where we detrained during the afternoon, after a journey of about twelve hours. After most welcome and refreshing tea, which we owed to the forethought of Captain Salter, the acting staff-captain, we marched to billets at La Houssoye, some five miles away, where C Company joined us early the following morning. We were now in the IX Corps, which formed part of General Rawlinson's Fourth Army. We were soon able to make ourselves comfortable, though the village was somewhat battered and contained very few inhabitants. When we moved further forward, it was, from a purely military point of view, a decided advantage to find no civilians at all. All around was a delightfully free rolling country, and we could wander anywhere according to our own sweet will, those lucky enough to have horses getting some lovely gallops across the chalk downs. This area had been too near the front line for the past few months for any work to be carried out on the land, and such crops as there were were now being harvested by soldier labour, mostly Canadian.

The enemy had been driven back from the neighbourhood during August by the Australians, who had had particularly hard fighting about Villers-Bretonneux, not many miles distant from where we were billeted, and the work of clearing the battlefield was already in hand. Gangs of Chinese were employed in the task, but we were not impressed by their industry. Everything had to be carried to dumps by the roadside, and no matter what the burden the only authorised way of carrying it was by putting it on the end of a pole, which the "Chink" carried over his shoulder. It seemed decidedly comical, to say the least, to see a man walk several hundred yards to retrieve a coat, for example, hang it on the pole, and walk several more hundred yards with it to a dump! Nevertheless, this seemed to be the recognised way of working.

Such training as we carried out was mostly in the attack and other operations, such as advanced guards, likely to be required in open warfare. Little was done in the way of bombing, which had had its day. There was a good deal of Lewis gun work, and field-firing practice in the shape of platoon attacks on strong points. Flags to represent tanks were introduced into the scheme with a view to giving some idea of how to follow up a tank and take possession of the ground it gained. A good deal of practice in map reading and compass work was carried out by officers and N.C.O.'s, which proved most useful in the days to come. Several officers and N.C.O.'s here enjoyed their first aeroplane flight through the kindness of the officer commanding a bombing squadron in the vicinity.

Orders for a move came after little delay, but with unexpected suddenness. We had to break off in the middle of a practice attack on September 18th, to prepare for our departure, and at 9 p.m. on the same day we left La Houssoye and marched to Bonnay, where we embussed for the forward area once more. Transport marched brigaded and was now under Lieutenant Toyne, who took charge when Lieutenant Tomlinson broke his collar-bone in a jumping competition a little while before at Vaudricourt. Somewhere about midnight the long procession of lorries moved off. The other two brigades of the division were being moved by the same means, and there is no doubt that the auxiliary 'bus companies were having a pretty busy time! In the darkness the journey seemed endless. It was too bumpy to allow even a doze, sleepy as most of us felt. The whole area was a desolate ruin, but in the darkness we were, of course, able to see little or nothing of it. For something like 40 miles, the Somme area, through which we were passing, was nothing but an immense wilderness—every village practically in ruins, and hardly sufficient remains in many cases to identify their position. In one case a sign-board had been put up to mark the site of the village, and on maps they were usually described as "— ruins of." Old trenches and barbed wire entanglements existed at various points. Not a scrap of ground was cultivated—all was wild and uncared for. Not a living soul was there except a few odd troops of our own, working mostly on roads or guarding dumps, and French, Italians, Portuguese and "Chinks" working on the railways. A few odd woods and shattered trees were practically the only things standing in this enormous tract of country. Later on we saw all this for ourselves when we used to cross this devastated area going on leave or for trips to Amiens, which a generous staff permitted us to indulge in occasionally. Much of the area had been fought over four times—firstly, when captured by the enemy in the original advance; secondly, when he withdrew to the Hindenburg Line early in 1917 and laid the whole place waste; thirdly, during his offensive of 1918; and, lastly, when he was driven out once and for all by British and other troops just before our arrival.

Eventually, about dawn on September 19th, the long train of lorries came to a halt, and we were dumped on the road about a mile west of a one-time village known as Poeuilly, to which we marched, and where we were told we had to bivouac.

It was a cheerless prospect to be turned loose into a bare field at 4.0 a.m. on a late September morning. Poeuilly, however, was found to contain a certain amount of useful material which very soon found its way to our field, and with the aid of a few trench shelters, and taking advantage of some trenches which were there, it was not long before we had put up some quite useful protection. Though chilly in the early morning the weather was quite seasonable, and on the whole we did not fare badly. Our transport arrived late the same day.

The Hindenburg Line lay a few miles in front of us, and some of its outer defences were already in our hands. On the afternoon of September 20th, we left Poeuilly and relieved the 2nd Royal Sussex in brigade reserve in trenches and dug-outs about Pontru, with battalion headquarters at Cooker Quarry, the 5th and 6th Battalions taking over the front line. At this point we were some seven miles north-west of St. Quentin, and two to three miles west of Bellenglise, on the St. Quentin canal. There was no great excitement during the three days we spent there except that we had rather bad luck with the transport. As the idea was rather pressed on us that we were now taking part in moving warfare, some of the horses and company limbers of bombs and small arm ammunition were taken forward to the edge of a small wood just behind battalion headquarters. Unfortunately this wood got shelled and several mules were knocked out, with the result that the ammunition was dumped, and the limbers and rest of the animals were sent back to Poeuilly.

On September 23rd we received orders for certain action to be carried out by us in connection with an attack which was to be launched the next day, when the 46th Division were to carry out a minor operation in conjunction with the 1st Division on their right. The Australians had pushed forward considerably on the left, and the line now bent back sharply, where the troops we had relieved had been held up by the village of Pontruet. The attack was planned both to straighten out the line and to get possession of the high ground on the right. The 138th Brigade, who had taken over from the Australians on the left, were ordered to capture the village of Pontruet, and for this purpose detailed the 5th Leicesters. The attack was to be carried out by an enveloping movement from the north, and the village was to be rushed from the east. Our 5th and 6th Battalions were to co-operate by occupying some trenches about Pontruet, and, on the night following, the 8th Battalion was to relieve the 5th Leicesters as far north as the inter-brigade boundary.

The attack was launched at 5 a.m. on September 24th, and though the 5th Leicesters made most strenuous efforts to attain their objectives, they just failed to achieve the full purpose for which they set out, and at the end of the day Pontruet was not ours. Our 5th Battalion on the right also had some stiff fighting, and suffered several casualties, taking their objective on the high ground south of Pontruet, and capturing about 100 prisoners. Late in the day our orders to relieve the 5th Leicesters were cancelled, and we had to take over from our own 5th Battalion, who were holding the western edge of Pontruet. This operation was completed just before dawn on the 25th, battalion headquarters being in a dug-out in the high ground south of Pontru. Fortunately we were there only two days, for the discomfort was very great, the dug-outs and cellars swarming with flies and vermin, and there was little other protection from the enemy shelling, which was fairly frequent. On September 26th we were relieved on an intensely dark night by the 1st Black Watch and went back to bivouacs just off the Vendelles-Bihécourt road, put up for us by the battle details, who had moved up from Poeuilly. They, together with the transport and quar.-master's stores, had had none too peaceful a time during the last few days. Having moved to Vendelles they were shelled out of it almost at the moment they arrived, but eventually found a quiet resting-place for a brief space at Bernes, where, in addition to ordinary stores, there were piled all the men's packs and spare kit, and numbers of Lewis gun boxes. All moves now were done in light fighting order and the quarter-master and quarter-master-sergeants had their time fully occupied in thinking how all the spare kit was to be got forward when it was wanted.

During our recent moves we had received a regular influx of new officers, no fewer than nine having joined between September 3rd and September 26th. They were 2nd Lieutenants G. Newton, John Henry Smith, A. N. Davis, R. N. Barker, T. F. Mitchell, W. J. Winter, R. S. Plant, P. A. Turner, and W. G. Jacques. We had lost 2nd Lieutenant Morris, who had gone to the 139th Trench Mortar Battery; and Company Sergeant-Major Slater and five N.C.O.'s who were sent to England as instructors. Slater was succeeded as company sergeant-major of A Company, by Sergeant Attenborough. Our battle casualties at Pontruet amounted to five killed and 24 wounded.

The men were now very fit and the battalion was on the top of its form. Our chief anxiety was whether after all we were to be in a real good push. We suspected that we might have been brought here to be whittled away in minor trench attacks, and that the opportunity of really showing what stuff the battalion was made of would never present itself. Our fears were not lessened when we saw how the 5th Leicesters and 5th Sherwood Foresters suffered at Pontruet, and we saw looming ahead what we imagined to be the never-ending luck of the 46th Division. Our fears were ill-founded. Better things were before us and arrived sooner than we expected.

CHAPTER 15

Bellenglise
September 26th, 1918—September 29th, 1918

A great effort was to be made to break the Hindenburg Line. Preliminary orders received on September 26th were to the effect that the 46th Division, as part of a major operation (simultaneous attacks by the British and French taking place at several other points), would at an early date cross the St. Quentin canal between Bellenglise and Riquerval bridge, and capture the Hindenburg Line. The general scheme was that the 137th Brigade were to capture the canal and hold the crossings, advancing as far as the brown line shown on the map, whilst the 139th Brigade on the right and 138th Brigade on the left, were to pass through them and consolidate up to and including the green line. If all went well the 32nd Division were to pass through and make further progress. The 1st Division were to protect our right flank, where the enemy were still occupying a large area of ground which might be decidedly dangerous to us, and in the event of the enemy withdrawing, they were to follow up and, if possible, capture Thorigny and the high ground round about it. On our left the 30th American Division, attached to the Australian Corps, were to seize the Bellicourt Tunnel (where the canal ran underground) and continue the attack in that direction. Tanks were to cross the canal by passing over the tunnel and come down to operate with the 138th and 139th Brigades and help them to reach their objectives.

In order to improve our position the 138th Brigade, who were holding the line running along the high ground just east of Victoria Cross Roads, carried out an attack on September 27th against the German trenches on the high ground north-east of Chopper Ravine. This was successful and the trenches were handed over to the 137th Brigade. Unfortunately, the following morning the enemy delivered a heavy counter-attack against the Staffords, and recovered so much ground that at night the latter had to withdraw from the portions still held and come back to our original line. This set-back, however, had no ill result.

Our preparations had to be made on the assumption that the attack would take place on the early morning of Sunday, September 29th, as it did.

From the line held by the division it was possible to get a good view of the canal and the ground beyond for some distance, and such reconnaissance as could be carried out in the time at our disposal was made by observation from this line.

Running diagonally across the front, through No Man's Land, down the slope to the Riqueval bridge, on the left, was a narrow road known as Watling Street. Immediately in front of our trenches was the ridge which we had had to evacuate, and from there the land again sloped down to the canal. Immediately the other side of the canal was the village of Bellenglise, about three-quarters-of-a-mile from our present front line, but looking much closer. The canal ran in a cutting, into which it was not possible to see, but from descriptions obtained from various sources it appeared that it had steep banks twelve to eighteen yards deep, and we were told that where there was water we might expect it to be seven to eight feet deep. As a matter of fact the canal in some parts was quite dry, and in other parts the

THE ST. QUENTIN CANAL, BELLENGLISE—LOOKING NORTH—1918

water was held up by big dams of concrete. When we did properly see it, it appeared to be more or less derelict. On the right towards Bellenglise it was mostly dry. Rising from the canal on the other side was a fairly gradual, but none the less decided, slope for some distance, fortified with lines of trenches, barbed wire and concrete machine gun emplacements, apparently a most unpromising position to attack—indeed, we thought it impregnable, and no doubt the Boche did so, too. It was an ideal spot for concealed dug-outs all along the canal banks. Many were found there, and Bellenglise itself contained a wonderfully constructed tunnel, estimated to be capable of holding at least a thousand men.

The problem of dealing with any water that might be found in the canal was a difficult but important one, as every preparation had to be made for getting across on the assumption that all the bridges would be destroyed. Accordingly the 137th Brigade were equipped with a number of collapsible boats and rafts, also mats for getting across any soft mud they might encounter, whilst almost at the last moment, numbers of lifebelts were sent up for their use, taken from the leave boats.

As it was doubtless realised that this great stronghold would require pounding almost to atoms, arrangements were made for getting together what must have been the largest array of guns that ever was collected, at any rate in such a short space of time. Battery after battery of every known calibre took up positions in one or other of the ravines and valleys behind the line. Indeed, there seemed no room for them all and many of them were practically in the open.

Behind the line an immense amount of railway and road work was being carried out in order to maintain supplies. Probably the most interesting piece of work was the relaying of the railway line from Roizel to Vermand, preparatory to its being continued into St. Quentin as soon as the latter should be liberated. We enjoyed watching the Canadian Engineers at work rebuilding bridges and bringing up and relaying fresh sleepers and metals, all the old ones having been removed by the enemy for several miles. The rapid reconstruction of the line was of vital importance, as it would form the main source of transport for all our supplies.

On the night of September 27/28th, we moved from bivouacs near Vendelles, and marched to our preliminary assembly position in some trenches near Red Wood, about half-a-mile north-west of that well-known landmark the Tumulus, a high chalk mound from which an excellent view could be obtained, but where it was not wise to pause to admire the scenery. Battalion headquarters was in a dugout at Hudson's Post, between Red Wood and the Twin Craters. This move was carried out without casualty, but the very dark night, coupled with a certain amount of gas shelling, and the absence of good guiding marks, made going somewhat difficult. A section from the 139th Trench Mortar Battery, which was to be attached to us for the battle, joined us just before the move.

The attack was to be carried out under a creeping barrage, and the objective allotted to us was the Yellow Line east of Bellenglise. The frontage allotted to the battalion was about 1,200 yards, and the advance in its final stages was to be carried out with two companies in the front line and two in support. In each case there were to be three platoons leading, with one in support, each front platoon thus having a frontage of about 200 yards. The distance between front and support companies was to be 200 to 250 yards. The artillery barrage was to move at the rate of 100 yards in four minutes, making long pauses after each objective had been gained in order to allow time for the rear troops to continue the advance. A machine gun barrage also was to be fired during the opening stages of the attack, and for this purpose our divisional battalion was strengthened by the addition of the 2nd Life Guards Machine Gun Battalion and the 100th Machine Gun Battalion. By a happy coincidence some South Notts. Yeomanry were included amongst these machine gunners. The Royal Engineers and Monmouth Pioneers, detailed to put emergency bridges on cork piers across the canal for foot traffic and artillery, were to follow in rear of the 137th Brigade, and immediately in front of us. Second Lieutenant Davis with ten men was to keep touch with the last battalion of the 137th Brigade, whilst 2nd Lieutenant Plant was detailed to act as liaison officer with the 137th Brigade headquarters. Second Lieutenant Bradish was to do similar duty with the 139th Brigade, and 2nd Lieutenant Winter with the 6th Battalion, who were to follow immediately behind us, the 5th Battalion bringing up the rear. Guides from each company were detailed to follow the 137th Brigade and direct their companies to the canal crossings. Flags were to be carried to mark battalion and company headquarters. In addition to red flares for notifying the position of the advanced troops to our 'contact aeroplanes,' a number of tin discs were issued, which were to be waved by the men carrying them so as to catch the eye of the observers. Success signals—rifle grenades bursting into white over white over white—were to be fired by the leading companies as soon as they reached their objective. Pack transport was arranged in readiness for taking forward ammunition, water and other supplies, if required, as soon as it was possible to get them across the canal.

Enough and more than enough work was entailed in all these details to keep us busy during the short time available before the attack. Nevertheless all was ready by the appointed time, and about 3 a.m. on the morning of September 29th, after a most welcome issue of rum, which fortunately arrived just in time, we began to move into our final assembly position on the eastern side of Ascension Valley. The valley never had been a place to linger in, as most nights and early mornings the Hun was in the habit of treating it liberally with high explosive and gas shells, and this occasion was no exception, a combination of the two making things very unpleasant. Further, it was a dark night, and, worse than all, a dense fog came down over everything, so that movement over these more or less open spaces with little or nothing to guide us was extremely difficult. However, in the end everyone got into position in good time and without accident. Fortunately most of the shells were then passing over us into the valley behind. Companies were drawn up as follows: Right Front (A Company), Captain Thomas; Left Front (B Company), 2nd Lieutenant Bloor; Right Support (C Company), Lieutenant Cairns, in the absence of Captain Miners on leave; Left Support (D Company), Captain White. Captain C. P. Elliott was acting as second-in-command, Major Andrews being away on leave.

Zero was fixed for 5.50 a.m., at which time the 137th Brigade were to advance from our front line. At the same time the 1st Division were to advance so as to protect our right flank up to a point near Bellenglise bridge.

Promptly at zero an uncanny stillness was broken by an inferno of noise. With a din and roar that can never be forgotten by those who heard it, one of the greatest concentrations of artillery the World had ever seen came into action. The crash and rattle were appalling. Sandwiched as we were, with machine guns blazing away just in front, and 18-pounders belching out fire just behind, it was perfect pandemonium. Speech was impossible. Though it was now practically daylight the fog was so intense that you could not see a yard in front of you. All over the battlefield it was the same. We could only imagine the difficulty with which the Staffords were going, if they were going at all, and we could see nothing. Our right company, A, had been detailed to assist that brigade to mop up the enemy trenches west of the canal, and on completion re-form in the old German front line, and await the arrival of the other companies. This company advanced in artillery formation as soon as the machine guns ceased firing, about 15 minutes after zero, and reached these trenches without accident. Little was found to be done there, and having distributed themselves in the trenches, they awaited the time for the general advance to begin. The rest of the battalion moved forward at the same time in a similar formation to Nib and Quill trenches on Hélène Ridge. Even for this short move direction could only be maintained by means of compasses. We made ourselves as comfortable as possible there, as we knew that we should have some time to wait before advancing further. In any case we were not to move without orders from brigade headquarters, and it was not intended that we should be involved in the actual fighting until the 137th Brigade were east of the canal, and then probably not for some time unless they were in difficulties. The Boche had put down a counter-barrage directly after our attack began, and a certain number of shells and some machine gun bullets fell about the ridge where we were, but caused us little inconvenience.

In spite of the fog wounded men were finding their way back, and odd lots of German prisoners were being brought back by escorts of Staffords. How they did it we never quite knew, but it was reported that in one case the escort of a party of prisoners having been lost in the fog, got a captured German officer to act as guide by marching due west on a compass bearing! For over three hours we were unable to get any definite news as to the progress of the battle. The first official message which reached our brigade headquarters to the effect that the 137th Brigade were across the canal, arrived at 8.30 a.m., and orders were at once sent to the three battalions to get on the move and keep in close touch. Unfortunately our telephone line to brigade headquarters was broken, and the message had to be sent by runners, who after experiencing the greatest difficulty owing to the fog, eventually reached us at 9.37 a.m. Orders were sent to companies as quickly as possible, and we moved off again in artillery formation, keeping direction with our compasses. Progress, of course, was extremely slow. By the time we reached the canal, which seemed much further away than we had imagined, the fog began to clear and caused us no more trouble. The canal was crossed by plank foot bridges, which, fortunately, were still more or less intact, and companies pushed on in a direction practically half-right towards the villages of Bellenglise on the right and La Baraque on the left.

Here our first real fighting began, considerable opposition being met with from isolated snipers and machine gun posts, particularly on the right, where A Company had a very rough time. Two platoons of that company, under 2nd Lieutenants Bradwell and Shackleton, worked their way along the bend of the canal sheltered by a large ditch, and rushed several pill-boxes from the rear. At one large concrete dug-out a Boche was discovered just emerging with his machine gun ready to fire. Bradwell stopped him with a revolver bullet through the chest. The bullet went through the next man behind him as well, and finished by lodging in the throat of a third—a very useful shot! A little later the same officer got a sniper, who was obstinately holding up the advance with a small group of men, by a rifle bullet neatly placed between the eyes at 300 yards. The left of A Company also met with opposition from machine gun nests in the ruins of the houses. Thomas himself, in rushing one machine gun, had no time to draw his revolver, but put one Boche out of action by a kick under the jaw. C Company reinforced A and shared with them the clearing of Bellenglise, but in doing so they also had a bad time. Stanley Cairns led them with great dash, only to be killed in an attack on a group of Boches who were holding up the left of A Company. They were, however, eventually rushed and all bayoneted. On the left some of B Company lost direction and strayed over to the 138th Brigade. Though the resistance on this flank was not so great it was not altogether easy going, and there was considerable shelling and machine gun fire. Bloor, in command, got badly wounded, and Rawding, his very gallant company sergeant-major also fell, dying the next day. Mobilised with the battalion he went out with it as a private and won promotion by sheer merit. All ranks of the battalion had the greatest regard for him and his loss was very keenly felt. D Company, under Captain White, ably assisted by 2nd Lieutenant Smith, acting as second-in-command, also gave a hand in the mopping up. Casualties were, of course, mounting, as there was heavy shelling going on most of the time, particularly on the eastern edge of Bellenglise. Eventually, however, the village was cleared and we got to our next starting-point, the brown line, with our right on the canal, at 11.30 a.m. This was only ten minutes after our scheduled time which, considering the almost insuperable difficulties caused by the fog, must be considered excellent. It meant, of course, that our barrage, which advanced again at 11.20 a.m. (five-and-a-half hours after zero) was slightly ahead of us, but that was now too late to be altered and we had to make the best of it.

At this point we were to have been joined by a company of five tanks, but they had not turned up. They arrived, however, a little later and were going forward to help the attack of the 6th Battalion, who followed us, when they were put out of action by enemy field guns firing from south of the canal and at point blank range. Our final advance, therefore, had to be continued without their help. We moved off this time in extended order and met with little opposition, though there was considerable machine gun fire from the south side of the canal, which was not particularly accurate and did little damage. We reached our final objective about 12.15 p.m., only a few minutes after scheduled time, and the 6th Battalion immediately pushed on through us.

Our right flank was somewhat exposed, as the enemy were still holding the ground south of the canal, and one or two feeble attempts at counter-attacks were made from that direction, but were easily broken up. The 1st Division had been unable to advance to connect across with us at Bellenglise, but by their demonstration they doubtless prevented the enemy from concentrating for a counter-attack in that quarter, which was a decidedly weak spot.

Our advance had been extremely rapid and to a certain extent our success was due to that fact. The enemy in many cases were taken before they had time to get to their battle positions. At the same time every member of the battalion was determined to get there. Particularly good work was done by Sergeant Peach, who was acting company sergeant-major of C Company, and himself accounted for three of the enemy at one post, by Sergeant Oldham, Lance-Seargeants Field and Illger, and Corporal Slater, when in temporary command of platoons, also by Sergeant Claxton, Corporals Gadsby, Skelton and W. Foster, Lance-Corporal R. Harvey. and Privates Cook, Titmus, Welbourne and Stapleton. Communication throughout the day was almost entirely by runners, who had an exceptionally strenuous time, but in spite of all their difficulties they never failed to get their messages through. Specially valuable work was done in this respect by Privates B. Smithurst, Feighery, Sully, Colton and Parker. The signallers had a thankless task in trying to keep their lines repaired. A special word of praise is due to Lance-Corporal J. North for his work in this connection. The medical officer, Captain Homan, had a difficult task in attending to the wounded in open trenches and often under heavy shell fire. He got great help from Padre Sturt, who was always rendering faithful service, and from a willing band of stretcher bearers, who worked unceasingly throughout the battle, notably Corporal Wrigglesworth and Privates Westnidge and Green. Company Sergeant-Major Stokes, who was acting as regimental sergeant-major, was also of the greatest service in looking after ammunition and other stores.

The sight presented by the enemy defences east of the canal gave no room for doubt that our guns had done most deadly work. The ground was literally torn to pieces, trenches and wire being blown to atoms in all directions, and there seemed to be scarcely a spot that had not been touched.

The prisoners taken by us numbered something like 300. There is no doubt that our bombardment had caused many of them to become more or less senseless. In many cases all they did was to retire to their dug-outs and await the end. Full dug-outs emptied themselves at the first word, and poured out their garrisons, which were as quickly marshalled by our men and led off to the prisoner cages in batches, 50 or more in a batch, and very often not more than one of our men in charge. In addition to prisoners we captured over 40 machine guns and 10 trench mortars. Guns did not come within our province, as they were all beyond our objective.

Our casualties, considering all things, were small, and this was doubtless due to the great rapidity with which the advance had been carried out. In addition to the two officer casualties, our losses during the day were 14 other ranks killed and 80 wounded.

The battlefield after the fog lifted presented a sight never to be forgotten. On the left, tanks could be seen working their way along the German trenches, followed by groups of infantry, who at once took possession of the ground gained. Behind, guns were limbering up and being got forward to fresh positions; pack ponies and limbers were being taken up with ammunition; parties of Boche prisoners were wending their way back from the front areas in batches of 10's, 20's, up to 200 or more, presenting a very bedraggled appearance. Many of them had been requisitioned for duty at the forward aid posts and were carrying back our wounded. Add to the whole, shells bursting here and there—one knew not when or where the next was coming and didn't care—and some idea may be formed of what the battlefield of Bellenglise looked like. It was like an enormous circus.

The 138th Brigade on the left met with equal success, but north of them the attack did not go so well, and at the end of the day the Australians and Americans, though in a satisfactory position for continuing the attack, were considerably behind their objective.

During the afternoon the 32nd Division came moving over the back areas by companies in artillery formation and pushed on through us, but there was no time that day for them to make any fresh attacks, and they had to be content with putting out outposts. There is no doubt that could their attack have been pushed on at once the fighting of the next few days would not have been necessary. As it was our line did not get further than the final objective of the 5th Battalion, and further preparation was required to push the Boche from the few remaining points that he still held in the Hindenburg Line. By the victory of the 46th Division on September 29th the main portion of that line had been absolutely smashed and the last great turning-point in the war passed, and from now onwards the final defeat of the enemy was but a matter of days. It must be confessed that the fog, which lasted practically the whole morning, largely accounted for our success. Without it it is very difficult to conceive how we could have managed to get possession of the canal and the high ground on the east of it. A naturally strong defensive line itself, it formed with the addition of the artificial defences made by the enemy, an almost impregnable position. general headquarters thought it *was* impregnable.

It has since transpired that our fears that our attack was only in the nature of a "demonstration" were only too well founded, as it appears to be a fact that we were not expected to cross the canal at all. Lieutenant-General Sir John Monash, who commanded the Australian Corps on our left, referring in his book, *The Australian Victories in France in 1918*, to the action of September 29th, says:

> Quite early in the day news came in that the IX Corps on my right hand had achieved an astonishing success, that Bellenglise had been captured, and that the deep canal had been successfully crossed in several places. It was the 46th Imperial Division to which this great success was chiefly due.—There can be no doubt that this success, conceived at first as a demonstration to distract attention from the Australian Corps' front, materially assisted me in the situation in which I was placed later on the same day.

For once general headquarters' arrangements for the 46th Division miscarried.

Sappers got the Riqurval bridge fit for transport early in the afternoon, and by 3.0 p.m. guns and other horse transport were passing over it. Later in the evening, after the 32nd Division had got clear, some of our transport and cookers came up, and our hardworking quarter-master-sergeants brought us very welcome and much-needed refreshment after a most strenuous day.

CHAPTER 16

Ramicourt and Montbrehain

September 30th, 1918—October 4th, 1918

September 30th was spent in dug-outs and trenches in the region of our objective of the previous day, between Bellenglise and Lehaucourt. Early that morning the 1st Division advanced and occupied Thorigny and Talana Hill, south of the canal, thus securing our right flank, the retreating enemy offering splendid targets for our Lewis guns. The same day St. Quentin fell to the French.

In the afternoon the 32nd Division moved forward to the attack, supported by cavalry, which it was hoped it would be possible to use if the infantry broke through the last remaining fragment of the Hindenburg Line. This was known as the Beaurevoir-Fonsomme Line and ran more or less north and south about midway between Joncourt and Ramicourt. It consisted of a strong barbed wire entanglement and a double line of shallow trenches about a foot deep, with concrete machine gun emplacements every 50 yards. The whole was in a very incomplete state, but at the same time constituted a strong line of defence. Unfortunately the 32nd Division were unable to break this line, which the enemy were holding in force. Similarly, the 1st Division on the right were unable to make any further progress, and the 2nd Australian Division met with no greater success on the left. In consequence the cavalry had to withdraw behind the canal.

The arrival of the cavalry a few days previously behind our lines had presented one of the most picturesque scenes one could wish to see. Two abreast they came in almost endless streams along the roads and side-tracks and passed on to forward positions behind the canal, and the sight was one never to be forgotten. Not less wonderful, perhaps, was the unceasing flow of transport of every conceivable kind backwards and forwards along the Vadencourt-Bellenglise road. The surface of the road was in excellent condition and in an incredibly short period the Sappers, who were now having very strenuous times, erected an Inglis bridge over the canal at Bellenglise, capable of carrying lorries and guns of all calibres. The way all this work was pushed on was little short of marvellous, and one could not help being struck by the enormous amount of organisation it all entailed, and the care with which every detail connected with the advance had been arranged.

The 139th Brigade were now temporarily attached to the 32nd Division, whilst the 137th and 138th Brigades were concentrated near the canal. We were supposed at this moment to be ready either for another battle or for moving forward according to the ordinary rules of warfare, with advanced guards and so on, if the enemy should give way. Preliminary orders were indeed received that portions of the brigade were to be employed as advanced guard to the corps, with their objective as Le Cateau.

With the object, therefore, of reorganising as far as possible, we were withdrawn from our position near Lehaucourt on October 1st, and moved about a mile north, to the trench system in Springbok Valley, just behind Magny la-Fosse. On the same day the transport, quarter-master's stores and battle details which had previously moved to a field near Hart Copse, a few hundred yards north-west of the Twin Craters, moved further forward and established themselves in Chopper Ravine, near the canal. This was not a specially comfortable spot, and the quarter-master's department was constantly put out of order by the arrival from time to time of odd shells from a German long-range gun. Several of the riding horses, the cookers and some of the ammunition and Lewis gun limbers were up with the battalion, so that the amount of transport left behind was not great. Both men and horses were now having a most strenuous time, and we were lucky at this juncture in getting back Captain A. Bedford from a tour of duty at home. He arrived on September 29th and was at once appointed transport officer. We had been obliged to leave behind at Bernes large quantities of stores, including packs and Lewis gun tin boxes, owing to lack of transport, and it was a most trying business, when everyone was wanting lorries, to get the extra transport necessary to bring them along. To make matters worse the Hun was just now particularly active with his aeroplanes, and with fine nights he made frequent trips over our lines, dropping bombs. When the nights were very dark he often used to let off brilliant white parachute lights, and as they descended he was able to get some view of the roads and transport lines and any movement there might be. Usually he flew extremely low, and there is no doubt that he did considerable damage; especially as there were such masses of troops and transport concentrated in a particularly small area. We unfortunately lost several horses, but casualties amongst personnel were insignificant. His best bombing effort was on the evening of October 3rd. Having evidently seen a large party of men near La Baraque cross-roads, the airman promptly made for them and let loose two bombs, which fell right amongst them. Between 40 and 50 were blown to bits, whilst nearly as many were badly wounded, and the rest scared out of their wits. What the airman doubtless did not know was that they were a party of Boche prisoners! Only about six British soldiers were killed. It made a ghastly mess at the cross-roads, which was a most uninviting spot to pass for days afterwards.

During the short time at our disposal we did the best we could to reorganise our somewhat reduced forces. In spite of our losses at Bellenglise we still had 46 officers and 752 other ranks, so were fairly well off. Second Lieutenant Winter was put in command of B Company, and Captain Miners, who had just returned from leave, resumed command of C.

On October 2nd orders were received that we were to take part in another big attack in conjunction with the 2nd Australian Division. Our divisional commander only received his orders for this attack at 4.30 p.m. on that day, and the operation was to take place early the next morning, so that there was very little time to get orders passed to the lower commanders and the necessary arrangements made. The orders were explained by the brigade commander to battalion commanders at a conference at brigade headquarters at Magny-la-Fosse about 9 p.m., and it was after 10 p.m. before Colonel Dempster was able to give his orders out to companies. The general scheme was that the 139th Brigade were to break through the Beaurevoir-Fonsomme Line and capture the villages of Ramicourt and Montbrehain, whilst the 137th Brigade on the right and the 2nd Australian Division on the left, were to attack at the same time, and the 1st Division, on the right of the 137th Brigade, were to capture Sequehart.

The objective of the 5th and 8th Battalions was the Red Line running north-west to south-east, just west of Montbrehain, the 5th Battalion being on the right and the 8th on the left, whilst the 6th Battalion was to pass through, capture Montbrehain and push out outposts as far as the "dotted blue line." This was something like 4,000 yards from our present outpost line. A company of nine tanks were to cooperate with the brigade, advancing immediately behind the first line. The attack was to be launched at dawn and was to be carried out under an artillery barrage which, after delaying six minutes on the opening line, was to move at the rate of 100 yards in four minutes. The delay was to enable the infantry to adjust their distance behind the barrage, which was to open a good deal further in front of them than usual, owing to the fact that the artillery had mostly to move into fresh positions, and we could not, therefore, risk getting up close to its assumed line, whilst allowance also had to be made for the attacking troops not being exactly in their right position, owing to the difficulty of forming up in the dark on an uncertain mark.

Our jumping-off line ran from near Joncourt cemetery to the railway cutting. The battalion frontage was approximately 1,000 yards and was divided into two company lengths. A (Thomas) on the right, and B (Winter) on the left were to lead, with C (Miners) and D (White) in support about 150 yards behind them. Second Lieutenant Plant was sent as liaison officer to the Australian battalion on our left, 2nd Lieutenant Newton to brigade headquarters, and 2nd Lieutenant Jacques to the 5th Battalion. Some additional work was to be thrown on C and D Companies, who were to follow up the 6th Battalion, mop up for them in Montbrehain and then return to the Red Line. There was no time for reconnaissance. All we knew of the country was what we had gathered from maps or our intelligence department. From personal observation we knew nothing. Even the front held by the 32nd Division was not at all certain. We did know, however, that the enemy were holding the Beaurevoir-Fonsomme Line in force and that the country was of a fairly open type, sloping gently down to Ramicourt in the valley and up again beyond to Montbrehain, which would probably be a difficult problem to tackle.

It was in these circumstances that we set out shortly before midnight in the pitch darkness from Springbok Valley. Guides from the 32nd Division met us at the entrance to Joncourt and conducted us to the forming-up line, A and B Companies throwing out a screen of scouts in front as a precaution before we formed up. Though this was a most precarious proceeding it was carried out successfully, and by 5.30 a.m. on October 3rd, all troops were in their assembly positions, leading companies extended in two lines and support companies in lines of "section-blobs." During this operation the enemy did a certain amount of shelling, but not enough to cause us any great trouble. There was some fog at first, and this in the early stages of the battle, combined with smoke from a screen put down by the artillery to hide the tanks, made direction somewhat difficult. Later on it cleared and the day became quite bright and fine.

There was not such a concentration of guns as we had had on September 29th, nor had we anything like so many heavies, though there was a certain number of them firing on a few special targets, such as villages and other points behind the lines. The Guards Machine Gun Battalion again helped with the preliminary barrage, which opened promptly at 6.5 a.m., just as it was beginning to get light. We adjusted our position to the line of bursting shells and followed on as soon as the guns lifted. The rate of progress, 100 yards in four minutes, was throughout found to be too slow in this more open fighting, and we were constantly either waiting for the barrage to move on or running into it—not at all a pleasant proceeding.

It was not long before we began to encounter, in addition to the enemy's counter-barrage, opposition of a serious nature from his infantry. The inevitable delay since we crossed the canal on September 29th had given the enemy time to bring up large reserves, and on this occasion the 46th Division had opposed to it four Boche Divisions— two tired and two fresh. Doubtless the enemy realised that every effort must be made to retain this, his last organised defence on this part of the front, and certainly the men holding the line we had to attack put up a most strenuous fight, and in hundreds of cases died bravely, fighting to the last.

The Beaurevoir-Fonsomme Line was strongly held. In addition to many machine guns in the line itself, there were also machine gun sections in rifle-pits immediately behind it. Unfortunately the barrage put down by our guns was somewhat thin. There had been no previous bombardment, and as a result we found that the defences of this line were practically intact. No machine gun emplacements had been touched and not a single gap made in the wire, which was very strong, and we had to manipulate it as best we could.

A good deal of resistance in the early part of the fight was met with from the neighbourhood of Wiancourt on the left, and the high ground south-east of Swiss Cottage, and it was found that the Australians had not been able to make much progress and were practically held up. This being the case it was realised that the village of Wiancourt, which should have been taken by them, would be a serious menace to our left flank, and it was, therefore, decided that we should go out of our way and take it in the general advance. Two platoons of A Company, with portions of B and D (companies having got somewhat mixed owing to loss of direction), penetrated into the village and opened heavy Lewis gun and rifle fire on its defenders, who offered a stubborn resistance, mainly from machine gun posts. Eventually some of them were seen to run back, and our line immediately rushed forward with the bayonet and killed or captured the whole of the garrison. Several were killed whilst still holding the handles of their machine guns. Company Sergeant-Major Attenborough, of A Company, here performed several gallant feats in leading rushes against machine gun groups, and later did most valuable work in trying to establish liaison with the Australians, who unfortunately, even after the capture of Wiancourt, were unable to advance so as to help us.

Meanwhile the right was not making much headway, and C Company, from support, had become one with the attacking company. The advance here being held up by machine gun fire, Lance-Corporal Vann with much gallantry crawled forward and managed to knock out the gun team which was causing most of the trouble. A trench something like 100 yards long, crowded with the enemy, was thus taken in the flank, and those who did not surrender were killed in trying to escape. They had, however, caused us many casualties, including 2nd Lieutenant Dunkin and Sergeant Hurt killed, besides many wounded. One of the most gallant N.C.O.'s in the battalion, Sergeant Hurt had already won the D.C.M. and M.M., and his death was a very great loss.

Similar actions had been taking place in other parts of the line. Again and again nests of machine guns were rushed at the point of the bayonet, which weapon undoubtedly did more deadly work on this occasion than on any other in our experience. Where they could not be taken by frontal attack, parties worked round their flanks and rushed them from the rear. The intensity of the fighting can be imagined from the fact that after the battle nearly 200 dead Germans were found along this line of trenches on the front of the 139th Brigade alone.

The main Fonsomme Line was now ours, though won at heavy cost. Direction had improved, though we were all too far to the left and much disorganised. We had to make the best of it and try to straighten out as we pushed on into the valley towards Ramicourt. Here we were met with fire from Boche guns firing from behind Montbrehain with open sights, causing many casualties. The position was as exposed as it could be, the only shelter being provided by one or two sunken roads. At the same time four or five of the tanks, which for some reason had got behind at the start, had now come up and did much useful work in the outskirts of Ramicourt, though the same Boche guns brought most effective fire to bear on them, one of them getting five direct hits. On the left, B Company, who under Winter's excellent leadership, had done much fighting, now mixed up with A and reinforced by D, were also suffering heavily from the enemy artillery fire, and advanced by section rushes covered by Lewis gun fire. It was here that 2nd Lieutenant T. F. Mitchell, commanding a platoon of D Company, which he led with supreme gallantry, caring nothing for his own safety, was mortally wounded, dying the next day.

Ramicourt was eventually reached by oddments of A, C and D Companies, the remainder of the battalion having got too far left, and passing through its northern outskirts. There were several machine guns in the village, and snipers were active from the windows of the houses. These were all successfully mopped up with the help of the 6th Battalion, who pushed up a company and their battalion head-quarters, as there were so few troops at this point, the 5th Battalion having edged off through the southern outskirts of the village. Jack White was seen in the village, wandering round quite unconcerned, revolver in holster—a small cane which he carried being apparently his most trusty weapon.

Having completed the capture of the village, which yielded a to-tal of something like 400 prisoners, the remnants of the troops there were gathered together and the advance continued. A machine gun nest at Ramicourt station having been rushed with the aid of a tank, we pushed on to our objective, which, except on the extreme left, we reached practically up to scheduled time, 10.30 a.m., most of the troops being disposed in sunken roads on the west of Montbrehain. It had not been a good day for the tanks, which in the end were all knocked out, though the last one working with the 5th Battalion on the right had a good run and knocked out no fewer than 16 machine guns before being put out of action.

As soon as the barrage lifted from the Red Line, the 6th Battalion began to push on. They had met with an appalling disaster soon after crossing the Beaurevoir-Fonsomme Line, where Colonel Vann, once more gallantly leading his battalion and in the forefront of the battle, was killed, shot through the head. The 5th Battalion too, lost Colo-nel A. Hacking, who was wounded in the arm. Thus two old officers of the 8th were put out of action almost at the same moment, both leading battalions in our own brigade. Alfred Hacking had done invaluable work during the few months he had commanded the 5th Battalion, and for his excellent leadership and gallantry during the fighting of September 29th and October 3rd was awarded the D.S.O. and Bar. Bernard Vann, affectionately known to some of his earlier friends as "Vasi," was described on one occasion by General Allenby, as the most fearless officer he had ever met, whilst a brother officer writes of him:

I can think of him only as a fighter, not merely against the enemy in the field, but a fighter against everything and everybody that was not an influence for good to his men. It was his extraordinary courage and tenacity which will be remembered by all who knew him: he inspired all by his wonderful example of courage and energy.

Wounded at least eight times, and awarded the M.C. and Bar, and the French Croix de Guerre with Palm, it was fitting that his constant gallantry and magnificent example should be further recognised—alas! after his death—by the award of the Victoria Cross.

On continuing the advance the 6th Battalion edged towards the south, going through the centre and right of Montbrehain, and leaving the northern portion alone. This left us considerably exposed, and an enemy machine gun firing from a position at the cross-roads on our left front, was doing much damage. White, Thomas and Miners held a hasty conference and decided to rush it, and the two former with a reconnoitring party went into the village to see if it could be outflanked from the region of the cemetery. At this moment a little "Joey" came in with "hands up," and it was decided to try a ruse. It was suggested to him that he should go and tell his friends to surrender, and after a little persuasion he went. The machine gun stopped firing and he approached the post and disappeared into the ground, thus telling us what we wanted to know—the way in. Action was taken at once to deal with it. Second Lieutenant Harrap, who had already done much valuable work, got together some Lewis guns and opened frontal fire on the position, whilst Miners and Sergeant Stimson worked round the flank from the village side and by a careful manoeuvre rushed on to the post the instant Harrap's guns stopped firing. Much to their surprise the post was found to be a quarry containing something like ten or a dozen machine guns and 60 or 70 men! A few bombs and revolver shots and the white flag went up. Harrap, who had rushed his men forward across the intervening 200 yards, was also at hand, and the capture of the post was complete. Second Lieutenant Barker's platoon (A Company) also assisted with rifle and Lewis gun fire, Barker himself being wounded.

Out of the medley of troops which collected there—of all battalions in the brigade—some attempt was then made to organise a company, and posts were pushed further forward. The rest of the village after a hard struggle fell into the hands of the 6th Battalion about the scheduled time, 11.30 a.m. Loud explosions, heard soon after the village was entered, were caused by the blowing up by the Boche of two houses in the main street near the church. Attempts were made to push out platoons to the "line of exploitation," beyond the village, but this was found to be impossible owing to heavy machine gun fire.

Both in Ramicourt and Montbrehain we found French civilians, whose pleasure at being at last released from the Hun terror knew no bounds. About 70 all told had remained behind, refusing to be evacuated by the Boche. They gave us a great welcome and in spite of shells and bullets, brought out coffee to our men as they passed by. Later, under the guidance of the brigade interpreter, M. Duflos, they were taken back to safer regions.

It soon became evident that further trouble was in store for us owing to the fact that our left flank was again in the air. The Australians were not up with us and we were very uncertain of their whereabouts, though apparently not altogether out of touch with them, for one of their officers, who was met in hospital later in the day, reported having received from someone in our battalion the laconic message: "We are at——. Where is the Australian Corps?" The enemy were still holding in force a position at no great distance from our left flank, and indeed, at one time were reported to be massing for a counter-attack which, however, did not mature. But on the right of the brigade the situation was far worse. There the 137th Brigade, after making some progress, had eventually to give ground, and their left was now considerably behind our right. We were thus in a most awkward salient with both flanks exposed. It was, therefore, not surprising to find soon after noon very evident signs of a real counter-attack being prepared against the brigade exposed right flank, and when a little later this attack was launched, the enemy managed to get round the south-east of Montbrehain and into that corner of the village in some strength, and it was decided to withdraw from it. This was successfully carried out under great difficulties, and eventually the brigade took up a line just east of Ramicourt, the 8th Battalion occupying the railway and sunken road north-east of that village. The enemy soon reoccupied the whole of Montbrehain, but was unable to advance further.

We were now very short of ammunition as no supplies had been sent forward. This was mainly due to the fact that we had depended on a supply tank, which did not fetch up quite where we expected. Fortunately no ill results accrued, but it taught the lesson that the supply of ammunition to advanced troops in moving warfare requires very careful prearrangement.

Company commanders again conferred and decided to alter their dispositions, and with a view to protecting our left flank, B and C Companies moved across to bridge the gap there, leaving A and D Companies in the railway cutting. In these positions we were left for the rest of the day more or less in peace.

In spite of a slight set-back it had been a glorious day for the 8th Battalion. There was really no comparison between this battle and that of September 29th. The attack on September 29th was undoubtedly more spectacular, but in our humble judgment, having regard to the extremely short notice received, the strength of the enemy and the many difficulties encountered, the breaking of the Fonsomme Line on October 3rd may truly be counted as one of the most gallant exploits of the whole war.

Where one and all did so well and so many gallant deeds were performed it is difficult to single out any for special praise, but it is desired to note specially the good work of the following in addition to those already mentioned: Sergeant H. Wilson, Lance-Sergeant Wicks, Corporal Clark, Lance-Corporal Creamer, and Privates Draper, Crowe, Slater, Wesley, Starr, Baxter, Jackson, and Martin. The day, however, had cost us much. Our casualties were one officer and 20 other ranks (including Sergeant Gurdens) killed, and three officers (2nd Lieutenants T. F. Mitchell, who died the next day, Barker, and F.T.W. Saunders), and 86 other ranks wounded.

Captain Homan had his regimental aid post with battalion headquarters in a dug-out in the sunken road near our jumping-off line. Here he and Padre Sturt worked for something like 24 hours on end, attending to the wounded, though both badly gassed, whilst a willing band of stretcher bearers again performed a prodigious amount of work under most trying circumstances. Particular praise is due to Corporals Wrigglesworth and J. Wright, and to Privates L. Thomas and F. Green, the latter of whom was awarded a bar and the former a second bar to his M.M., for gallant work on this occasion.

It was impossible to estimate the actual number of prisoners captured by us, as there was one "pool" for the whole brigade, but undoubtedly we had a very large share of the total, which was 36 officers and nearly 1,500 other ranks; in addition to which large numbers were left on the ground dead. Of machine guns too, we captured a very large number, but owing to the impossibility of collecting them, little idea of the total could be formed.

During much of the day horse artillery and numbers of light rapid-moving tanks, known as whippets, had been waiting in the valleys

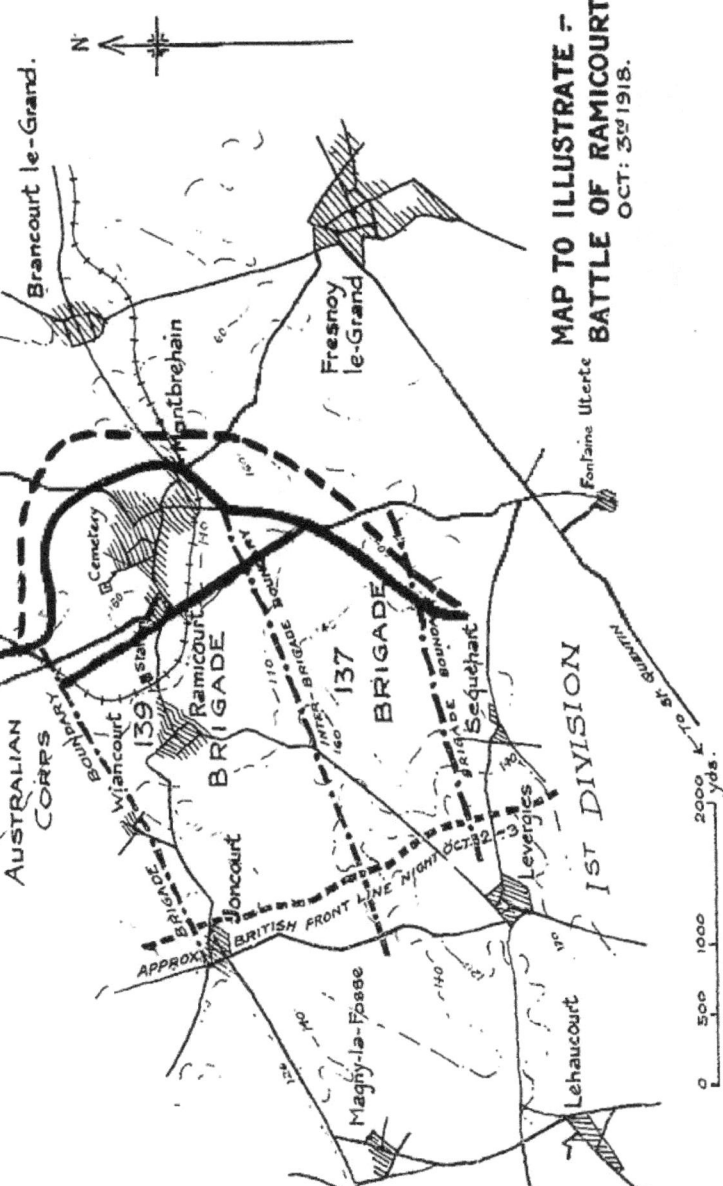

MAP TO ILLUSTRATE :-
BATTLE OF RAMICOURT
OCT: 3RD 1918.

behind Joncourt, ready to push on once the line was broken, and endeavour to make a clean break through. Unfortunately their services could not be used, and once more they had to withdraw.

Late at night we got news that we were being relieved by the 4th Leicesters. They turned up alright to take over from B and C Companies, but owing to some error failed to relieve A and D, who were left holding the line, with little ammunition and no rations, and were not relieved until the afternoon of October 4th, when they made their way back to the valley just in front of Magny-la-Fosse and joined the rest of the battalion in tents and bivouacs put up by "Tony" Bradish and Hallam, with the help of the battle details. "Bedder" too, was there, with Regimental-Quarter-Master-Sergeant Pritchard (who during these strenuous times had to carry on without a quarter-master), and the four quarter-master-sergeants, all of whom did their utmost to make everyone comfortable.

CHAPTER 17

The Last Fight
October 4th, 1918—November 11th, 1918

Such impromptu cleaning up as was possible, was carried out during what remained of October 4th, and we felt much better. We also carried out a certain amount of reorganisation of companies, which were now thinning rather more rapidly than we cared for, but the opportune arrival of 85 reinforcements at this moment, helped us considerably. The enemy caused a certain amount of annoyance, and a few casualties, by every now and then firing in our direction with a high-velocity gun, and at night dropped a few bombs uncomfortably near, so that it was not quite as peaceful as we should have liked.

The next morning we were rather disturbed at hearing that there was more work to be done. The 32nd Division on our right had suffered heavy casualties in trying to get hold of Sequehart, and the 139th Brigade was now detailed to relieve some of their exhausted troops. At this moment our brigade was attached to the 6th Division. Rapid reconnaissance was made during the day, and at night we relieved the 97th Brigade. So heavy had their casualties been that our three companies for the front line and support each relieved a battalion. These were Dorsets, Highland Light Infantry and Royal Scots.

The line taken over ran through the village of Sequehart, and was the extreme right of the British front, next to the French. C Company were on the right, D on the left, astride the cross roads, with B in support and A in reserve. C Company had the unusual privilege of forming an "international post" with the French, and Corporal Simpson, who spoke the language, was put in charge of our part of the garrison. We cannot say that after our visits to the French headquarters, we felt we quite knew where their front line was, but possibly it was our fault. When they suggested "we are here," we certainly thought they were somewhere else, but we managed very well, and materially assisted them in an attack on the 7th, by conforming to their movements and giving them flank support, and their commanding officer expressed his grateful thanks for our help.

We have before spoken of "Bloody Ypres." The officer commanding D Company is reported to have applied the superlative of the same expressive word to this sector, but then he had cause for doing so, for during the two days the battalion held it, his company headquarters got five direct hits. Perhaps under such circumstances, he was slightly embittered! During the time we were there, the enemy hardly ceased to shell the village—not desultory shelling, but veritable barrages from end to end. It had already changed hands three times, and we wondered if they were going to try and turn us out! Signs of fierce struggles were on every hand. In the streets and all around lay bodies still unburied, both of our own and the enemy's. It was a ghastly place to be in. signallers and linesmen had a particularly rough time, and lines were down almost continuously.

October 6th, was a particularly bad day, as we lost Colonel Dempster and the second-in-command (Captain C. P. Elliott), both wounded. They had gone to see how things were going on in the forward area, and on returning to headquarters, which was in a dugout behind Levergies, they were unfortunate enough to be in the neighbourhood of a dump of shells by the roadside at the same moment as a Hun gunner dropped a shell right on the dump. The result was that both these officers began to soar skywards, as if off for their *harp and wings divine*, but eventually found themselves on mother earth once more, the commanding officer badly shaken and cut about the face, the strap of his tin hat broken by the force of the explosion, and Pynsent Elliott finding that for some little time he would have to take his meals off the mantelpiece! The commanding officer was anxious to be allowed to remain with us, but eventually was persuaded otherwise, and they both left for the dressing station, and Major V. O. Robinson, M.C., of the 6th Battalion, was sent to take over temporary command.

The following night we were relieved by the Monmouths, who had orders to clear out the Boche from some machine gun nests on the Sequehart–Mericourt road the next morning, in conjunction with an attack by the 6th Division on the left, and French on the right. Relief was complete about midnight, and we marched back to Lehaucourt, where we spent the following day. On October 9th, Colonel Dempster returned, though not looking at all well. Major Robinson remained with us as second-in-command, as Major Andrews had left a few days previously, to attend the senior officers' course at Aldershot. A day or two later Captain Miners was appointed adjutant, and was succeeded in command of C Company by 2nd Lieutenant Druce.

Things were now moving rapidly. Although the gallant attack by the Monmouths had been repulsed with heavy casualties, their action had enabled the 6th Division to get on, and eventually surround the enemy and capture the lot. The enemy then withdrew more quickly, closely followed by the 138th Brigade, who led the pursuit. On October 9th, we moved to Levergies, and the next day to Mericourt, where we went into bivouacs. This village was just on the west of Fresnoy-le-Grand, which was entered by the 138th Brigade the same morning.

We now took a little more interest in life. Everyone was feeling better for the rest, and found the rapid movement quite entertaining, especially as we were now approaching civilisation again. Fresnoy was the first town of any size that we reached; though showing distinct signs of shelling here and there, it was not badly damaged. It was interesting to see the Boche war savings campaign posters, and probably the most interesting specimen, painted all over the gable end of a house, represented "John Bull" on his island, tearing his hair in a perfect frenzy, with "U" boats all around him! Here, too, there were many inhabitants, who were of course delighted to see us. Much of the land was under cultivation, and we had really come to the end of that desolate region which was so distasteful to us all.

On October 12th, we moved a further step forward, and that afternoon reached Jonnecourt Farm, between Fresnoy and Bohain. Just before leaving we had all welcomed back Colonel Currin, more or less recovered from his wound, and with his arrival Colonel Dempster left us. Jonnecourt Farm was somewhat damaged, and said to be mined, so we put up our bivouacs and tents in the open just by it. The farm had been captured only a few days before by our cavalry, and we had the uncongenial task of burying the bodies of those who had been killed in the attack. We now had a few days peace, and were able to refit, bath at the old German baths in Fresnoy, which were excellently fitted up, and reorganise our diminished forces. A pleasing little ceremony was performed here, when the "congratulatory cards" from the divisional commander for the N.C.O.'s and men, who had been recommended for good work during the recent fighting, were presented to them by the commanding officer at a battalion parade, ending up with the battalion marching past the recipients whilst the band played the regimental march.

We were not left here for long, there being more dirty work to be done yet. The 138th Brigade had been joined by the 137th Brigade, and together they were now held up about the Bois-de-Riquerval, east of Bohain, where some tough fighting had been going on, the enemy rear-guard making a stout defence, so as to give his main body time to get away. With the object, therefore, of clearing the whole of this front and pushing the enemy back to the Sambre-Oise canal, a general attack was arranged to take place on October 17th, by the IX Corps in conjunction with the French on the right, and the Americans on the left, the 46th Division being ordered to clear the enemy from the Bois-de-Riquerval and the Andigny-les-Fermes ridge.

On October 16th, we received orders for the attack, which was to take place early the following morning. The 138th Brigade were to attack on the left of the 139th Brigade whilst the 137th Brigade were to hold their present line on the right. The attack of the 139th Brigade was to be on a one battalion front, and we were selected to carry out the attack, with two companies of the 5th Battalion in close support, the remainder of the brigade being in reserve. The objective (the blue line) was the line of the Andigny-les-Fermes-Bohain road, the consolidation of which was to include two strong points, one being the hamlet of Regnicourt. Royal Engineers were allotted to us to help in the consolidation, and posts were to be pushed forward south of this road. The two companies of the 5th Battalion had two tasks allotted. One was to move through our right company, after the objective had been captured, occupy a small length of trench there, and seize a small wood, so as to protect our right from possible counter-attack from Hennechies Wood. The other was to follow our centre company, mop up any enemy left in the elements of trenches in that company's area, and help to mop up Regnicourt itself.

Tanks were to assist in the operation, one moving down our right boundary, and helping to mop up the trenches on the extreme right, and two others working along the high ground on the left, and assisting if required in the capture of Regnicourt, proceeding thence to help the 138th Brigade at Andigny-les-Fermes.

A glance at the map will show that the attack was at right angles to the general line of our advance, which was north east. It was therefore impossible for our guns to fire the normal barrage, and the attack had to be carried out under an enfilade barrage, working forward on the leap-frog principle. This was difficult to lay correctly, and the greatest care had to be taken that troops forming up were well clear of it. After three minutes on the opening line it was to advance at the rate of 100 yards every three minutes. One round of smoke shell was to be fired at each lift, which obviously would not be so easy to identify as in the case of an overhead barrage. A smoke curtain was also to be fired on the northern edge of the Forêt d'Andigny. The Life Guards Machine Gun Battalion were to help with their barrage, also a company of the 6th Machine Gun Battalion. Three sections of our own machine gun battalion were allotted to us, to be used mainly in defence against possible counter-attacks, and a section from the 139th Trench Mortar Battery, to assist in the capture of Regnicourt.

In order to help matters on our front a "Chinese" or "dummy" attack was arranged to take place on the front of the 137th Brigade on the right. Dummy tanks and figures were to be placed in position during the night, so as to appear at dawn as if attacking the Bois-de-Riqerval from the west, whilst a rolling barrage was arranged to move through the wood in order to give a further idea of an attack being in progress there, and, it was hoped, bring down some of the enemy's barrage in that quarter.

During the afternoon of October 16th, a reconnaissance was made by the commanding officer, second-in-command, and company commanders. During this operation, which was interrupted by a fierce bombardment of our lines, an old lady could be seen quietly moving her household effects on a wheelbarrow down that portion of the Vaux-Andigny road running between our lines and the enemy's.

Leaving our surplus stores, bivouacs and other paraphernalia at Jonnecourt Farm, we moved off about 10.30 p.m., Colonel Currin having previously harangued us in no uncertain way, and in a manner truly characteristic. On reaching the outskirts of Bohain, we turned off to the right and proceeded by a track previously taped out by the Royal Engineers, so as to relieve the roads of traffic, and avoid going through the town. On reaching the quarry east of Bohain, just off the Bohain-Vaux-Andigny road, we halted, and had an excellent issue of hot porridge, tea and rum—our cookers having gone up to that point beforehand. Pack mules and limbers with ammunition and other stores, were a little further behind, but near enough to be got forward quickly if required during the battle. On this occasion the ammunition supply was well arranged, thanks to the good work of "Bedder" and "Tommy" Tomlinson, who got pack mules forward in the attack with Lewis gun drums just at the right moment, to the accompaniment of some very expressive language on the part of the transport men.

We moved on again between 2 and 3 a.m., and without difficulty reached and formed up on our jumping-off line, which had been previously taped out by the brigade major, Captain Grinling, about 70 yards south of the Bohain-Vaux-Andigny road. We had three companies in the front line, A (Toyne, in the absence of Thomas on leave) on the right; B (Geary) in the centre; and C (Druce) on the left; whilst D (Warner), in support behind C Company, was in the vicinity of Vallée Hasard Farm. Battalion headquarters and the regimental aid post were at a house near the road. A and B Companies each had attached half a section of Royal Engineers from the 465th Field Company. Two companies of the 5th Battalion were in rear, and the rest of that battalion were more or less dug in under the woods on our right. The 6th Battalion were in reserve north-west of the road. All troops were in position by 3.45 a.m. on October 17th. Our actual forming up line was in the area of the 6th Division, who had been holding the front we were attacking; they withdrew from this line some time before zero so as to give us a free course.

The frontage allotted to us was about 1,200 yards, each of the leading companies thus having approximately 400 yards. This was a long space to cover, especially now that our numbers were so diminished that we had been forced to reduce platoons to three sections instead of four. Each of the leading companies had three platoons in the front line, with sections in blobs, and one platoon in support, whilst D Company was formed in a rectangle with a platoon at each corner, and company headquarters in the centre, the three sections of each platoon being arranged in a kind of arrowhead.

Zero was 5.20 a.m. The barrage came down punctually, and we started forward to our last attack. There was a certain amount of mist which developed into a dense fog, and was doubtless intensified by our own smoke shells. A troop of our cavalry in the vicinity of the Vaux-Andigny road put their gas masks on, and were last seen moving along the road in that "get-up."

It is pretty safe to say that everyone was lost almost immediately, and as a consequence we wandered out of our course, a fact which was destined to give us much trouble. It was also impossible to judge the lifts of the barrage, so that there was great confusion, and things for a long while did not go at all well. On this occasion, too, compasses do not appear to have proved of great avail. C Company on the left kept going for some time alright, and got possession of some high ground after overcoming, under the excellent leadership of 2nd Lieutenant Druce, some opposition from machine gun nests, though some of these were missed owing to the fog. Then they wandered off in an easterly direction and got on to the 138th Brigade area on our left, and later, when the fog cleared, they found themselves nearly at Andigny-les-Fermes. B Company in the centre went on until they were held up by unbroken wire, and heavy machine gun fire from the Regnicourt ridge, and from a clearing in the centre of the battalion area. Their commander, Captain Geary, was killed by machine gun fire after leading his men with the greatest bravery. On many previous occasions he had done excellent work, and his loss was most keenly felt. A Company on the right soon lost touch with B, but got on until they reached a position near the railway track, in spite of having had a very nasty time and many casualties from the machine guns in the same clearing.

D Company lost touch with everyone at first, and got completely split up. Company headquarters were lucky enough to run into a Boche machine gun post, which they cleared with much skill, capturing 11 men, and putting the two guns out of action. Then they decided to try and find battalion headquarters, as they concluded they must have got too far forward. By a somewhat circuitous route they eventually succeeded in doing so, and found that Colonel Currin had also had difficulty in getting to his advanced headquarters, which was no more than a map reference. Of the rest of D Company, three platoons got across to the right of our front and did good work there, particularly 2nd Lieutenant Newton and his platoon, who were of great assistance to A Company. A great feat was performed by some members of the other platoon of D Company, who had kept their direction on the left towards Regnicourt. Having run up against a couple of machine guns, Sergeant Robinson and Lance-Corporal Harper went forward to reconnoitre the position, and finding it strongly held, went back for the rest of the platoon. With a combination of fire and movement they succeeded in getting round the flank of the post and rushing it. Lance-Corporal Harper, who stood up when only a few yards from the post in order to be able to aim more accurately, was shot through the head, and Lance-Corporal Coombes at once rushed forward, shot six Germans with his revolver, and finished off the last man who was trying to run away with his Lewis gun.

When news of all these happenings duly reached him by runners, stragglers and other means. Colonel Currin collected all the oddments who had wandered to his headquarters, and sent them forward under Major Robinson to push the enemy out of the clearing between B and C Companies. The fog had to a certain extent cleared by this time, but it was still not easy to keep direction. Very soon, however, it lifted altogether, and the party found itself on the western edge of the clearing and fired at by the enemy both from the clearing and from the ridge towards their right front, from which the enemy were also firing into the rear of B Company, who had gone past them.

The party now advanced by bounds, and was throughout most gallantly led by Major Robinson, who went out absolutely unarmed, but later managed to get a Boche pistol lent him, which he very soon lost. Knowing him as we do we are not surprised that such a small matter did not worry him in the least! Eventually they got possession of a trench on the ridge, which afforded them a certain amount of cover. The garrison of this trench, about 10 men with a machine gun, were very fortunate in receiving quarter, as they fired on our advancing line up to the last minute, and then threw up their hands. Most of the trouble now came from machine guns about half right, and it was determined to round them up. At this point Sergeant Winson, of C Company, did most excellent work. Regardless of all risk he kept his Lewis gun trained on the enemy, whilst a party worked round their right flank, first by crawling over to a small clearing, and then rushing the post from there. This manoeuvre was entirely successful, six machine guns, and about 40 prisoners being captured.

At the same time that part of C Company, which had wandered away to the left, turned back and moved towards the high ground east of Regnicourt. The enemy in the clearing now realised that they were more or less surrounded, and after little more resistance surrendered, 27 machine guns and 140 prisoners being taken from this small area. A Company of the 5th Battalion under our old regimental quartermaster sergeant, now Captain Dench, arrived shortly afterwards and took up a position in the clearing as a reserve.

A Company on the right had fared very badly, having met with heavy machine gun and rifle fire and suffered many casualties, including their commander. Lieutenant Toyne, who was wounded, and 2nd Lieutenant Jacques, killed, leaving the company under the command of 2nd Lieutenant Shackleton. Eventually, owing to their exposed position they had to retire slightly, but later were reinforced by two companies from the 5th Battalion, and together they were able, after some very stiff fighting, to dislodge the enemy and get their objective. Lieutenant Thomas of the 465th Field Company, Royal Engineers, did some very gallant work here in reorganising parties and leading them forward in attempts to get on, and the greatest praise is due to him for his splendid efforts.

Major Robinson's party, after getting the ridge, pushed on to Regnicourt village, where they found some of the Leicesters, who had wandered on to our front. Just beyond, one of our tanks had broken down, and had a very rough time before its crew could be rescued. It was now about 10.15 a.m. Captain Warner was put in charge of the front line with orders to consolidate, and he accordingly reorganised the odd parties of men he found under his command, and began to establish strong points south of the Andigny-les-Fermes-Bohain road. Some trouble was caused at this time by a German field gun inside Hennechies Wood, which was firing on these parties at point blank range. Once its position was located, however, it was not long before our gunners forced it to withdraw, and the posts were eventually established.

About 11 a.m. the enemy were seen massing for a counter-attack about 1,500 yards away on our right front, but we got the guns of the whole "group" turned on to the area in a very short time, and the Boches were completely broken, only a half-hearted attempt being made, and only one man reaching our lines.

By noon the enemy in the Forêt d'Andigny must have begun to feel that with the 138th Brigade—who had now captured the village of Andigny-les-Fermes—on their right flank, and the 137th Brigade and ourselves on their left, it was time they were moving, for a patrol which we pushed out towards the wood found it occupied only by a few odd machine guns. Major Robinson himself took charge of this patrol, which consisted of a platoon of B Company, under Company Sergeant-Major Cobb. On one or two occasions, owing to their small numbers they had to creep round to avoid these machine guns, but they escaped without accident, and after proceeding a distance of something like 2,000 yards in a south-eastern direction, they eventually found a French post about 100 yards south of Forester's House. The *poilus* were delighted to see them, and showed their appreciation by giving our men the whole of the contents of their water bottles.

About 5 p.m., companies having been to some extent reorganised, an outpost line was formed running due north and south from Hennechies Wood, east of Regnicourt, and joining up on the left with the 138th Brigade. Later on, the 137th Brigade moved up a battalion through the wood to fill the gap between our right flank and the French.

During the attack we captured something like 220 prisoners, and nearly 100 machine guns, besides inflicting many other casualties. Our own losses, too, were heavy—the heaviest in officers that we had experienced in the recent fighting. Besides Geary, we lost 2nd Lieutenants Plant and Jacques killed, and Lieutenants Toyne and Whitelegge, and

MAP TO ILLUSTRATE THE BATTLE OF REGNICOURT.

N

Oct. 17th 1918.

Vaux Andigny

6th DIVISION

138 INFANTRY BRIGADE

Andigny-les-Fermes.

Vallée Hasard

139 INFANTRY BRIGADE

Farm

Regnicourt

S.1
S.2
S.3

Bois de Riqueval

Forêt d'Andigny

137 INFANTRY BRIGADE

Bohain

0	500	1000	2000

yds.

SCALE.

A.B.C&D. COYS FORMING UP POSITIONS.

Z. CLEARING WHERE "D" COY CAPTURED 2 MACHINE GUNS.

Y. COPSE, WHERE Major Robinson's Party was held up.

2nd Lieutenant John H. Smith wounded, whilst in other ranks we lost 25 killed or died of wounds, and 54 wounded, including Seargeants Oldham, Sharrock and Wicks. Deeds of gallantry were conspicuous on all sides, and especially good work was done by several N.C.O.'s in charge of platoons. Amongst the following, who did particularly well and have not already been mentioned in connection with the Battle of Regnicourt, are several who had previously displayed conspicuous courage in other recent battles: Seargeants Shepperson, Sharrock, Wallis, Scrimshaw, and H. Wilson; Corporals Watson and Francis; Lance-

Corporals Slater, Creamer (killed), Robinson and Beech, and Privates Wesley, Houghton, Martin, Draper, Jackson, Berresford, C. Smith, Vipond, Lees, Turpin and Roe.

In a way it was an unsatisfactory day, and we feel we have hardly had our deserts for the gallant work done by all ranks against an enemy holding in much greater strength much more strongly fortified positions than had been anticipated. The fighting was extremely hard, if anything harder than at Ramicourt, and the greatest possible credit is due to all for the gallant way they fought, and the great dash and determination they displayed to get their objective. Regnicourt is apt to be looked on as a small matter, but for the 8th Battalion it was one of the most strenuously fought battles of the war.

About midnight, we were relieved by the 6th Battalion, and rested for the night just behind Regnicourt. The following day, as the brigade had been squeezed out of the line altogether by the further retirement of the enemy, we were able to withdraw, and in the evening marched back to Fresnoy. We were met on the road by our drums, under the leadership of Corporal (shortly to become Sergeant-Drummer) Coupe, who had got them to a wonderful state of perfection. They cheered everyone up, and considerably helped the last part of the march. We were glad to see General Harington waiting for us just before reaching the village, and his brief "Well done, Sherwoods" as we passed, was the fullest appreciation of our efforts that we could wish for.

We now had several days complete rest, and were fortunate in getting, almost at once, a draft of 120 reinforcements, mostly men of the Northumberland Hussars, who had not previously seen service abroad. They were a good lot, and with their addition we felt more like ourselves once more; in fact our paper strength now totalled 34 officers, and 745 other ranks. We had quite a pleasant time doing a little training, as well as reorganising and cleaning, and devoting the afternoons to football.

The fighting moving further off each day, we had to move forward on October 29th to Bohain. This was carried out as a brigade march, and we entered Bohain with bands playing, and the civilian population in the streets to welcome us. The town had been knocked about very little, and the billets were extremely comfortable. Our training here included a route march across the scene of our recent fighting, in order to imbue the newly arrived with a sense of the honour they should realise had been done them in posting them to such a fine battalion!

A great drawback to our advance all this time was the business-like way in which the Boche had mined the roads and blown up railways. Every railway and river bridge had been systematically blown up, and mines had been put at every cross roads, and usually in the deep cuttings and high embankments, so as to give the maximum of trouble in filling and getting past. In many cases, these mines had actually been blown and all we found were huge craters. In a few cases delay-action mines had been laid, which did not explode for some little time. All this gave our Sappers much work to do in reconnoitring road crossings, and other points for signs of mining where they were not blown, or in arranging for temporary roadways to be constructed, or craters to be filled in where they had been exploded. But on a larger scale the enemy's very clever system of working his delay-action mines on the railways, was the biggest nuisance we had to contend with. The railway having been repaired well forward, a mine would suddenly go up miles behind, thus preventing trains getting on to the appointed railhead, and so causing endless worry to the authorities who had to arrange for our supplies coming up. To them this disorganisation must have been extremely disconcerting, and it went on altogether for nearly a month. The mines were so cunningly concealed that it was impossible to locate them. In spite of everything supplies reached us in some marvellous way without a hitch.

On November 3rd, in order to support the 1st and 32nd Divisions, who were to attack the line of the Sambre-Oise canal on the following day, and to exploit the success if they broke through, we moved to the little village of Escaufort. It was a heavy march, the roads were bad, and we arrived late in the evening soaked through to spend a dreary night in poor billets, many of which had suffered during the bombardment of the last few days, and in bivouacs. Early the following morning we pushed on to St. Souplet, where we prepared to stay for the night in a few old barns. Later in the day, however, news was brought that the attack had been successful, and we moved on to Catillon, on the canal. Transport, quarter-master's stores and battle details moved to Mazinghien. The same night we got orders that we were to pass through the 1st Division and 138th Brigade, and take up the pursuit, the following day.

We had been informed that owing to the blowing of the bridge over the canal at Catillon, we should have to make a detour of several miles with cookers and Lewis gun limbers to get across by a pontoon bridge, in order to arrive at our point of assembly on the Catillon-La Groise road, which was only about 1,000 yards away! We determined to see if we could not find some other means of doing this, and thanks to a reconnaissance by Major Robinson, we found that it was possible for infantry to cross the canal over debris from the blown up bridge, though the transport would have to go round. This was a great boon, as it enabled us to get breakfast before starting considerably later than would otherwise have been necessary. Captain A. Bedford arrived with the rations about 3.0 a.m., we had breakfast at six, and at eight moved off, being across the canal, and in our proper position by 8.30. Limbers and cookers joined us about nine, A Company's cooker having fallen overboard in crossing the pontoon bridge but having been extricated without damage. We were the only battalion in the brigade that day to start out with a full stomach and our day's rations with us!

Late in the afternoon we moved into poor billets in the village of Mezières, where we stayed the night, and were joined by transport, stores and battle details. Bedford worked uncommonly well, as did also the quarter-master's branch, in getting up rations, which they had to man-handle over the canal crossing—still impossible for traffic—and reload into our transport limbers. For all their efforts we were duly thankful.

On November 6th, the 5th Battalion were to attack as the 6th had been held up just west of Prisches, and we were to move up in support. The method adopted was for the attacking troops to pass round the village, whilst the support battalion, pushing one company on the road as an advanced guard, moved by platoons at about 50 yards interval. This was now true open warfare, and there was no organised line of defence. The day's objectives were Prisches and Cartignies. After an early start we continued our march towards Prisches, the attacking troops meeting with little opposition, and our advanced guard, A Company, were quickly in after them. The enemy had gone and we had got possession by 10.30 a.m.

We shall never forget the reception by the inhabitants of Prisches! We were the first of the relieving troops they had seen, and their feelings at being thus released after four years of oppression and slavery at the hands of the Hun, found expression in many demonstrations of joy and gratitude. Civilians of all ages came out to greet us. Their national flags—Heaven only knows where they came from or how they were concealed from the enemy—were displayed on all sides, and even before the enemy were clear of the village the *tricolour* was floating from the church tower! It was truly a wonderful sight, and a day never to be forgotten. We were surrounded by offers of coffee and fruit, cider and cognac, plentifully mingled with the tears and kisses of the grateful inhabitants. Indeed, so insistent were they that progress became difficult. We eventually, however, managed to establish battalion headquarters in a farmhouse at the east end of the village, where we again had a great reception, and stayed for some refreshment during a temporary hold-up of the advanced troops.

The attacking troops were to push on through the next village, Cartignies, and establish an outpost line on the other side of it. So rapid was the retreat, and so certain were we of success, that whilst at Prisches we despatched Bradish and a party of N.C.O.'s to get our billets there for the night! In the afternoon we were able to push on with the rest of the battalion, B Company forming the advanced guard. On arriving at Cartignies we were met by Bradish, who informed us that he had made arrangements for billeting us, but that half the village was still in the hands of the enemy, who were firing on the 5th Battalion with machine guns. The commanding officer whilst reconnoitring near the church, soon discovered this for himself, so withdrew diplomatically, deciding that it was not "our war" just then. Accordingly we got into our billets and posted sentries and Lewis guns at windows and other points for our protection. Owing to some of the Staffords who were also in the village, deciding to hold their outpost line in the village, instead of on the other side the river, the clearing of the village was a longer process than it should have been. It caused us no trouble, but we doubt if Tomlinson and Tebbutt would have slept so comfortably had they known that their billet was in No Man's Land! However, all was well; we had had another great reception from the delighted inhabitants, and after a long and tiring day we were soon asleep in good, comfortable billets.

For the next three days we stayed there, being joined by the transport and stores, battle details and several officers from England, who had never been out before.

The Hun was now going away rapidly, and it was very doubtful if we should be required again. We never were, and were glad to find we had done with him.

There was talk of an Armistice, and we were also warned that German envoys were expected, and might come through our lines. This they did not do and we were not sorry.

On November 10th, we had to move out of Cartignies to a small village, Boulogne-sur-Helpe, near by—the most easterly point the battalion ever reached.

November 11th came in just the same as any other day, but quite early a wire from brigade headquarters stated that the Germans had agreed to our armistice terms, and the Great War was over.

CHAPTER 18

Home Again

November 12th, 1918—July 5th, 1919

For the next few days we lived in an atmosphere of uncertainty. Were we to be one of the chosen divisions to go forward as part of the army of occupation, or were we to be left to spend weary months scavenging in the fair land of France? There may have been a few who did not want to go on, thinking they would probably lose their chance of an early return home, but in the main we were anxious to push on and satisfy our souls by actually setting foot on German soil as part of the conquering army. Our hopes fell from day to day as we heard no orders to prepare to move forward, and eventually, much to our regret, we learnt that after all we were not going to Germany. It was nearly the end of November when we received the following letter from General Sir H. S. Rawlinson, commanding the Fourth Army:

It is a matter of very deep regret to me that the 46th Division is not accompanying the Fourth Army to the frontier. I desire, however, to place on record my appreciation of the splendid performances of the division during the recent operations, and to congratulate all ranks on the conspicuous part they have played in the battles of the 100 days. The forcing of the main Hindenburg line on the canal, and the capture of Bellenglise rank as one of the finest and most dashing exploits of the war. The attacks of October 3rd, and the subsequent operations about Bohain, together with the later advance towards the Sambre canal, constitute a record of which all ranks of the division may justly feel proud. I offer to all ranks my warmest thanks for their great gallantry, and to the leaders and staffs my admiration of their skilful direction and staff work throughout these battles. To every officer, N.C.O., and man of the division, I offer my warm thanks and hearty congratulations, and trust that at some future time they may again form part of the Fourth Army.

On the day after the armistice, Major-General Boyd came to see us, and presented some medal ribbons, and in the afternoon an entertaining football match between officers and N.C.O.'s was won by the latter, the officers in a few cases having some difficulty in staying the course.

We left Boulogne-sur-Helpe on November 14th, and marched *via* Cartignies to Landrecies—a town which had seen much of the recent fighting, as well as having played a prominent part in the early days of the war. The whole of the 139th Brigade was concentrated here, and as our stay was likely to be a lengthy one, we soon set to work to make ourselves comfortable. Most of the battalion were billeted in one of the French barracks, D Company being allotted a school near by. Though the town had been considerably damaged by shells, our billets were more or less watertight, and in fairly good order. The transport and quarter-master's stores were also in the town close to the barracks.

On Sunday, November 17th, a church parade of the whole division was held at Landrecies, as a thanksgiving service, and afterwards the major-general distributed medal ribbons. He paid us a high compliment as we marched past after the ceremony, when he said that in all his military career he had never seen a battalion march past in better style!

The work of clearing the battlefield in the area round about Landrecies began at once. We did four hours a day at this work on four days a week, and on the other two days carried out ordinary military training. Education classes were also started and carried on for several months, and though the numbers who attended were not large, there is no doubt that very much useful work was done in this way. Lieutenant C. M. Bedford was responsible for the educational work at first, handing it over later to Lieutenant Tebbutt. Afternoons were invariably spent in recreation, inter-battalion and inter-company soccer matches, cross-country runs, and other sports. there were also rugger teams in the division, and later a brigade hockey team was formed. A few lucky ones got trips in Colonel Barron's ambulances to Brussels, Amiens, Valenciennes, and other towns of interest within reach, but this luxury did not last long. A recreation room at the barracks was started for reading and indoor games, whilst Lieutenant Pennington got an extraordinarily good concert party going, which was known eventually as The Penguins and gave entertainments to several other units. "Robbo" managed to scrounge a piano for them from a ruined house in the town, and during the dark nights we had much to thank them for. Later on there were whist drives, and some of the gayer element even went to dances, classes in which gentle art were held by the 6th Battalion. Padre Sturt, in addition to giving valuable help with the education classes, started a debating society, at which many entertaining topics were discussed.

On November 29th, the first batch of miners left for demobilisation, an urgent call having been made for these men owing to the coal shortage. The batch included several old hands, who had crossed to France with the battalion in 1915. The remainder were sent off in December, during which month we lost no fewer than 230.

In the afternoon of December 1st, we were honoured by a visit from the king, the Prince of Wales, and Prince Albert. They were received by Major-General Boyd and the Mayor, and afterwards walked through the town surrounded by masses of troops of the division. It was all delightfully informal; they had a wonderful reception, and at times found it difficult to get on.

A week later, on December 8th, we were delighted to see a representative from our own county, in the person of the Duke of Portland. He was accompanied by Colonels Mellish and Foljambe, the Bishop of Southwell, and Major E. T. Baines, whilst Padre Hales, who was now deputy chaplain general of a neighbouring corps, also came over for the ceremony. The opportunity was taken of getting the duke to present medal ribbons to some officers and men who had been awarded decorations during the recent fighting. This was done at a battalion parade, at which the duke gave a short address, saying that he had brought from the home county congratulations and greetings on our work during the last few months. After the parade the battalion marched past the duke headed by the brigade band.

The following week a colour party consisting of Captain White, 2nd Lieutenant James H. Smith, Company-Sergeant-Major Cobb, Sergeant Martin and Sergeant Skelton, having been sent to Newark for the special purpose, arrived with the colours, which remained with the battalion for the rest of our stay in France.

Amongst numerous officers who joined us in these days we were particularly glad to welcome our old friend Torrance, who at once resumed the duties of quarter-master.

The last item of interest in the great year 1918, was the celebration of Christmas. The only drawback on this occasion was that we were not able to celebrate it until Boxing Day, owing to the non-arrival of the necessary feeding stuffs and drinks. Something had gone wrong in the back regions, a thing which had been going on for some time, as canteen stores were always short, and rations at no other period of the war were so scarce or poor. We poured curses on the Royal Army Service Corps, and all connected with them, but to no purpose. Boxing Day, however, will live long in our memory. There was plenty of food and drink, and all sorts of other good things, towards the purchase of which we had been largely helped by money presents from friends at home. Each company had its own dinner, followed by a concert. The major-general visited every company, and was greeted with the greatest enthusiasm. He wished every one a happy time and prosperity in the New Year. The children of Landrecies also had a treat, being given a special show by the divisional cinema, and a sumptuous feed, and we venture to think they will not forget Christmas 1918 for many a long day—they had certainly not had one like it during the previous four years. Colonel Barron and his excellent quarter-master, Major Moreton, of our field ambulance, were largely responsible for the feed, whilst we helped to buy toys.

It took us some time to get over Christmas. In fact, Christmas at Landrecies in 1918 lasted several days, and was full of incident! As soon as the New Year came in—on January 3rd, 1919—we moved once more to Prisches, where a fresh area was allotted us to clear. Here we carried on in much the same way as at Landrecies, but owing to demobilisation having become more general, we were losing men daily and our numbers were gradually but surely dropping. Early in the New Year Major Robinson left us to rejoin the 6th Battalion, and Major Andrews resumed duty as second-in-command.

On February 19th, we began a westward move to be nearer railhead, marching that day to Bazuel, and the following day to Bethencourt, near Caudry, from which place we were destined finally to be scattered to the four winds. From here we sent back most of our horses and mules, with others from the brigade, to an auction sale at Prisches, where they were sold in a most entertaining manner by a French auctioneer at good prices to the local inhabitants. Our transport vehicles were sent to the divisional park at Caudry.

The same sort of work and play and demobilisation continued, and at the end of April we were left with only nine officers and 52 other ranks. Officers and men who were not demobilised went mostly to the 51st and 52nd Sherwood Foresters (Young Soldiers Battalions), or to prisoners of war camps at Nancy and Péronne. Eventually in June, Colonel Currin and the cadre left for England, leaving behind only a baggage guard under Captain Warner, who came home in July. Colonel Currin and his party arrived at Newark late on June 21st, and the official welcome took place on June 23rd, when the mayor met them at the town hall, and the colours were once more placed at the Drill Hall. With the colonel were Regimental Sergeant-Major Mounteney, Company Quarter-Master Sergeant Bee, Sergeant Blunt, Lance-Corporal Tuckwood, and Private Durand. With the exception of two short periods when he was away sick or wounded, Regimental Sergeant-Major Mounteney served with us the whole of our stay in France. Both in and out of the line he rendered most valuable service to the battalion, and even in the darkest hours we were always sure of his cheerful help.

On July 5th, a memorial service was held at Southwell Cathedral, for the Nottinghamshire men who had fallen in the war. After the ceremony, the men of the battalion who were present, were entertained to tea in the schools at Southwell, and Colonel Huskinson took that opportunity of thanking the ladies of the county for their kind help during the war. We feel sure, that though on this occasion they are put last, they will none the less accept our kind appreciation of all the work they were at such pains to do, and for the thousands of comforts they got together and sent out to us.

From the time we left England to final disembodiment no fewer than 193 officers, and 2,650 other ranks served with the battalion. There were 21 deaths from sickness and four fatal accidents. Battle casualties amounted to 26 officers, and 447 other ranks killed, or died of wounds, and 64 officers, and 1,400 other ranks wounded. Such a tragic total, however, cannot wholly be a measure of the trials and vicissitudes of three-and-a-half years' fighting. If in this record we have succeeded in conveying an impression to those who were not so fortunate as to be with us, or in reminding those who were, of courage, dogged perseverance, and unselfish devotion to duty in action, of pleasures, humour and happier times at rest, our efforts may not, perhaps, be without value in the days that are to come.

Speak!
Was our course well run?
Is there aught wherewith to upbraid us?
Have we fled from the thunder of battle, or flinched at
the lightning's track?
Answer!
What need of answer?
By the God of Truth who hath made us,
Thou knowest the Flag went forward, and never a foot went back!

The Last Muster, by J. S. Arkwright

APPENDIX I.

ROLL OF HONOUR

List of those who were Killed, or Died of Wounds or Sickness.

OFFICERS.

1915.

April 22—2nd Lieut. J. R. Eddison
June 6—Capt. H. G. Wright
,, 15—Lieut. A. F. O. Dobson
,, 15—2nd Lieut. W. H. Hollins
Oct. 13—2nd Lieut. R. E. Hemingway
,, 14—2nd Lieut. E. F. S. Handford
,, 14—Capt. H. B. S. Handford
,, 14—2nd Lieut. E. S. Strachan
,, 15—Lieut.-Col. G. H. Fowler
,, 25—2nd Lieut. G. H. Fisher
Nov. 12—Lieut. C. M. Houpton

1916.

Jan. 1—Major J. P. Becher
Dec. 20—2nd Lieut. L. E. King-Stephens

1917.

March 4—Lieut. R. A. Abrams
April 23—2nd Lieut. W. P. Duff
,, 23—2nd Lieut. E. Hopkinson
Aug. 30—2nd Lieut. D. Tanner
Oct. 27—2nd Lieut. J. H. Hofmeyr

1918.

April 29—Capt. H. K. Simonet
Sept. 6—2nd Lieut. C. J. Elly
,, 29—Lieut. S. E. Cairns
Oct. 3—2nd Lieut. A. D. H. Dunkin
,, 4—2nd Lieut. T. F. Mitchell
,, 17—Capt. A. E. Geary
,, 17—2nd Lieut. R. S. Plant
,, 17—2nd Lieut. W. G. Jacques

OTHER RANKS.

1914.

Sept. 28—Drummer R. Baker
Nov. 17—Pvte. S. Skelton

1915.

April 6—Pvte. J. Hyde
,, 11—Pvte. P. Richardson
,, 12—Pvte. D. Smith
,, 12—Pvte. A. Frary
,, 13—Pvte. W. R. Copley
,, 15—Pvte. A. E. Hopewell
,, 20—Pvte. H. Trickett
,, 20—Pvte. J. Wright
,, 21—Pvte. T. Murden
,, 21—Pvte. A. Bates
,, 21—Pvte. F. Adams
,, 21—Pvte. J. Berresford
,, 21—Sergt. G. Wilmore

April 21—Pvte. T. H. Mayman
,, 22—Pvte. H. Sketchley
,, 23—Pvte. H. Stevenson
,, 23—Pvte. W. Taylor
,, 24—Pvte. W. Hunt
,, 24—Pvte. C. Redmile
,, 24—Pvte. W. Godfrey
,, 24—Pvte. C. Hibbert
,, 24—Pvte. R. East
,, 24—Pvte. J. Bonner
,, 24—Pvte. H. Grant
,, 24—Pvte. H. Husband
,, 24—Pvte. W. Johnson
,, 24—Pvte. W. Pattison
,, 24—L.-Corpl. W. Ashley
,, 24—Pvte. A. E. Hincks
,, 24—Pvte. H. Randall
,, 24—Pvte. E. Worthington

April	29—Pvte. J. Brindley	
„	30—Pvte. H. Foster	
„	30—L.-Corpl. E. Markwell	
May	2—L.-Corpl. C. Land	
„	2—Corpl. E. Parker	
„	8—Pvte. H. Kirk	
„	8—Pvte. A. V. Soar	
„	8—L.-Corpl. W. H. Ridgard	
„	10—L.-Corpl. A. Priestley	
„	17—Pvte. E. Eaton	
„	24—Pvte. W. Widnall	
„	24—Pvte. T. Hardy	
„	25—Pvte. H. Spademan	
June	5—Pvte. R. Mills	
„	6—Pvte. T. Massey	
„	12—Pvte. F. Paling	
„	14—Corpl. C. J. Wilson	
„	15—Corpl. F. Wilcox	
„	15—Pvte. A. E. Armitage	
„	15—Pvte. F. Hill	
„	15—Pvte. B. Cox	
„	15—Pvte. P. May	
„	15—Pvte. R. W. Moakes	
„	15—Pvte. W. Richardson	
„	15—Pvte. O. L. Bryan	
„	15—Pvte. A. Cook	
„	16—Pvte. G. Richardson	
„	24—Pvte. W. H. Hird	
„	27—L.-Corpl. J. Churn	
„	27—Pvte. F. Edwards	
„	27—Pvte. C. E. Stones	
July	12—Pvte. E. Robinson	
„	16—Pvte. G. Tinker	
„	16—Corpl. F. Godson	
„	18—Corpl. E. Dewsnap	
„	20—Pvte. E. Richardson	
„	21—Pvte. C. Taylor	
„	21—Pvte. G. Hinton	
„	22—Pvte. J. Bowskill	
„	25—Pvte. J. Watson	
„	30—Pvte. J. W. Jubb	
„	30—Pvte. J. Rudkin	
„	30—Pvte. F. Walster	
„	30—Pvte. C. Thorpe	
„	30—Pvte. R. Downham	
„	30—Pvte. S. Oliver	
„	30—Pvte. R. Huckerby	
„	30—Pvte. F. Ingham	
„	30—Pvte. F. Parker	
„	30—Pvte. C. Lines	
„	30—Pvte. A. Woodhead	
„	30—Pvte. A. Coy	
	30—Pvte. J. Rossington	

July	30—Pvte. A. R. Walker	
„	30—Pvte. H. Taylor	
„	30—Pvte. H. W. Raynor	
„	31—Corpl. S. Humberstone	
„	31—L.-Corpl. I. Webster	
„	31—Corpl. R. J. Hotson	
„	31—Pvte. T. Davidson	
August	1—Pvte. J. Hopewell	
„	1—Pvte. H. H. Turner	
„	4—Pvte. J. W. Lee	
„	5—Pvte. C. Crampton	
„	7—Pvte. H. Moore	
„	7—Pvte. A. Scott	
„	8—Sergt. A. Phillipson	
„	8—L.-Corpl. P. Scott	
„	8—Pvte. A. Smith	
„	8—Pvte. F. Gumsley	
„	8—Pvte. E. King	
„	13—L.-Sergt. E. Layhe	
„	14—Pvte. G. E. Fletcher	
„	14—Pvte. A. Walsham	
„	14—Pvte. W. Kirkham	
„	14—Corpl. G. C. Higham	
„	17—Pvte. J. A. Saunders	
„	30—Pvte. G. W. Cartwright	
„	30—Pvte. G. Richards	
Sept.	3—Pvte. H. Key	
„	10—Pvte. L. Smith	
„	12—Pvte. A. Wesson	
„	16—Pvte. W. T. Marshall	
„	19—Pvte. G. Barker	
„	25—L.-Corpl. T. Humphrey	
„	25—Pvte. L. Hayes	
„	28—Pvte. R. Gray	
„	29—Drummer J. Newton	
Oct.	5—L.-Corpl. E. Hale	
„	5—Pvte. J. R. Roe	
„	5—L.-Sergt. C. E. Harrison	
„	8—Pvte. N. Chadbourne	
„	14—Sergt. C. E. Cox	
„	14—L.-Corpl. A. Spencer	
„	14—Corpl. J. C. Simpson	
„	14—Pvte. E. Mecklenburgh	
„	14—Corpl. W. Wardle	
„	14—L.-Corpl. E. Clay	
„	14—L.-Corpl. W. J. Herepath	
„	14—L.-Corpl. A. H. Hardy	
„	14—Pvte. A. Baldwinson	
.	14—Pvte. H. L. Smith	
„	14—Pvte. E. Kirk	
„	14—Pvte. J. W. Renshaw	
„	14—Pvte. C. Stimson	
„	14—Pvte. S. P. Huggins	
.	14—Pvte. L. H. Flint	

1915—contd.

Oct. 14—Pvte. F. W. COLEMAN
,, 14—Pvte. G. SIMMS
,, 14—Pvte. A FOTHERINGHAM
,, 14—Pvte. S. H. LISTER
,, 14—Pvte. A. PETTINGER
,, 14—Pvte. A. HAZZARD
,, 14—Sergt. M. MILLBAND
,, 14—L.-Corpl.H.E.WOODHEAD
,, 14—Pvte. J. DODSWORTH
,, 14—Corpl. J. SHARMAN
,, 14—L.-Corpl. B. C. VICK
,, 14—Pvte. A. HAZLEWOOD
,, 14—Pvte. H. COOK
,, 14—Pvte. C. S. HARRISON
,, 14—Pvte. H. WILKINSON
,, 14—Pvte. A. EYRE
,, 14—Pvte. E. C. PHILLIPSON
,, 14—Pvte. W. ANTHONY
,, 14—Pvte. F. FARRAND
,, 14—Pvte. A. B. SMITH
,, 14—Pvte. W. THOMPSON
,, 14—Pvte. G. SEYMOUR
,, 14—Pvte. F. BRYAN
,, 14—Sergt. H. HALL
,, 14—Pvte. A. MOYSES
,, 15—Pvte. W. RADFORD
,, 15—Sergt. G. F. FOSTER
,, 15—Pvte. S. BROUGHTON
,, 16—Pvte. R. TAYLOR
,, 18—L.-Corpl. F. J. LOWE
,, 22—Pvte. A. WOOLLEY
,, 27—Pvte. E. CHILVERS
,, 30—Pvte. R. HURT
Nov. 22—Sergt. A. SHEPPARD
Dec. 2—Pvte. C. H. CLIFFE
,, 8—Pvte. C. REDFERN

1916.

March 20—Pvte. J. EVANS
,, 21—Pvte. F. FOOTITT
,, 25—Pvte. E. GILBERT
,, 28—Pvte. C. E. ELLIS
April 4—Pvte. J. E. EASTON
,, 4—Pvte. A. WRIGHT
,, 4—Pvte. F. JOHNSON
,, 4—Pvte. J. W. HEMPSALL
,, 5—Pvte. E. A. HILL
,, 15—Pvte. G. WILCOCKSON
,, 15—Pvte. L. CHANDLER
,, 17—Sergt. W. H. MARKHAM
,, 17—Pvte. W. NORTH
,, 17—Pvte. E. H. MUTTON
,, 18—Pvte. H. ELLIS

April 18—Pvte. E. NELSON
,, 18—Pvte. W. ROBINSON
,, 18—L.-Corpl. J. FOOTITT
,, 18—Pvte. G. MARRIOTT
,, 18—Pvte. G. H. JOHNSON
,, 18—Pvte. L. J. MOORE
,, 20—Pvte. H. HICKING
,, 20—Pvte. T. B. TERRY
,, 25—Pvte. C. WELLS
June 3—Pvte. H. SKILLINGTON
,, 20—Pvte. A. E. PULFORD
,, 20—Pvte. J. FOGG
,, 20—Pvte. G. A. BINGLEY
,, 20—Pvte. L. TYERS
,, 20—Pvte. T. STOUT
,, 24—Pvte. A. FROGGATT
,, 24—Pvte. J. W. MOOR
,, 24—Pvte. A. ENGLISH
,, 24—Pvte. T. COPE
,, 25—Pvte. M. JOHNSON
,, 25—L.-Corpl. A. E. SOOLEY
,, 26—Pvte. E. TOYNE
,, 26—Corpl. W. G. MOORE
,, 26—Pvte. E. JUDSON
,, 27—L.-Corpl. A. A. GRANT
,, 27—Pvte. F. W. BONSER
July 1—Pvte. F. CLARKE
,, 1—Corpl. E. ALLEN
,, 1—Pvte. J. W. EDWARDS
,, 1—Pvte. G. SEAGRAVE
,, 1—Corpl. S. MATTHEWS
,, 1—Corpl. J. J. ALVEY
,, 1—Pvte. T. F. BARLOW
,, 3—Pvte. A. BOUSFIELD
,, 6—Pvte. G. TALBOT
,, 10—Pvte. G. JEFFERY
,, 12—L.-Corpl. W. YOUNG
,, 13—L.-Corpl. E. PRIDE
,, 13—Pvte. W. E. BEARDSLEY
,, 14—Corpl. A. E. PALING
,, 17—Pvte. J. F. WOOD
,, 24—Pvte. J. R. SEYMOUR
August 8—Pvte. J. BURKE
Sept. 21—Pvte. A. STOCKS
Oct. 7—Pvte. W. HAMMOND

1917.

Jan. 24—Pvte. J H SPENCE
,, 24—Pvte. J. STAFFORD
,, 24—Pvte. R. KNEE
Feb. 12—Pvte. F. ROBERTSON
,, 16—Pvte. F. W. BEIGHTON
,, 17—L.-Corpl. E. SLACK
,, 17—Pvte. J. W. SHARMAN

1917—contd.

Feb. 17—Pvte. F. MAKIN
,, 17—Pvte. G. ADDISON
March 4—L.-Corpl. R. MARRIOTT
,, 4—Pvte. H. RIMES
,, 4—Pvte. J. MYATT
,, 4—Pvte. P. FAULKNER
,, 4—Pvte. F. S. COOPER
,, 5—Sergt. J. HENLEY
,, 5—Pvte. S. J. PREECE
,, 6—Pvte. J. H. HASLAM
,, 15—Pvte. C. H. BRYAN
April 21—Pvte. G. STUBBINS
,, 21—Pvte. J. E. WILKINSON
,, 21—Pvte. L. BURROWS
,, 23—Corpl. W. STREET
,, 23—L.-Corpl. R. VACEY
,, 23—L.-Corpl. J. HINCHLEY
,, 23—L.-Corpl. W. WARD
,, 23—Pvte. W. BARWISE
,, 23—Pvte. G. GARBETT
,, 23—Pvte. G. H. SMITH
,, 23—Pvte. E. GOODACRE
,, 23—Pvte. E. R. HEWSON
,, 23—Pvte. J. HOLWELL
,, 23—Pvte. T. H. JONES
,, 23—Pvte. G. MILLER
,, 23—Pvte. F. PHILLIPS
,, 23—Pvte. W. STEELE
,, 23—Pvte. H. BARNES
,, 23—Pvte. S. HODGKINSON
,, 24—Corpl. A. COX
,, 26—Pvte. J. NICHOLSON
May 8—Pvte. D. McGLURE
,, 10—Pvte. R. SHORT
,, 10—Pvte. C. PERKINS
,, 11—Pvte. F. W. BROWN
,, 11—Pvte. G. NICHOLLS
,, 12—Pvte. A. L. VARLEY
,, 12—Pvte. J. SINCLAIR
,, 12—Pvte. R. TURNER
,, 19—Pvte. J. K. STRACHAN
,, 28—L.-Corpl. H. NEWMAN
,, 28—Pvte. R. MORRIS
,, 29—Pvte. F. MARSHALL
,, 30—Pvte. L. HOUFTON
,, 30—Pvte. T. SHERRATT
,, 30—Pvte. H. SIMPSON
,, 30—Pvte. S. MORLEY
June 2—Pvte. W. GALE
,, 3—Pvte. S. PEACH
,, 6—Pvte. A. L. REEKIE
,, 8—Pvte. J. H. WHITEHEAD
,, 8—Pvte. G. W. HENLEY

June 8—Pvte. G. S. REIACH
,, 8—Corpl. F. S. PICKERING
,, 8—Pvte. T. CLARKE
,, 9—Pvte. A. FITZHUGH
,, 22—Pvte. W. N. STONE
,, 22—Pvte. J. W. BRADBURY
,, 22—Pvte. A. SIMPSON
,, 22—L.-Corpl. E. JOHNSON
,, 22—Pvte. A. MAWSON
,, 23—Pvte. T. GROSSE
,, 23—Pvte. H. F. BUCKLER
,, 23—Corpl. A. HUMBERSTONE
,, 23—Pvte. G. F. COLLINS
,, 23—Pvte. J. BUSWELL
,, 26—Pvte. C. E. ALLEN
,, 26—Pvte. J. H. FOX
,, 26—Drummer S. R. WILLINGHAM
July 1—Pvte. P. N. COUPE
,, 26—Pvte. G. H. STUBBINS
,, 28—L.-Corpl. A. HUNTBACH
,, 28—L.-Corpl. W. BULMAN
,, 30—Pvte. G. F. ALLEN
August 4—L.-Corpl. H. TAYLOR
,, 5—L.-Sergt. S. BOWLER
,, 30—Corpl. H. WRIGHT
Sept. 2—Pvte. A. ROBERTSON
,, 3—Pvte. A. P. FRETTINGHAM
,, 12—Pvte. H. WILSON
,, 12—L.-Sergt. J. BLYTHE
,, 12—L.-Corpl. H. C. KEY
,, 13—Pvte. L. LILLEY
,, 13—Pvte. G. DARWIN
,, 13—L.-Corpl. C. PARKIN
,, 13—Pvte. W. S. BELL
,, 13—Pvte. W. A. BECKETT
,, 13—Pvte. W. C. RANDALL
,, 13—Pvte. E. STEWART
,, 13—Pvte. S. THORNE
,, 29—Pvte. T. GILBERT
,, 29—Pvte. H. C. SMEDLEY
Oct. 4—Sergt. W. H. DRABBLE
,, 4—Pvte. G. H. WEST
,, 4—Pvte. A. LOVEGROVE
,, 5—Pvte. H. SHUFFLEBOTTOM
,, 14—Pvte. J. BENNETT
Nov. 2—Pvte. E. SHARPE
,, 4—Pvte. H. SYSON
,, 23—Pvte. W. BLACKSHAW
,, 28—Pvte. H. FOX
Dec. 6—Pvte. W. J. PALMER
,, 9—L.-Corpl. A. DEAN
,, 11—Pvte. H. MOULT
,, 21—Pvte. G. LARGE

1918.

March 17—Pvte. F. L. CHAPMAN
,,   22—Pvte. S. S. IVES
,,   22—Pvte. J. THOMPSON
,,   22—Corpl. H. TYNE
April 8—Pvte. C. SCHOLES
,,   18—Corpl. G. CAUDWELL
,,   18—Pvte. C. H. ARAM
,,   18—Pvte. A. LEADER
,,   28—Pvte. E. CROSS
,,   28—Pvte. F. TOWNSEND
,,   29—Pvte. G. F. GARRATT
May   5—Pvte. A. E. CLIFF
,,   5—Pvte. A. H. WHEWAY
,,   9—Pvte. E. H. ASLING
,,   15—Pvte. A. BEASTALL
,,   18—Pvte. H. COOPER
,,   19—Pvte. A. ARMSTRONG
June   15—Pvte. W. H. BALDWIN
,,   15—Pvte. W. BUCKLEY
,,   16—Pvte. G. R. ATKINSON
,,   16—Pvte. A. LOVER
,,   19—Pvte. W. CLARKE
,,   23—Pvte. W. TUDBURY
,,   29—Pvte. C. J. RICKETT
July   10—L.-Corpl. H. SMITH
August 7—Pvte. G. CHADWICK
,,   13—Pvte. J. G. BOOTHBY
,,   14—L.-Corpl. F. PECK
,,   17—Pvte. G. ROWLEY
,,   26—Pvte. S. BERRY
,,   28—Pvte. E. POWELL
,,   28—Pvte. G. WILLIAMSON
,,   29—Pvte. J. A. RILEY
,,   29—Pvte. G. STENDALL
,,   29—Pvte. G. RENSHAW
,,   29—Pvte. F. H. HEIGHWAY
Sept. 22—Pvte. G. F. ROGERS
,,   25—Corpl. A. E. LAMBERT
,,   25—Pvte. W. ROGERS
,,   26—Pvte. W. J. PHIPPARD
,,   26—Corpl. J. W. ELCOCK
,,   29—Pvte. I. EVANS
,,   29—Pvte. T. RENNIE
,,   29—Corpl. H. RUSSELL
,,   29—L.-Corpl. J. HOE
,,   29—Pvte. J. E. TINKLER
,,   29—Pvte. G. S. GOODBOURNE
,,   29—Pvte. F. CONWAY
,,   29—L.-Corpl. T. H. SWANN
,,   29—Pvte. F. KEY
,,   29—Pvte. E. LEEK
,,   29—Pvte. J. RICE

Sept. 29—Pvte. C. E. GODDARD
,,   30—Comp. Sergt.-Major J. F.
                              RAWDING
,,   30—Pvte. E. WALKER
,,   30—Pvte. T. JOHNSON
Oct.   1—Pvte. A. WATSON
,,   3—Pvte. J. E. SMITH
,,   3—L.-Corpl. G. T. TOLLY
,,   3—Pvte. G. BALLINGTON
,   3—Pvte. D. IRVINE
,,   3—Pvte. S. SPENCER
,,   3—Pvte. J. TAYLOR
,,   3—Sergt. C. H. GENDERS
,,   3—Pvte. J. HOLMES
,,   3—Pvte. J. R. RUSH
,,   3—L.-Corpl. A. MANTLE
,,   3—Pvte. H. F. RUSSELL
,,   3—Pvte. F. W. LAMBERT
,,   3—Pvte. H. KEECH
,,   3—Pvte. H. G. HANDLEY
,,   3—Pvte. S. GUY
,,   3—Sergt. S. HURT
,,   3—Pvte. J. SULLEY
,,   3—Pvte. W. BARKSBY
,,   3—Pvte. J. W. NORTH
,,   3—Pvte. A. GOLDSMITH
,,   3—Pvte. A. E. WARD
,,   3—Pvte. J. MOON
,,   4—Pvte. F. J. LEWIS
,,   4—L.-Corpl. C. H. CHADBOURNE
,,   7—Pvte. A. CLEMERSON
,,   8—Pvte. H. SILVESTER
,,   9—L.-Corpl. A. H. PENFORD
,,   12—Pvte. W. WALTERS
,,   13—Pvte. A. S. ROBERTS
,,   14—Pvte. C. E. HALLAM
,,   17—Pvte. W. GODSON
,,   17—Pvte. J. BAILEY
,,   17—Pvte. G. E. SMITH
,,   17—Pvte. G. E. P. DENNIS
,,   17—Pvte. H. ADLINGTON
,,   17—Pvte. S. SEAL
,,   17—Pvte. H. SIMMONS
,,   17—Pvte. T. W. HORNE
,,   17—Pvte. F. WOODHEAD
,,   17—Pvte. A. JONES
,,   17—Pvte. J. W. STEWART
,,   17—Pvte. G. FLOYD
,,   17—Pvte. F. N. GUTTRIDGE
,,   17—Pvte. T. TURNER
,,   17—Pvte. A. DIGGLE
,,   17—Pvte. E. GODDARD
,,   17—L.-Corpl. F. H. CLARKE

251

Oct.	17—L.-Corpl. W. C. CREAMER	Oct.	18—Pvte. A. BACON
,,	17—Pvte. G. WILDSMITH	,,	22—Pvte. G. W. ROLLETT
,,	17—L.-Corpl. J. F. HARPER	,,	23—L.-Corpl. L. HORTON
,,	17—Pvte. G. WELBOURNE	,,	23—Pvte. B. A. CUTLER
,,	17—Pvte. G. REDFERN	,,	24—Pvte. A. GITTENS
,,	18—Pvte. T. SEDGEWICK	Nov.	1—Pvte. W. J. COATES
,,	18—Pvte. J. ROBINSON	,,	5—Pvte. C. WAGSTAFF
,,	18—Pvte. C. WHITTAKER	,,	11—Pvte. T. S. HANDY
,,	18—Corpl. A. C. SCOTT	,,	13—Pvte. R. HAND
		Dec.	24—Pvte. H. BUZAN

Officers who were Killed or Died of Wounds whilst serving with other Units.

2nd Lieut. A. D. BAILEY
2nd Lieut. F. E. KEBBLEWHITE
2nd Lieut. F. M. CORRY.

Lieut. C. H. HICKS
Lieut.-Col. B. W. VANN

Other Ranks who were Killed or Died of Wounds, after being granted Commissions in other Units.

Comp. Sergt.-Major J. A. GREEN
Comp. Sergt.-Major F. SPENCER
L.-Corpl. F. L. WILSON
L.-Corpl. F. B. GILL

Comp. Sergt.-Major E. HAYWOOD
Comp. Sergt.-Major W. H. M. HOTSON
Pvte. J. A. CHRISTIE

252

APPENDIX II.

HONOURS.

BAR TO D.S.O.

Lieut.-Col. J. F. DEMPSTER   Lieut.-Col. R. W. CURRIN

D. S. O.

Lieut.-Col. J. E. BLACKWALL   Major J. P. BECHER
Major A. L. ASHWELL   Major R. J. WORDSWORTH
Rev. J. P. HALES

2ND BAR TO M. C.

Major V. O. ROBINSON

M. C. AND BAR.

Capt. B. W. VANN

M. C.

2nd Lieut. J. S. C. OATES   Capt. J. B. WHITE
Capt. A. HACKING   2nd Lieut. J. BLOOR
Capt. W. C. C. WEETMAN   2nd Lieut. W. J. WINTER
2nd Lieut. W. P. DUFF   Capt. A. B. MINERS
2nd Lieut. E. HOPKINSON   2nd Lieut. F. L. HARRAP
Capt. A. E. GEARY   Lieut. S. E. CAIRNS
Capt. J. W. TURNER   2nd Lieut. T. F. MITCHELL
2nd Lieut. A. C. FAIRBROTHER   Capt. St. G. L. M. HOMAN, R.A.M.C.
Capt. H. DE C. MARTELLI   Rev. D. E. STURT
Capt. H. K. SIMONET   Capt. C. G. DRUCE
Major A. ANDREWS   Capt. E. W. WARNER
Capt. E. A. HUSKINSON   2nd Lieut. J. F. SHACKLETON
2nd Lieut. S. BRADWELL   Capt. A. BEDFORD
2nd Lieut. JAMES HOWARD SMITH   Lieut. A. G. T. LOMER
Capt. G. THOMAS

O.B.E. AND M.V.O.

Major G. S. HEATHCOTE

O.B.E. AND BREVET MAJORITY.

Major G. CLARKE

O.B.E.

Lieut.-Col. C. J. HUSKINSON
Lieut.-Col. R. F. B. HODGKINSON

D. C. M. AND BAR.

Comp. Sergt.-Major F. ATTENBOROUGH

D. C. M. AND M. M.

L.-Sergt. C. CLAXTON   Pvte. G. H. WESLEY

D. C. M. AND M. S. M.

Comp. Sergt.-Major J. F. RAWDING

D. C. M.

Regimental Sergt.-Major W. MOUNTENEY
Sergt. A. SHEPPARD
Corpl. H. TYNE
Sergt. E. GRANTHAM
Pvte. J. NICHOLSON
Corpl. W. E. BOOT
Sergt.-Drummer W. CLEWES
L.-Sergt. T. TURGOOSE
Pvte. R. KEELING

Comp. Sergt.-Major E. HAYWOOD
Sergt. C. E. CROOKS
Sergt. H. SCRIMSHAW
Sergt. J. L. PEACH
Corpl. R. FRANCIS
Comp. Sergt.-Major A. COBB
Comp. Sergt.-Major W. STOKES
L.-Corpl. W. BEECH
Sergt. H. WILSON

M. M. AND 2 BARS.

Pvte. L. THOMAS

M. M. AND BAR.

Pvte. F. GREEN

M. M. AND M. S. M.

Pvte. J. NELSON

M. M.

Sergt. J. T. TEMPLEMAN
Corpl. W. H. LACEY
Corpl. S. MATTHEWS
L.-Sergt. T. MARTIN
Pvte. G. F. HOLBERY
Sergt. C. GRAINGER
L.-Corpl. H. J. WALSH
Corpl. H. HICKMAN
Corpl. C. E. BRYAN
Corpl. J. W. WILSON
Sergt. W. L. GREEN
Sergt. L. BELL
Sergt. C. T. BLUNT
Comp. Sergt.-Major E. E. DEVERALL
Sergt. J. G. COLLINS
Sergt. W. G. OLDFIELD
Corpl. T. W. LOWE
Pvte. W. HEATH
Sergt. J. HENLEY
Corpl. W. STREET
L.-Corpl. W. TEARE
Corpl. C. HAGUES
Sergt. R. H. BOLTON
L.-Corpl. J. F. STEWART
Pvte. G. F. GARRATT
Sergt. W. H. MARTIN
L.-Sergt. R. TURNER
Pvte. G. WILDSMITH
Pvte. W. H. TAILBY
Pvte. G. STAMFORD
Pvte. G. COOK
L.-Sergt. W. FIELD
L.-Sergt. F. ILLGER
L.-Corpl. J. NORTH
Pvte. G. FEIGHERY

Pvte. B. SMITHURST
Pvte. W. TITMUS
Pvte. A. W. COLTON
Pvte. C. WELBOURNE
Pvte. G. SULLEY
Corpl. S. SLATER
Corpl. W. FOSTER
Pvte. W. PARKER
Pvte. A. W. STAPLETON
Corpl. R. HARVEY
Sergt. J. STIMSON
Pvte. E. CROW
Sergt. C. VANN
L.-Corpl. S. SLATER
Corpl. J. WRIGHT
Pvte. J. W. STARR
L.-Corpl. F. BAXTER
Corpl. W. CLARK
Sergt. W. WRIGGLESWORTH
Sergt. C. SHARROCK
Pvte. W. H. MARTIN
Sergt. H. SHEPPERSON
Sergt. A. WINSON
Pvte. J. ROE
L.-Corpl. J. U. COOMBS
Pvte. F. DRAPER
Pvte. A. JACKSON
Pvte. A. TURPIN
Pvte. N. LEES
Pvte. J. VIPOND
Pvte. W. HOUGHTON
Pvte. W. G. NICHOLSON
Pvte. C. SMITH
Pvte. H. BERESFORD
Corpl. S. GADSBY

Pvte. W. Westnidge
Corpl. G. Skelton

Pvte. E. Mosgrove

M. S. M.

Comp. Sergt.-Major A. Mabbott
Sergt. T. Taylor
Sergt. J. Eggleston
Sergt. R. Harvey

Regtl. Qtr.-Mtr. Sergt. F. A. Pritchard
Comp. Qtr.-Mtr. Sergt. H. J. Wilson
Comp. Qtr.-Mtr. Sergt. G. E. Bee
Comp. Qtr.-Mtr. Sergt. W. I. Dale

Mentioned in Despatches.

Lieut.-Col. G. H. Fowler
Major J. P. Becher
Major A. L. Ashwell
Major R. J. Wordsworth (2)
2nd Lieut. J. S. C. Oates
Capt. E. C. A. James
Capt. E. N. T. Collin
Capt. B. W. Vann
Capt. A. Hacking
Capt. J. W. Turner
Lieut.-Col. J. E. Blackwall
Rev. J. P. Hales (2)
Lieut.-Col. C. J. Huskinson (2)
Capt. C. L. Hill
Major G. Clarke
Lieut. W. H. B. Rezin (2)
Hon. Lieut. and Quarter-Master F.
TORRANCE
Capt. R. Whitton
Capt. C. G. Tomlinson
Lieut. C. H. S. Stephenson
Lieut.-Col. R. W. Currin
Capt. N. L. Hindley

Lieut. S. Sanders
Sergt. E. Grantham
Comp. Sergt.-Major J. F. Rawding
Sergt. J. T. Templeman
Sergt. C. T. Blunt
Pvte. F. Holland
Regtl. Sergt.-Major W. Mounteney
Sergt. A. Phillipson
Pvte. S. Boothby
Pvte. C. Redfern
Corpl. G. Caudwell
Pvte. H. Needham
Comp. Sergt.-Major T. Powell
Comp. Sergt.-Major J. T. Slater
Sergt. R. F. Bescoby.
Regtl. Qtr.-Mtr. Sergt. F. A. Pritchard
Sergt. R. Harvey
L.-Corpl. W. Beech
Comp. Sergt.-Major E. E. Deverall
Corpl. E. Dexter
Sergt. F. Losley
L.-Sergt. J. Wicks

FOREIGN DECORATIONS.

French :—

Légion d'Honneur (Chevalier).

Lieut.-Col. J. E. Blackwall

Croix de Guerre.

Capt. B. W. Vann
Capt. W. C. C. Weetman
Comp. Sergt.-Major A. Cobb

Pvte. F. Holland
Sergt. T. Oldham

Belgian : —

Croix de Guerre.

Regimental Sergt.-Major W. Mounteney

Russian :—

Medal of St. George (4th Class).

Drummer J. Newton
Drummer W. Robb

Corpl. J. Sharman

www.ingramcontent.com/pod-product-compliance
Lightning Source LLC
Chambersburg PA
CBHW032039080426
42733CB00006B/130